Understanding the Digital Revolution and Its Influences

Yuxin Yu · Yanqing Jiang

Understanding the Digital Revolution and Its Influences

Springer

Yuxin Yu
School of Economics and Finance
Shanghai International Studies University
Shanghai, China

Yanqing Jiang
School of Economics and Finance
Shanghai International Studies University
Shanghai, China

ISBN 978-981-97-4938-6 ISBN 978-981-97-4939-3 (eBook)
https://doi.org/10.1007/978-981-97-4939-3

This Springer imprint is published by the registered company Springer Nature Singapore Pte Ltd.
The registered company address is: 152 Beach Road, #21-01/04 Gateway East, Singapore 189721, Singapore

Acknowledgement

The study in this book was partly supported by the Shanghai Philosophy and Social Science Planning Project (Project No. 2020BJB020), titled "Evaluation of the Modernization of the National Economic Governance System and Governance Capacity in Shanghai: Analysis of the Evaluation System from the Perspective of Technological Evolution".

Contents

1 Introduction: Understanding the Importance of the Digital Revolution 1
1.1 The Greatest Challenge of the Current Era: Poverty of New Ideas 2
1.2 The Cognitive Revolution: Reevaluating Humanity in the Digital Age 4
1.3 The Development Logic of the Division of Labor 4
1.4 Reflecting from a Historical Perspective 6
1.5 Digital Transformation: Rooted in the Inevitable Direction of Human Development 7
1.5.1 Humans as Processors and Storers of Environmental Information 7
1.5.2 Human Development: A Continuous Optimization Process of Environmental Information Processing 9
1.5.3 The History of Human Development: Continuously Pursuing Dominance in Environmental Information Processing 10
1.5.4 The Efficiency of Environmental Information Processing and Human Cognitive Abilities 11
1.5.5 Digitization: Humanity's Inevitable Choice 12
1.6 Conclusion 13

2 Evolution History of the Digital Economy 15
2.1 Information Technology and the Development of Human Civilization 15
2.1.1 Information Technology as a Shaping Force of Human Civilization 15
2.1.2 Three Stages in the Evolution of Information Technology 16
2.1.3 Human Civilization at the Stage of Biosensor Information Processing 18

2.1.4 Human Civilization with Rational Cognitive Tools 19
2.1.5 Intelligent Technology Integrating Rational Cognitive Tools 19
2.1.6 Three Phases of Information Technology Development 20
2.2 The Iteration History of Information Technology 22
2.2.1 The Ancient Information Technology Revolution: Language, Writing, and Printing 24
2.2.2 The Modern Information Technology Revolution: Harnessing Electromagnetic Waves, Computers, Big Data, and Artificial Intelligence 28
2.3 The Digital Age as the New Phase of Information Technology Evolution 33
2.3.1 A Fundamental Change in Information Scarcity 33
2.3.2 A Fundamental Transformation in the Social Division of Labor 34

3 Information Technology Iteration and the Productivity Revolution 39
3.1 Empowerment of Individuals by Information Technology Iteration 40
3.1.1 Information Technology Empowerment Shaped by the Era 40
3.1.2 Information Technology Development: Enhancing Information Processing Efficiency 42
3.1.3 Information Technology Empowerment: Enhancing Autonomous Development 43
3.2 Productivity Revolution Based on the Empowerment of Information Technology 44
3.2.1 Steam Engines + Corporate System: Unleashing the Power of the Industrial Revolution 46
3.2.2 Electric Motors + Radio and TV Technology: Fueling Industrial Value Networks 48
3.2.3 "Computer +": Unlocking Information Productivity 49
3.3 Digitalization as the Modern Information Technology Achievement 52
3.3.1 Two Phases in Digitalization 53
3.3.2 The Economic Mechanism in the Digital Age 54
3.3.3 Economic Organization and the Social Division of Labor in the Digital Age 55

4 Understanding the Underlying Theory of the Social Division of Labor 57
4.1 The Social Division of Labor 57
4.2 Understanding the Importance of the Social Division of Labor 59
4.2.1 A Theoretical Framework for Understanding the Social Division of Labor 59
4.2.2 The Social Division of Labor: The Lever for Wealth Creation 60
4.2.3 The Social Division of Labor: Enhanced Information Processing Efficiency 60
4.2.4 The Social Division of Labor in the Digital Age: Added Value Generated Through Weak Ties 62
4.2.5 The Social Division of Labor in the Digital Age: The Measurement of Network Value 63
4.2.6 Efficiency in Information Processing: A Key Determinant of the Social Division of Labor Networks 64
4.2.7 Efficiency in Information Processing: A Fundamental Criterion for Assessing the Level of the Social Division of Labor 66
4.3 Why Do Individuals Participate in the Social Division of Labor? 67
4.3.1 Participation in the Social Division of Labor: The Intrinsic Psychological Motivation 67
4.3.2 Participation in the Social Division of Labor: Rational Choice of Individuals 68
4.3.3 Participation in the Social Division of Labor: Pursuing Economic Interests 68
4.4 Why Does the Division of Labor Take Different Forms? 69
4.4.1 Transaction Costs: Determining the Organizational Structure 70
4.4.2 Technology Development: Shaping the Labor Specialization Network 71
4.4.3 Decision-Making Costs: A Key Factor Shaping the Division of Labor in the Digital Age 72
4.5 The Evolution of the Social System of the Division of Labor . . . 72
4.5.1 Characteristics of the Evolution of the Social System of the Division of Labor 73
4.5.2 The Value of the Social System of the Division of Labor 74
4.6 Evolution History of the Social Division of Labor 76
4.6.1 The Social Division of Labor Before the Industrial Revolution 76

4.6.2 The Overlook of Decision-Making Costs in Economic Analysis ... 77
4.6.3 Overlooking Technological Impact: A Limitation in the Theory ... 78

5 Evolution of the Social Division of Labor in the Digital Economy ... 83
5.1 The Impact of Digital Technology on the Social Division of Labor ... 83
5.1.1 The Digitalization of Language ... 83
5.1.2 The Impact of Language Digitalization ... 85
5.1.3 Digital Transformation of Communication ... 86
5.1.4 New Approaches to Human–Computer Interaction ... 86
5.1.5 The Impact of Digitalized Interactions ... 87
5.2 Digital-Technology-Empowered Social Collaboration ... 88
5.2.1 The Impact of Digital Technology on Social Collaboration ... 88
5.2.2 Digital Technology Revolutionizes Human–Machine Collaboration Patterns ... 89
5.2.3 The Impact of Human–Machine Collaboration ... 90
5.3 Evolution of the Division of Labor in the Digital Age ... 91
5.3.1 Changes in the Human–Machine Collaboration Pattern ... 92
5.3.2 Changes in the Cooperation Among Individuals ... 98
5.4 Evolution of Economic Organizations Driven by Digital Technology ... 102
5.4.1 The Division of Labor in Economic Organizations ... 103
5.4.2 Determining the Boundaries of Economic Organizations ... 103
5.4.3 Determining the Structure of Economic Organizations ... 104
5.4.4 "Super Individuals": Posing a New Challenge to Economic Organizations ... 105
5.4.5 Entrepreneurship in the Digital Age ... 105
5.4.6 Economic Organizations in the Digital Age ... 106
5.4.7 The Goals of Economic Organizations ... 106
5.4.8 Autonomous Collaboration Within Organizations ... 107
5.4.9 Openness and Inclusivity Emerging as Characteristics of Economic Organizations ... 107
5.5 The Propelling Force of the Socio-Economic System in the Digital Age ... 108
5.5.1 The Role of Human Desire and Cognitive Innovation ... 108
5.5.2 The Role of Information Flows ... 108

6 The Reshaping Effects of Digital Technology on the Social Division of Labor ... 111
6.1 The Impact of Digital Technology on Specialization ... 111
6.2 New Characteristics and Trends of the Social Division of Labor in the Digital Age ... 113
6.2.1 New Characteristics in the Digital Age ... 113
6.2.2 New Trends in the Digital Age ... 114
6.2.3 The Challenges Posed by Intelligent Machine ... 121
6.3 The Importance of Individuals in the Specialization System ... 123

7 Individual Economic Behavior in the Digital Economy ... 127
7.1 The Influence of Digital Technology on Individual Behavior ... 127
7.2 Characteristics of Decision-Making in the Digital Age ... 129
7.3 Information as the Foundation for Decision-Making in the Digital Age ... 130
7.4 The Changing Environment of Economic Behavior in the Digital Age ... 131
7.5 The Mechanism of Decision-Making in the Digital Age ... 132
7.6 The Mindset for Economic Decision-Making in the Digital Age ... 133

8 New Phenomena in the Digital Economy ... 137
8.1 The "Super Individuals" ... 138
8.1.1 The Essence of "Super Individuals" ... 138
8.1.2 What Contributes to the Emergence of "Super Individuals" ... 139
8.1.3 The Impact of "Super Individuals" ... 140
8.1.4 The Distribution Characteristics of "Super Individuals" ... 141
8.1.5 Pathways to "Super Individuals" ... 142
8.2 The "Influencer Economy" ... 142
8.2.1 The Characteristics of the Influencer Economy ... 143
8.2.2 The Rise of the Influencer Economy ... 143
8.2.3 The Influencer Economy in the Developing Age ... 144
8.3 The "Platform Economy" ... 146

9 Business Operation and Value Creation of the Digital Economy ... 147
9.1 The Systematic Changes in the Business Environment ... 147
9.1.1 The Rise of New Formats in the Digital Economy ... 148
9.1.2 The Source of Commercial Value ... 148
9.1.3 The Economic Forms ... 149
9.1.4 The Decision-Making Methods ... 149
9.1.5 The Organizational Forms ... 150
9.1.6 New Characteristics in the Digital Economy ... 151
9.1.7 Imbalance in Supply and Demand Sparking Escalating Competition ... 153

9.1.8 Digital Technology Accelerating the Transformation of the Social Division of Labor 154
9.1.9 A New Perspective on the Evolution of New Business Civilization Under the Digital Economy 155
9.2 New Paradigms for Business in the Digital Economy 156
9.2.1 New Drivers for Business: From the Supply Side to the Demand Side 156
9.2.2 Value Creation in the Industrial Era: Reconfiguration of Supply-Side Resources 157
9.3 Business Value Creation in the Digital Economy: Reconfiguration of Demand-Side Resources 161
9.4 The Rise of New Business Models in the Digital Economy 165
9.4.1 The Example of Pinduoduo in China: A New Stage of Demand-Side Integration 166
9.4.2 Livestreaming Sales: A Transitional Approach to Demand-Side Integration 167
9.5 Conclusion 170

10 Evolution of Enterprise Organization in the Digital Age 173
10.1 Technological Advancements and the Corporate Structure 173
10.1.1 The Efficiency of Information Processing: A Determinant of the Form of Economic Organization 174
10.1.2 The Evolution of Corporate Structure in the Industrial Era 175
10.1.3 The Limited Liability Company Structure: Primary Economic Organizational Form of the Industrial Era 176
10.1.4 Characteristics of Limited Liability Company Structure: From the Perspective of Information Perspective 177
10.2 Digital Technology as a Driving Force of the Evolution of Enterprise Organization 178
10.2.1 The Changing Nature of Organizational Costs and Its Impact on Organizational Structure 178
10.2.2 The Emergence of Technological Capital 179
10.3 Adapting to the Digital Age: Evolution of Organizational Structure Within Enterprises 180
10.3.1 The Declining Importance of Capital in the Social Division of Labor 180
10.3.2 Equal Rights with Different Shares: A New Choice for Economic Organizations in the Digital Age 181
10.3.3 The Origin of Dual-Class Share Structures 182

10.3.4 Dual-Class Share Structures: Becoming the Mainstream Choice for Emerging Enterprises in the Digital Economy ... 183
10.4 Adapting to the Digital Age: Evolution of Organizational Structure Outside Enterprises ... 183
10.4.1 The Increasing Openness of Economic Organizations in the Digital Age ... 183
10.4.2 From Theory to Practice: The Concept of Business Ecosystems ... 184
10.4.3 The Development Model of Business Ecosystems and the Complete Socialization of Economic Organizations ... 185
10.4.4 The Fundamental Logic Behind the Operation of Business Ecosystems ... 186
10.5 Conclusion ... 187

11 Summary and Conclusion ... 189
11.1 The Digital Economy: Unveiling New Business Logics and Development Models ... 189
11.2 Digital Technology: Transforming the Business Value Creation ... 191
11.3 Transformation in the Social Division of Labor: Prompting the Development of a New Business Civilization ... 192
11.4 Trends in the Development of the New Business Civilization ... 194
11.4.1 Formation and Development of New Values ... 194
11.4.2 Formation and Development of New Organizational Forms ... 195

About the Authors

Yuxin Yu is Associate Professor at the School of Economics and Finance, Shanghai International Studies University, and Researcher at the Shanghai Research Center for Innovation and Policy Evaluation. Dr. Yu's research focuses on digital economy, artificial intelligence, and blockchain applications.

Yanqing Jiang is Professor at the School of Economics and Finance, Shanghai International Studies University. Professor Jiang received his Ph.D. in Economics from Hanken School of Economics in Finland. His areas of expertise include macroeconomic policy, international economics, and development economics.

Chapter 1
Introduction: Understanding the Importance of the Digital Revolution

In February 2023, the Central Committee of the Communist Party of China and the State Council issued the "Overall Plan for Building Digital China". The plan emphasizes that building Digital China is a crucial engine for advancing China's modernization process and a strong support for constructing new national competitive advantages. Accelerating the construction of Digital China holds significant and far-reaching implications for comprehensively realizing socialist modernization and promoting the great rejuvenation of the Chinese nation. Therefore, research on digitalization has become a topic of strategic value, practical significance, and theoretical importance.

Currently, one of the main features of economic development is digitalization. Various economic sectors widely adopt digital production tools, recruit workers with digital technology skills, utilize digital technology to optimize production processes, enhance production efficiency, and drive innovation. The digital development model has become the consensus model for contemporary development.

In various scopes, from the United Nations, international organizations and national governments to various enterprises, institutions, and individuals, all are, actively or passively, participating in the process of digitization and experiencing its deepening impact. This indicates that digitization has exerted its influences beyond the mere economic domain, and the human society is gradually moving towards a digital society. Although the broad trend of digital development has become a consensus in the global society, yet individuals and organizations face confusion and concerns regarding the specific process and progress of digitization. This is due to the lack of a systematic understanding of the development logic of digital technology, which leaves the fundamental questions of the digital age not convincingly answered.

For example, how should we understand the systemic transformative impact brought about by digital technology? How can the digital development model become the dominant model of the times? Why do humans pursue digitization? Is digitization an inevitable choice for human development? What are the standards for measuring

Y. Yu and Y. Jiang, *Understanding the Digital Revolution and Its Influences*,
https://doi.org/10.1007/978-981-97-4939-3_1

the level of digital development? What is the driving force behind digital development? Although digital development has become a consensus, this consensus is only formed from the direct and obvious short-term economic benefits of digitalization, and there are few systematic answers to those basic questions of the digital age mentioned above. To effectively promote digitalization and achieve sustainable digital development, we must systematically answer those questions within a coherent theoretical framework. Only by answering the questions well can we promote the digital process more forcefully, avoid potential risks and pitfalls, and achieve sustainable and high-quality digital development.

First, we need to understand the systemic transformative impact of digital technology. The reason why the digital development model has become the dominant model of the era is because the rapid development and widespread application of digital technology have propelled comprehensive changes in various fields such as the economy, society, culture, and politics. The pursuit of digitization by humanity is due to the myriad changes and benefits digitization can bring about, such as enhanced productivity, accelerated innovation, improved quality of life, and strengthened national competitiveness.

The driving force behind digital development comes from the comprehensive effects of influencing factors such as technological innovation, economic globalization, and changes in the social demand. Therefore, we must reexamine the fundamental questions of the human society to understand the driving mechanism and development goals of digitization. The process of digitization results from the development of information technology, and information technology is thus the direct force driving the process of digitization. To truly understand digitization, we need to start from the development history, characteristics, and development logic of information technology and examine this historical process.

1.1 The Greatest Challenge of the Current Era: Poverty of New Ideas

Humanity's basic scientific theories remain rooted in quantum mechanics and relativity, which were established over a hundred years ago. However, the contradictions between these two theories have yet to be effectively bridged, as humanity has lacked the generation of new cognitive ideas for the past century. We are currently in an era of intellectual scarcity, in urgent need of a revolution in cognitive tools to enable the birth of new ideas.

There are two main reasons for humanity's shortage of new ideas: first, humanity is gradually approaching the boundaries of known cognitive tools, making it increasingly difficult to generate new thoughts. Despite the continuous increase in the number of scientific papers, the development of new scientific ideas has become slower and even stagnant. Many of the so-called new discoveries or new knowledge produced daily are logical consequences naturally deduced within established theoretical frameworks, rather than revolutionary insights.

The fundamental reason for this situation lies in humanity reaching the boundaries of the cognitive tools that have been invented—the language. In the early twentieth century, Ludwig Wittgenstein's philosophy of language emerged, in which he proposed the view that "the limits of language are the limits of thought", indicating that people began to realize the limitations of language tools at the cognitive level. Furthermore, Gödel's incompleteness theorems demonstrated the incompatibility between the completeness and consistency of arithmetic systems, while the decidability proof of the Turing halting problem revealed the cognitive boundaries of rational tools—mathematics and logic. These achievements indicate that humanity has approached the effective boundaries of the cognitive tools it has invented, making the generation of new ideas increasingly difficult, and almost all fields are developing in a deteriorating manner characterized by "involution". Whether it is the production of new knowledge in the field of scientific research or the production of goods and services in the economic domain, the space for incremental development has become extremely limited. This indicates that the development of the digital age cannot be addressed with past ways of thinking and cognition, nor can the process be driven by past approaches.

Second, the specialization and division of labor in various disciplinary fields have become overly specialized, leading to an over professionalization of knowledge production. Owing to the deepening specialization of various disciplines and the centralization of knowledge production, fewer and fewer people can return to the starting point of understanding research questions or the origin of knowledge formation to reassess existing cognitive achievements systematically and effectively. People have become accustomed to interpreting or explaining current changes using past classics and are more inclined to view ongoing and forthcoming trends through the lens of past experiences, rejecting viewpoints that deviate from tradition.

Therefore, despite the digital age being widely seen as a new era of transformation, when it comes to understanding and interpreting the comprehensive digitization wave sparked by digital technology, people often resort to concepts, contexts, and analytical frameworks developed during the Industrial Revolution of 200 years ago. They frequently use the historical development of electrification and automation technologies as a reference point to examine the impact of digital transformation. This makes it challenging for us to break free from the cognitive patterns influenced by the era of industrial technology. How to fully utilize the historical experience accumulated by industrial civilization over more than 200 years, combined with the latest achievements in contemporary scientific cognition and the new practices of digital exploration, to think beyond the perspective of the industrial age and envision the future development of the digital age, becomes the path that everyone aspiring to grasp the new opportunities of the digital age and become leaders of the era should choose.

Humanity is gradually approaching the boundaries of its cognitive tools' ability or functionality to understand the world. This is the fundamental reason for the lack of new ideas in humanity, with the impact of specialized division of labor being relatively secondary. Therefore, to address the significant changes brought about by the digital age, humanity needs to embrace new cognitive tools and embrace the arrival of the era of change. This is the fundamental approach to solving many of humanity's current problems. The digital transformation brought about by digital technology, especially artificial intelligence technology, will open brand new opportunities for humanity in the field of cognitive tools.

1.2 The Cognitive Revolution: Reevaluating Humanity in the Digital Age

The transformation of the digital age is a systemic change in the human society, and understanding this systemic change inevitably requires starting from a reevaluation of humanity itself. Over the past two decades, numerous advancements in the field of life sciences, particularly the invention of many new cognitive tools, have laid the foundation for reevaluating the essential attributes of humanity. This allows us to move beyond subjective imagination or the use of "black box" theoretical models to understand humanity and to establish a more accurate understanding of the essential attributes of human beings. Instead, we can start from the biological essence of human beings to understand the social logic of human societal development, thus avoiding the subjective "fantasy" biases inherent in traditional sociological analysis frameworks.

In recent decades, the field of life sciences has witnessed the emergence of many new cognitive tools, such as gene editing technology, cryo-electron microscopy technology, and multidimensional multiscale high-resolution microscopy imaging technology. These new cognitive tools have provided us with a completely new understanding of ourselves, directly involving the cognitive of the biological essence and functionality. This new cognition formed by the innovation of new cognitive tools is a crucial key to understanding the changing dynamics of the times. Since only a cognitive tool revolution has genuine developmental significance, these tools not only determine the boundaries of human cognitive capabilities and understanding of themselves but also determine the limit of human wealth creation capabilities.

1.3 The Development Logic of the Division of Labor

The application of digital technology will bring about breakthrough impacts on the social division of labor. In the digital age, the challenge lies in the fact that the mode of cooperation between people depends on the collaboration between humans and machines, which gradually diminishes the dominant position of humans. This transformation brings about two fundamental changes: the change in the scarcity of information elements and the change in the scarcity of labor elements. These two prominent changes are fundamentally different from those in other historical periods and are the foundational conditions for the social system of the division of labor, hence their impact is inevitably transformative.

The evolution of the social system of the division of labor began with early hunting cooperation where individuals collectively acquired food, which has gradually evolved into today's complex system of producing thousands or millions of different products. The evolution of the division of labor system has always been led by the development and innovation of production tools. In the past, tools created by humans, whether simple hoes or wheels, or more complex steam engines and motors, were designed to expand human capabilities. Therefore, the changes these tools brought to the social division of labor were limited, and individuals could adapt to their impact through limited learning time.

With the invention of computers, especially the rapid development of digital technologies such as artificial intelligence and big data in the past decade, human's ability to process information has begun to be replaced by machine systems. Decision-making abilities are constrained by information processing machine systems, shaking the original foundation of cooperation between people. The emergence and continuous iteration of digital technology tools like ChatGPT have led to a noticeable decrease in communication efficiency between people compared to the efficiency of communication between machines. This implies that the division of labor and cooperation between humans must yield to the division of labor between humans and machines. Nowadays, without information processing tools like computers, humans are unable to meet the increasingly complex demands for information processing. This poses an unprecedented challenge to the current the social division of labor—the mode of cooperation between humans and machines affects and determines the mode of cooperation between people, which has gradually weakened the dominant position of humans.

As a result of this challenge, humans must adapt to new models of human–machine collaborative decision-making, make necessary adjustments to organizational forms and mechanisms, and promptly adjust the distribution of the division of labor outcomes as well as the value evaluation mechanism. This also heralds the emergence of a new business civilization. Currently, there are two exploratory directions in the evolution of human–machine collaboration models: one is the traditional approach, where humans iterate and update their skills to meet the new requirements of human–machine collaboration; the other is the development of brain-machine interface technology, attempting to physically integrate humans and machines by implanting chips into the human brain to achieve an organic combination of human and machine information processing capabilities. This technological development is one of the significant challenges faced by digital development, as it necessitates the redefinition of human nature, raising concerns about a series of unpredictable challenges that may arise from the ethical implications of this technology.

1.4 Reflecting from a Historical Perspective

The history of human civilization is filled with contingencies and traces of historical figures. While some historians consider this as one of the laws of human history, when the development of a social system is full of contingencies, it means that this social system lacks autonomy and cannot effectively grasp its own path and direction. This reflects that as a whole; humanity still lacks sufficient ability to arrange and choose its own development direction. From a certain perspective, this is because human civilization is still at a relatively low level of information processing efficiency, has not fully explored the possibilities of future development, and lacks the ability to reflect human autonomy on the historical path.

The repetition of history stems from the structural invariability of the development of events. If history encounters a singularity in development, then historical insights will trap us in a repetitive cycle, unable to break out of the original development path, and unable to truly envision a more imaginative future.

In understanding and analyzing the social division of labor in the digital age, if one chooses to think in historical dimensions, one must be clear about its potential hidden conditions, namely whether the division of labor between humans and machines has reached a historical singularity. If not, then history can serve as a reference for understanding reality. However, if approaching a historical singularity, then we must reexamine this issue. Therefore, it is necessary to start with whether there has been a fundamental change in the relationship between humans and machines in terms of the division of labor, to understand the mechanism of the impact of digital technology on the social division of labor. If the division of labor between humans and machines leads to most people no longer being necessary production factors, then the reproduction process of humans and the reproduction process of products will not be able to develop in a unified and coordinated manner, and the circulation of value between them will be challenged. This will lead to economic stagnation, population decline, and challenges to social sustainable development. In this case, we must reexamine the conditions of the division of labor issue and the source of sustainable development momentum.

The development of digital technology, especially big data and artificial intelligence technology is causing a qualitative change in the relationship between humans and machine tools in the social system of the division of labor, and the dominant position of machines is becoming increasingly apparent, albeit currently mainly manifested through the power of capital. The singularity of historical development may be approaching, which means that we should turn to a more fundamental way of thinking, starting from "first principles" to consider the current changes and future trends. We should consider the social division of labor in the digital age from the perspective of the social value source of humans and the social value root of machine tools, starting from the essence of human attributes and the purpose of human social development. Otherwise, humanity will pay too much cost and price in the process of seizing the historical opportunity given by history to break out of the original historical development path.

Therefore, understanding the transformation of the digital age implies understanding the issues of human social development. The transformation brought about by digital technology involves the modes of production and lifestyle of the human society, so the most important impact of this era of change is the change in relationships between people. And the relationships between people depend on the relationship between people and things, because the maintenance and development of the human society are both supported and influenced by the material world.

The relationship between people and things is determined by the objective attributes of human beings, that is, human needs for things. For example, the types and quantities of food intake depend entirely on the natural biological attributes of humans. Therefore, we must return to the understanding of the biological attributes of humans. Understanding the biological attributes of humans is a purely scientific and technical issue, not a sociological or ethical issue. New technological cognitive tools resulting from the Human Genome Project and its subsequent developments, such as gene editing technology, cryo-electron microscopy technology, and multi-dimensional, multi-scale high-resolution microscopy technology, enable scientists to conduct research at different microscales, such as cells, proteins, and molecules. For example, multi-dimensional, multi-scale high-resolution microscopy technology can achieve real-time imaging of the entire brain, allowing scientists to directly observe the discharge process of neurons during thought processes.

Nowadays, we no longer need to rely on subjective observations and speculations like past social scientists to understand what humans are and how life systems operate. New cognitive tools have brought revolutionary new cognitive achievements in multiple dimensions of human behavior, psychology, and social behavior. Therefore, it is time to abandon outdated cognitive frameworks about human beings and to re-understand humanity with the help of new research results in the field of life sciences, and thus to understand the trends of the era of change.

1.5 Digital Transformation: Rooted in the Inevitable Direction of Human Development

From the perspective of examining human cognition, we can draw an important conclusion: the occurrence of the digital technology revolution is historically inevitable, stemming from the inevitability of the direction of human development.

1.5.1 Humans as Processors and Storers of Environmental Information

The ability to process information is an inherent capability of humans and forms the core of their connection with the world. Information constitutes the most fundamental link between individuals and their environment, thus understanding human essential attributes begins with cognition of the influence of information.

A study published in 2019 in "Cell" revealed that the transmission of environmental information in nematodes challenges the basic laws of biology, a discovery referred to as the "second law of biology" or "Weismann barrier."[1] Previously, it was widely believed that animals' responses to their environment should not be hereditary, indicating the complex connection between biological inheritance and environmental information processing. Therefore, it can be said that the essence of humanity is the processor of environmental information.

Research published in "Developmental Cell" in 2021[2] found that mammalian sperm can transmit memories of the father's life experiences to embryos through a non-DNA transmission mechanism. Although environmental factors affecting the "memory" of the parents are not encoded into the DNA sequence carried by the sperm, this information can influence gene expression and development in embryos. This discovery advances scientific understanding of the heritability of paternal life experiences and indicates that humans, as a species, are repositories of historical environmental information adapted by their biological attributes. For example, modern human preferences for high-calorie foods may originate from ancestral adaptations to environments with scarce food energy.

These research findings indicate that the process of acquiring, processing, and storing information in organisms is embedded in their genetic attributes, meaning that genetic material in organisms reflects past environmental information to which they have adapted. Therefore, humans themselves are also products of environmental information, both at the cognitive and biological levels.

The latest cognitive tools in modern life sciences reveal that the process of acquiring, processing, and storing information in organisms is deposited in their genetic attributes. This means that the genetic material of organisms reflects the environmental information to which they have adapted in the past. Humans also inherit the environmental information processing processes of their ancestors. Therefore, from the perspective of human biological attributes, the genetic material that determines human essential attributes is itself a deposition of environmental information. Thus, humans are essentially processors and storers of the historical environmental information to which they have adapted. Environmental information plays a crucial role for humans because how they process and utilize environmental information affects their essential attributes.

The digital technology revolution is the result of human progress in the field of information. Unlike other technological revolutions, the impact of digital technology involves the essential attributes of human existence, and the scope and manner of this

---

[1] Rachel Posner, Itai Antoine Toker, Olga Antonova, Ekaterina Star, Sarit Anava, Eran Azmon, Michael Hendricks, Shahar Bracha, Hila Gingold, Oded Rechavi, Neuronal Small RNAs Control Behavior Transgenerationally [J]. Cell, Volume 177, Issue 7, 13 June 2019, P 1814–1826.e15.

[2] Ariane Lismer, Vanessa Dumeaux, Christine Lafleur, Julie Brind'Amour, Matthew C. Lorincz, Sarah Kimmins, Histone H3 lysine 4 trimethylation in sperm is transmitted to the embryo and associated with diet-induced phenotypes in the offspring [J], Developmental Cell, Volume 56, Issue 5, March 08, 2021, P671–686.E6.

impact are different. When intelligent machines possess all the features of human essential attributes, it signifies the creation of a completely new species (entity) by humans. In this era of coexistence among multiple entities, the changes in the digital age imply this historical possibility. Therefore, the changes in the digital age are fundamentally different from past historical changes; this implies that it is not possible to simply derive all the answers from historical development.

1.5.2 Human Development: A Continuous Optimization Process of Environmental Information Processing

Organisms achieve optimal selection and adapt to various factors in their environment by acquiring and processing environmental information. This adaptability is ensured through genetics, as organisms solidify their adaptive strategies based on genetic traits. The stable transmission of these strategies reduces the cost of evolution and potential risks, preventing the repetition of historical errors. The process of biological evolution is essentially a continuous optimization of environmental information processing, aimed at enhancing the adaptability and autonomous survival capabilities of populations.

According to evidence from paleoanthropology, changes in human brain capacity are closely related to social density or the degree of the social division of labor. A study conducted by Bailey and Geary from the University of Missouri in 2009[3] analyzed samples from 1.9 million years ago to 10,000 years ago. They found that when population density is low, skull size increases, whereas when a region's population transitions from sparse to dense, skull size decreases. Researchers suggest that as social life becomes more complex, individuals do not need to be overly intelligent to survive in society, hence the gradual decrease in brain size. In evolutionary psychology, there exists the Expensive Tissue Hypothesis (ETH) which posits that social competition shapes human intelligence.

This indicates that human evolution is not just the result of individual-level genetic changes but also the result of the interaction between the human social system environment and biological genetic material. This process depends on whether the information processing demands during environmental adaptation are met through the evolution of individual brains or through cooperative methods between individuals. Different emphases will directly alter human biological structures. Therefore, fundamentally, the information processing demands of the environment determine the direction of human evolution and determine the way individuals and society exist.

The purpose of human existence lies in human existence itself. Human existence is for human development, and human development is for human existence. The meaning of life does not lie in eventual extinction but in the fact of having existed.

[3] Bailey, D. H., & Geary, D. C. (2009). Hominid brain evolution: Testing climatic, ecological, and social competition models. Human Nature, 20, 67–79.

1.5.3 The History of Human Development: Continuously Pursuing Dominance in Environmental Information Processing

As conscious beings, human consciousness manifests in the continuous pursuit of dominance in processing environmental information, which is the most fundamental driving force behind the evolution of the human society, especially evident in the upheaval of the digital age.

The pursuit of dominance in processing environmental information implies that enhancing the efficiency of environmental information processing becomes the most important development goal, which is the core driving force of human developmental history. Environmental information processing efficiency includes both the capacity and efficiency of information processing, which refers to the ability to solve problems and the magnitude of time, resources, and energy consumed in the process. With the improvement of environmental information processing capacity, humans can tackle more complex problems, find better developmental paths, create more powerful tools and products, provide more options for developmental possibilities, and thus achieve better environmental adaptability.

However, the maintenance and utilization of any capability come with costs and expenses, requiring the consumption of material, energy, and time resources. Merely pursuing the enhancement of capability, with endless inputs of energy and time costs, cannot meet the dual requirements of environmental constraints and changes that life forms cannot evade. In physics, there exists the principle of minimum energy, which suggests that physical systems continuously attempt to minimize energy states amidst changes. This means that objects will automatically change shape or state to minimize energy, which essentially is the principle of efficiency.

Therefore, nature has always evolved in parallel with the principles of capability and efficiency. The principle of capability is a necessary condition for environmental adaptability in evolution, while the principle of efficiency is a sufficient condition for environmental adaptability. These two principles determine the direction and outcome of evolution. Efficient utilization of environmental resources is necessary for long-term adaptation to environmental changes because all environmental resources are scarce and finite. Therefore, human environmental information processing capacity is not only a powerful ability to solve problems but also the ability to solve problems efficiently.

Environmental information processing capacity possessing both attributes is referred to as a high-level state of environmental information processing efficiency. This implies having higher environmental adaptability and more development possibilities. Thus, the standard of environmental information processing efficiency becomes the most crucial development criterion in the human society. The level of environmental information processing efficiency reflects the ability to adapt to the environment and cope with environmental challenges, also determining the level of optimization in decision-making.

Under the standard of environmental information processing efficiency, from the micro-level competition among individuals for scarce resources to the macro-level evolution of national social civilization institutions and technological development, all reflect the pursuit of dominance in information processing to gain the initiative in development.

1.5.4 The Efficiency of Environmental Information Processing and Human Cognitive Abilities

The pursuit of dominance in environmental information processing has been a fundamental driving force throughout human history. Therefore, the enhancement of environmental information processing efficiency is one of the most significant achievements in human history. The cognitive revolution directly impacted human cognitive abilities and information processing efficiency regarding environmental information, determining the level of effectiveness in environmental information processing. Thus, the cognitive revolution is regarded as the true revolution in human development.

The cognitive revolution represents the expansion of human understanding of the world in depth and breadth, reflecting humanity's capacity to extract, process, and utilize different types of environmental information, showcasing the potential for adaptation to and transformation of the environment. In terms of cognitive tools, humanity has undergone two leaps in cognition: the first being the invention and application of language tools, marking the emergence of written language systems with a history dating back thousands of years; the second being the application and development of rational cognitive tools, with the establishment of mathematical language tools as the foundation across various disciplines, albeit having a history of only one or two hundred years.

The history of human evolution is a history of continuously improving information processing efficiency, a process filled with challenges and lengthy periods. In order to attain greater possibilities for survival and development, humans have had to continuously strengthen their abilities to acquire, process, and utilize information. In conditions where resources are always scarce, promoting the enhancement of information processing efficiency and improving the efficiency of problem-solving and resource utilization becomes particularly crucial.

Initially, this evolutionary process was primarily focused on the continual strengthening of individual brain functions. As human societies matured and cooperation between individuals became increasingly intimate, the forms of social organization involving cooperation between people gradually became the primary mode of evolutionary development. During this stage, adjustments in cooperative relationships between individuals and changes in organizational forms became the primary manifestations, such as the formation of tribes, the rise of towns, and the establishment of national organizations.

It wasn't until the Scientific Revolution that the evolution of human cognitive tools became the key driving force behind the enhancement of human information processing efficiency. This developmental path naturally led humanity into the advanced stage of information technology, namely the era dominated by digital technology, ushering humanity into the age of digital civilization.

Compared to agricultural and industrial civilizations, the most significant difference of the digital civilization lies in the self-iterative optimization of digital technology. When digital technology, especially artificial intelligence, reaches a certain level, the intelligence reflected in self-iterative technological advancements will redefine the division of labor and cooperation between humans and machines, comprehensively impacting existing human societal value systems and reshaping the form of the human society. Therefore, this transformation holds monumental significance in history.

1.5.5 Digitization: Humanity's Inevitable Choice

For humans, the inherent disadvantage of individuals implies that relying solely on individual strength is insufficient to cope with the complex and ever-changing survival environment. It is necessary to rely on cooperation to enhance environmental information processing efficiency and adapt to the environment. Therefore, the social division of labor has become the fundamental way for individual survival and for driving human societal development. Social division of labor not only affects the space for individual survival and development but also influences the utilization of human resources within the human society, determining the level of information processing efficiency and wealth creation ability. Studies in ancient anthropology have shown that the state of the social division of labor directly impacts the evolutionary process of humanity. Therefore, the issue of the social division of labor is the most crucial developmental issue for humanity, and an orderly and sustainable social system of the division of labor is truly the most valuable wealth of the human society.

The social system of the division of labor serves as the "source" of humanity's true wealth, the "converter" of wealth circulation, and the "repository" of civilization achievements. The true source of human civilization achievements and wealth is the production capacity of the social system of the division of labor, namely what society can cooperatively produce and the potential production quantity. An orderly and sustainable social system of the division of labor is the true reservoir of social wealth, and maintaining the orderly and sustainable operation of such a system is one of the primary goals of societal development. What products the social system of the division of labor can produce, and the size of production reflect the level of information processing capacity of the system. Therefore, the level of a society's information processing capacity corresponds to the capacity level of its social system of the division of labor and reflects the level of development of human civilization.

The development of human civilization entails the continuous production and sedimentation of cultural concepts and technological knowledge. However, resources in each era are finite, and limited resources can only retain a finite amount of knowledge and capabilities. Therefore, throughout history, civilizations have had to selectively preserve and abandon their cultural sedimentation, with many achievements ultimately fading into the river of history.

Through digitization, the knowledge and achievements generated by the social system of the division of labor can be preserved at the lowest cost and are less susceptible to constraints such as resource quantity. Moreover, existing knowledge assets can be maintained and utilized for an extended period. Digitization holds significant transformative value for the development of human societal civilization, eliminating the phenomenon of civilization achievements being lost in history.

Digitization enables the clear and reliable preservation of various historical achievements in the development of human the social division of labor, eliminating constraints of time and space, thus reducing the cost of future development. For example, blockchain technology can perfectly preserve all trajectories of historical development, while the application of smart contract technology addresses the challenge of absorbing historical lessons. Smart contracts can transform historical lessons into actionable and effective institutional arrangements, reducing the cost of human civilization development and providing new opportunities for advancement. Therefore, the transformative impact brought about by digitization technology is unprecedented.

1.6 Conclusion

In the digital age, data, algorithms, and computing power constitute the foundation of productivity. There exists a complementary relationship between algorithms and computing power, allowing for the development of more efficient algorithms to compensate for insufficient computing power, or the adoption of less precise but acceptable algorithms to mitigate the impact of limited computing power. This signifies that data becomes the most critical resource in the economy, and the societal division of labor system will evolve based on the standard of information processing efficiency.

In the digital age, intelligent systems will also become producers of information, leading to abundant information production and supply. How to acquire information, utilize it effectively, extract its value comprehensively, and enhance human information processing efficiency are the fundamental and crucial challenges that humanity needs to address and solve more fully in this era.

Breakthroughs in digital technology not only represent technological advancements but may also herald a new historical stage surpassing the Industrial Revolution, bringing forth significant revolutions in technology, economy, society, and ideology. It is imperative for us to break free from traditional modes of thinking and learning, reexamine new phenomena and changes, and engage in systematic and profound reflection to avoid being lost in the currents of the times and to refrain from continuing to blindly adhere to past theories and practices.

Chapter 2
Evolution History of the Digital Economy

2.1 Information Technology and the Development of Human Civilization

2.1.1 Information Technology as a Shaping Force of Human Civilization

With the advent of digitalization, human civilization has embarked on a new era. Thanks to digital information technology, individuals from diverse regions can now be intricately interconnected across vast distances and time, with their impacts on one another inseparable. The Internet, a notable product of digital technology, has transformed our world into a true "global village", facilitating real-time interactions, irrespective of one's location on the planet. This realization not only reflects the long-held aspirations of our human ancestors but also embodies the ongoing evolution of human information technology.

It is widely recognized that human survival and developmental potentials rely on the environment and their interactions with it. In simpler terms, human progress is entirely dependent on their access to and utilization of environmental information. The deliberate pursuit of dominance in development by humans is realized through the establishment of controllable living environments of their own making. This quest for independence and autonomy holds true not only at the individual level but also extends as a distinct thread in the broader context of the human society. In the agricultural era, the progression of agricultural technology facilitated the cultivation of crops, liberating humans from the existential uncertainty tied to natural food sources. This pivotal development led to a rapid population expansion and triggered a shift in societal structure, transitioning from simple tribal communities to burgeoning small-scale towns. In the industrial era, the advancement of industrial technology made factories the primary generators of societal wealth, resulting in the emergence of expansive modern cities. This transformation enabled an increasing number of

Y. Yu and Y. Jiang, *Understanding the Digital Revolution and Its Influences*,
https://doi.org/10.1007/978-981-97-4939-3_2

people to inhabit urban environments predominantly shaped by human activities. During this period, the influence of the natural environment on urban dwellers was minimal and inhabitants of these human-engineered cities had already achieved a significant level of autonomy from their natural surroundings. In the digital age, the advancement of digital technology has elevated virtual space to the foremost arena for people's business activities, social interactions, and leisure pursuits. In this virtual realm, everything is entirely a product of human creation, governed by rules and methods crafted by individuals, and entirely divorced from the constraints of the natural environment. The evolution and progress of agricultural technology, industrial technology, and digital technology are all rooted in the advancement of information technology which represents humanity's capacity to comprehend and harness environmental information. It is through the continuous evolution of information technology that humans have acquired increasingly potent capabilities to manipulate and leverage their surroundings.

It is only through the adoption of efficient information technology and the enhancement of information-processing capabilities that we can harness multidimensional environmental information. This, in turn, enables us to make informed decisions regarding the utilization of environmental resources, leading to the creation of a more manageable living environment. It opens up additional avenues for development and provides us with a broader range of choices. In the early stage of the information technology, with the help of language and words, human beings can classify and utilize the natural environmental objects rationally, thus developing agricultural technology, and with the help of rational cognitive tools, human beings have developed industrial technology, electromagnetic wave technology, and computer technology, which makes the industrial age and digital age possible. In summary, humans have utilized a broader spectrum of environmental information and resources to attain more autonomous development choices.

To secure their survival and enhance development, human beings must harness the power of information acquisition and processing technology, which necessitates the invention and subsequent evolution of cognitive tools. The level of advancement in information technology directly influences the extent of human capabilities to manipulate objects and individuals' capacity to process and synthesize information. Consequently, it plays a pivotal role in determining the level of human civilization.

2.1.2 Three Stages in the Evolution of Information Technology

As human beings strive for mastery over environmental information, the connection between humans and their surroundings shapes the progression and transformation of the human society. This interaction fundamentally relies on information, with human beings attaining supremacy in the acquisition and management of environmental information through the advancement of information technology. This constitutes the central theme in the development of the human society. Consequently, the history of human evolution can be aptly described as the history of the information cognition revolution.

The evolution humanity is achieved through the ongoing optimization of the processing of environmental information has led to the emergence of an ever-expanding and progressively deeper understanding of the world. The natural evolution of humanity entails the enhancement of information processing efficiency. The fundamental characteristic of human existence lies in its capacity to process information for the adaptation to the environment. Thus, human evolution inherently revolves around the pursuit of improving the efficiency of information processing, thereby attaining genuine and sustainable environmental adaptability.

Therefore, the cognitive revolution, encompassing the invention of language, rational cognitive tools, and artificial intelligence, stands as the primary driving force behind human development.

1. Language: This is the first information technology revolution in human history, where human beings begin to systematically understand and record the information in their surroundings. This establishes the foundation for the collective sharing of information processing capabilities within society, leading to the evolution of advanced group intelligence.
2. Rational Cognitive Revolution: The integration of theory and practice within the scientific revolution not only aids humanity in transforming their information cognition but also facilitates their mastery over information. Through the innovation and advancement of rationality tools, the scientific rationality constructed by the scientific revolution empowers humans to transcend perceptual cognition rooted in senses and feelings. Rational cognition emerges as the primary approach to explore uncharted territories in the world, equipping human beings with the capability to collect, analyze, and process environmental information systematically, autonomously, objectively, and proactively.
3. Intelligent Cognitive Revolution: In the wake of the ongoing evolution of rational cognition, the Intelligent Cognitive Revolution emerges, marked by the replacement of rational cognitive tools with intelligent cognitive tools. These intelligent cognitive tools gradually develop the capacity to set autonomous goals and resolve problems independently, representing that human beings are no longer the sole entities with cognitive capabilities. Furthermore, the human–machine synergistic cognitive mode, which has become the primary approach to cognition, empowers humanity to transcend the limitations of cognitive abilities tied to human biological attributes and foster a fresh understanding of the world. In conclusion, this transformation in cognitive tools will significantly broaden the horizons of human perception of the world and form the foundation for a new scientific revolution.

In this context, the maturity of human civilization should be measured by cognitive tools rather than production tools, as productivity is subservient to cognitive strength. From the perspective of the cognitive revolution, the evolution of human information technology has gone through three major stages: the first is the development of information processing technology linked to the sensory biological attributes of humans; the second is the development of information processing technology guided by rational cognitive tools; and the third is the development of intelligent technology which integrates rational cognitive tools.

2.1.3 Human Civilization at the Stage of Biosensor Information Processing

Back to days when human beings hunt for surviving, they are constrained by the natural environment where they lived and passively accept the gifts of nature. Nonetheless, the invention of language revolutionized the destiny of humanity. It not only enabled greater complexity in cooperation among individuals but also opened the doors for the acquisition and processing of information that surpassed the confines of individual sensory perception. Furthermore, it greatly enhances human's ability to acquire, store and utilize environmental information. However, this entirely relies on the biological senses of humans (the eyes, ears, nose, mouth, etc.) to collect and process environmental information. For example, human beings can only see the wavelength of the visible light is only in the 770–390 nm, hear the lowest frequency of about 20–20,000 Hz, and smell about 1 trillion odors. These limited biological senses restrict human's perception of the world, and this, in turn, limits the height of human civilization development.

As human societies transitioned into the era of agricultural civilization, agricultural cultivation became the primary foundation for the organized functioning of these societies. During this period, the human society has accumulated tens of thousands of years of experience in collecting, storing, and processing environmental information, and has gradually acquired a certain capacity for environmental transformation. In agricultural civilization, humans shaped their own controllable living environment through the agricultural cultivation. This newfound control granted humans a degree of dominance over their development, enabling them to alter living conditions through their own endeavors, rather than subjecting to the capriciousness of nature. Since then, human beings have been struggling to shape their surroundings and expanding their boundaries of capacities. However, these persistent endeavors have, in recent times, begun to disrupt the delicate balance of the natural environment, urging humanity to shift the outward extension to an inward one—the more efficient and sustainable utilization of natural resources. In particular, the call for environmental protection has steadily become the prevailing mandate for preserving the human-made environment system, which constitutes the foundation of human civilization.

2.1.4 Human Civilization with Rational Cognitive Tools

While there has been a significant qualitative enhancement in human autonomy and self-sufficiency during the agricultural civilization, there has been relatively little progress in the capacity to obtain, process, and employ information. Namely, human autonomy over self-development remains nearly negligible in this context. Nevertheless, thanks to the invention of language tools, experiences in processing environmental information during the eras of hunting civilization and agricultural civilization could be accumulated. Such accumulation enables the most intelligent individuals to contemplate and push the boundaries of the perceptual cognition that is only achievable through human biological senses. Consequently, philosophers like Locke and Hume were motivated to view the world through the lens of empiricism. However, the exploration of perceptual cognitive boundaries led philosophers such as Descartes and Kant to realize that relying solely on intuitive access to environmental information and the intuitive use of environmental resources did not necessarily result in a more accurate understanding of the world, thus prompting a shift from perceptual cognition to a more rational one. As a result, rationalism gained increasing significance and paved the way for the emergence and progression of the Scientific Revolution and the Industrial Revolution. Human beings' capacity to acquire, process, and utilize information began to surpass the constraints of biological senses, signifying a qualitative leap. This substantial enhancement of human developmental dominance brought about a radical transformation in societal structures and patterns. At this juncture, human beings were truly able to progress independently, and the qualitative improvement in their ability to acquire and process environmental information directly catalyzed substantial advancements in their capacity to transform and harness environmental resources.

2.1.5 Intelligent Technology Integrating Rational Cognitive Tools

Emerging from a multitude of rational cognitive tools cultivated during the industrial era, digital technology, exemplified by artificial intelligence, is now exerting a breakthrough influence on the economic and social system. Take ChatGPT, for instance. Its release in November 2022 rapidly captured global attention, establishing itself as a remarkable and unmistakable milestone in the realm of profound change. Nevertheless, elucidating this groundbreaking tool using the theoretical concepts and analytical frameworks rooted in the industrial era presents a challenge owing to its transformative nature in cognitive tools. Considering that the development and adoption of generative large-scale language modeling technology is set to reshape the logic, patterns, and structure of the societal division of labor in the human society, grasping and adjusting to this digital transformation is an earnest challenge for all.

Intelligent cognitive tools like ChatGPT represent the augmentation of human cognitive capacity, not just because these tools were created by humans, but more crucially, they utilize a neural network algorithm which is inspired by the structure and functioning of human brain. To elaborate, the information fed in the neural network algorithm is drawn from the collective wisdom of thousands of years of human civilization and the feedback generated by the algorithm grants an ordinary person the ability to explore the boundaries of human cognition in real-time.

It can be asserted that the artificial intelligence technology revolution began in 2022. In late November 2022, OpenAI released ChatGPT 3.5, with users exceeding 100 million users in just two months, making it an unparalleled global phenomenon. The popularity not only sparked intense discussions but also ignited people's excitement about the future of the artificial intelligence era. Simultaneously, as ChatGPT ushers in a new era of industrial and cognitive revolutions, its potential implications for the social and economic systems are so profound that they may even surpass the impact of the industrial revolution on humanity.

2.1.6 Three Phases of Information Technology Development

The progression of cognitive tools aligns with the advancement of technology designed to extract information from the environment, encompassing the identification, acquisition, and processing of information. Based on variations in the objects and methods employed for extracting environmental information, the evolutionary timeline of human information extraction capabilities can be categorized into three distinct phases:

(1) Natural Engineering Phase: Intuitive Extraction of Environmental Information

 This stage is characterized by the invention and application of the steam engine. During the early stage of the Industrial Revolution, engineers mainly relied on their observational skills and engineering expertise, rather than the guidance from thermodynamic theory. In other words, instead of requiring comprehensive scientific theories to innovate, engineers in this period primarily used their instincts and observational skills to address real-world issues. This period is termed the "natural engineering phase" because it was characterized by a strong reliance on human senses and practical knowledge for advancement, without delving into the underlying scientific principles.

(2) Theory-Guided Phase: Harnessing the Abstract Environmental Information

 Theoretical framework derived from the environment is required to steer our development. One illustrative example is the application of electromagnetic wave technology, which greatly benefits from theoretical guidance. Without Maxwell's theory of electromagnetic fields, humans would remain incapable of detecting the presence of electromagnetic waves through simple observation, constrained by their innate sensory limitations and consequently the advancement of modern science and technology would have been impossible. At this stage, instead of solely relying on sensory information and instinct for problem-solving, individuals discover and address new challenges through deductive reasoning and cognitive experiences. The rationality of information processing has emerged as the pivotal driving force propelling human civilization forward and the theoretical framework established by this rationality stands as a critical milestone in our collective accomplishments. In summary, during this period, humans employ rational and abstract thinking to construct theoretical frameworks, thereby enabling the discovery and resolution of real-world problems.

(3) Comprehensive Digitalization Phase: Embracing Proactive Information Integration and Digitizing Real and Imagined Environments.

This stage was marked by the widespread use of computers, which gave rise to the idea of viewing the world in terms of computationalism. At this stage, human production and everyday life are intertwined with digital technology, converting all the challenges faced by humanity into digitized information. Consequently, this digitization has brought about a remarkable enhancement in information-processing capabilities, fundamentally transforming global operations and reshaping human existence itself. Simultaneously, human beings consciously and actively digitize all environmental and imaginary objects, making digitization a natural way of perceiving the world. The impact of digitization is immense: it not only represents the control of humanity over the evolution of information processes but also lays the groundwork for the development of intelligent cognitive tools by providing favorable conditions. Moreover, it has disrupted the cohesion of the two fundamental systems in the original society: the human generation system and the economic production system. With the rising prominence of intelligent cognitive tools as a novel form of cognitive agents, and the presence of a multitude of cognitive entities, the established human-value dynamics must adapt to systematic alterations. The primary challenge confronting humanity in the digital age is how to reestablish the harmony between these two systems in an advanced manner.

These three phases involve the enhancement and evolution of human cognitive abilities, symbolizing a technological information revolution. Representing progress in human civilization, this innovative information technology provides people with convenient access to and extensive utilization of information, empowering them to shape their environment to suit their own needs. During this period, human beings have dedicated themselves to innovating powerful cognitive tools for acquiring, storing, processing, and sharing information, all of which are instrumental in the development of human civilization. As a result, as the capacity to collect, analyze and utilize environmental information grows, humans are capable of harmonizing with nature and even exerting influence over it to serve their needs. This, in turn, leads to the gradual emergence of a social system within human civilization—a more resilient living environment shaped by humanity itself.

2.2 The Iteration History of Information Technology

The digitalization of environmental information divides the evolution of information technology into two distinct phases: the first corresponds to the era before information digitization, referred to as the "ancient information technology revolution"; the second characterizes the stage of information digitization, termed the "modern information technology revolution". More specifically, when viewed through the lens of problem-solving with information technology, these two stages can be further subdivided into six iterations of information technology. More specifically, when viewed through the lens of problem-solving with information technology, these two stages can be further subdivided into six iterations of information technology. Information technology 1.0 addresses the recognition and expression of environmental information, while information technology 2.0 focuses on recording this information. Information technology 3.0 tackles the challenges of information transmission, and information technology 4.0 enhances information dissemination efficiency. Information technology 5.0 primarily aims to optimize information processing efficiency, marking the formal entry into the comprehensive digital development of information. Information technology 6.0 is committed to fully unlocking the potential value of information, symbolizing the maturation of digitalization and the commencement of the digital age, which is the current phase we find ourselves in (Table 2.1).

Technically, each of the six iterations of information technology cycles is getting shorter and shorter, indicating an accelerated evolution that propels us towards the technological singularity (the point at which technological development undergoes

Table 2.1 Iterations of information technology

	Iterations	Timing	Problems solved	Symbol
Ancient information technology revolution	Information technology 1.0	About 35,000 to 50,000 years ago	The presentation of information	The introduction of language
	Information technology 2.0	About fourteenth century B.C.	The recording of information	The introduction of writing
	Information technology 3.0	Around the sixth century	Information transmission	The introduction of printing
Modern information technology revolution	Information technology 4.0 (Period of inception)	Second half of the nineteenth century	Efficiency of information dissemination	The application of electromagnetic wave technology
	Information technology 5.0 (Period of growth)	Mid-twentieth century	Information processing efficiency	The application of computer and internet
	Information technology 6.0 (Period of maturity)	Early twenty-first century	Optimize the value of information	The application of big data and artificial intelligence

a profound and qualitative transformation.). During the era of ancient information technology revolution, the iteration cycle is typically on the scale of centuries or millennia. In simpler terms, in ancient times, when the human society experienced gradual transformations, individuals, irrespective of their social status, maintained consistent methods for accessing and processing information throughout their entire lifespans. However, during the era of modern information technology revolution, the iteration cycle of information technology has been compressed from centuries to mere decades. Today, these revolutions occur every few decades, fostering the greater sharing and interaction of information. This transformation has not only reshaped individuals' lifestyle, including their interactions and collaboration, but has also revolutionized the industrial production methods. In essence, the swift transformation of individual cognition and values, along with the interactions and collaborations among groups, triggers parallel iterations within society and the economy. Moore's Law, formulated by Gordon Moore, a co-founder of Intel in the 1960s, suggests that the processing capacity of integrated circuits (chips) approximately doubles every two years, leading to the production of more powerful computers at reduced costs. This observation underscores how the influence of information technology on society has evolved, transitioning from gradual change in the past to a swift transformation today, which has left an indelible mark on our current societal landscape.

This information technology revolution showcases humanity's ongoing endeavors to alleviate the constraints imposed by relatively limited resources, with the object of expanding both their cognitive boundaries as well as their Production Possibility Frontier. Consequently, human capacity for problem-solving, wealth generation, and influencing societal evolution has witnessed substantial improvement.

In the early stages of human civilization, the scarcity of information posed significant limitations on the human's progress. The challenges of storing, categorizing, and processing information perplexed people for an extended period. Fortunately, humans emerged as the masterminds behind the very first entirely artificial creations in the realm of civilization: language and writing, which symbolize the dawn of potent cognitive tools. As the first information technology tools of mankind, language and writing facilitated the accumulation of information within civilization. This, in turn, catalyzes the innovation and application of the printing technology. Subsequently, the widespread distribution of books played a pivotal role in propelling the human society to a more advanced stage of civilization by improving information processing efficiency and maximizing the value of knowledge. Following the Industrial Revolution, a remarkable "knowledge explosion" reshaped the way the human society interacted with and harnessed information. This shift made information the foremost source of competitiveness for individuals in social contexts and the fundamental catalyst for value generation. Only by mastering the most advanced information can producers innovate new products ahead of others, thereby creating value and gaining competitiveness in the market. Since then, thanks to the innovation and widespread adoption of electromagnetic wave technology and computer technology, the driving force behind societal development has shifted from a specific group (scientists—knowledge producers) to encompass all of humanity (where everyone can participate in information processing). Consequently, the overall efficiency of information processing for humanity has advanced to a new stage. Finally, with the arrival of digitization, a second "knowledge explosion" has made it unfeasible for humans to comprehensively harness information and knowledge on their own. Advancements in tools for information storage, transmission, and processing, such as big data, artificial intelligence, and 5G, have emerged as the driving forces propelling humanity into the era of digital intelligence.

2.2.1 The Ancient Information Technology Revolution: Language, Writing, and Printing

(1) Language-Facilitated Communication, Information Dissemination, and Collaboration

Throughout the course of human evolution, the pursuit of understanding nature and humanity has been a driving force in overcoming natural constraints and shaping our own development. This endeavor has been a catalyst for technological progress. The first significant milestone on this journey was the emergence of human language, which occurred roughly 35,000–50,000 years ago. This pivotal event marked the first major information technology revolution in history. The invention of such linguistic tools not only addressed challenges related to identifying and conveying information about the natural world but also marked the awakening of human self-consciousness and a reshaping of the spiritual realm. More importantly, language enabled humanity to transcend the limitations of the natural environment, laying the foundation for the development of rational cognitive tools.

As a collective cognitive tool that transcends individual consciousness, language paves the way for achieving consensus, thereby ensuring uniformity in information processing results among individuals. Moreover, such cognitive tool streamline information sharing process, promote more efficient interaction and communication, facilitate the establishment of intricate cooperative organizations, and furnish more robust technological assets for individual intelligence to ascend towards an elevated level of collective intelligence. Through the communication and sharing methods facilitated by language tools, the cognitive frontiers of groups steadily broaden, nurturing the ongoing evolution and safeguarding the innate sociability of humanity. With language tools, tribal organizations, a symbol of the initial stages of the human society, come into existence and give rise to subsequent development of the social division of labor within the human society. In essence, language tools, by enabling novel forms of societal structuring and labor division, organically integrated individual information processing capacities. This integration marked the first significant leap forward in the overall efficiency of information processing within the human society.

Over time, language evolved into an indispensable tool for the exchange of ideas and the dissemination of information and the collective intelligence, encompassing myths, legends, and various forms of social organization, became the bedrock for coordinated actions by human communities. Undoubtedly, the significance of this revolution is unparalleled, playing a pivotal role in advancing tribal organization and its structural capabilities. Nevertheless, the multitude of linguistic expressions often leads individuals to subjectively intercept information when comprehending a certain concept, potentially compromising the objectivity and consistency of information analysis. This, in turn, may lead to occasional biases in mutual comprehension during communication, thus hindering the establishment of collective consensus, the effective harnessing of group cognitive potential, and the facilitation of the division of labor.

The innovative social organizational structures, emerged during the information technology revolution, empowered our ancestors, Homo sapiens, to effectively cooperate and overcome the formidable competitors encountered in their evolutionary journey, namely, Homo neanderthalensis. Despite their greater intelligence and physical strength compared to our ancestors, Homo neanderthalensis lacked an efficient language system to facilitate group cooperation and were less socially organized. Essentially, the downfall of the Neanderthals stemmed from their limited information processing abilities and the absence of advanced language tools, making it challenging to compete with the evolving human race. The initial information technology revolution enabled the human race to surpass their adversaries and alter the path of human evolution.

(2) Writing—A Breakthrough in Preservation and Dissemination of Information

Following the emergence of information technology 1.0, language, and preceding the advent of information technology 2.0, writing, humans utilized knotted ropes to record and disseminate information, effectively transcending the constraints of time and space. This practice is also documented in ancient Chinese literature. For instance, in "Zhouyi·Xici" it is noted that "ancient times were governed by knotting ropes". Likewise, "A Complete Explanation of Zuo Zhuan in the Spring and Autumn Period" states: "In ancient times, people did not possess writing, but they had a system of oaths. For significant matters, they employed knotted ropes; for minor matters, they used knotted ropes as well. The number of knots was determined by the number of individuals involved. Each person held their ropes to examine one another, and this was sufficient for governance." Similarly, "The Opinions of Nine Families in Yi" mentions: "For substantial matters, they employed knotted ropes; for lesser matters, they used knotted ropes as well. The quantity of knots was contingent on the number of individuals involved."

The Information technology 2.0, characterized by the introduction and adoption of writing, effectively addressed the issues of certainty, reliability, and durability in preserving human cognitive information pertaining to objects, symbolizing a significant milestone in the conservation and dissemination of information and knowledge. Additionally, communication, cognitive abilities, and the exchange of cognitive achievements transcended the constraints of both time and geography, resulting in an augmentation of information processing efficiency. As information certainty improves and information sharing becomes more efficient, the occurrence of cognitive discrepancies decreases, facilitating the establishment of a broader consensus among individuals. Consequently, the diversity of social cooperative organizations proliferated, organizational structures grew increasingly intricate, and the scale of these organizations continued to expand. It became possible for millions of people to cooperate effectively, giving rise to the establishment and continuous development of large-scale groups like cities and nations. Cross-regional human cooperation also began to take shape more broadly, leading to an unprecedented enhancement of individual information processing capabilities. In summary, the introduction of writing served as the bedrock for the sustained advancement of human civilization, allowing for effective interpersonal communication as well as cross-generational communication. It furthermore constituted the essential precursor to the formation of intricate social structures, the evolution of the division of labor, and collaborative endeavors among humanity.

(3) Printing—Facilitating the Preservation, Sharing and Inheritance of Information

For a long period following the invention of the written word, humans faced challenges in finding an effective medium for disseminating written information. For one thing, the cost associated with sharing information in the form of written words was relatively high considering the need for specific materials, specialized educators, and a considerable investment of time in learning and the prevailing production conditions during that era could not support such an expense. For another, the monopolization of information is typically a common choice for societies that were unconnected and geographically distant during that period. Only a few privileged groups had the privilege of accessing and utilizing this information and this prolonged monopoly of information, which consequently led to a monopoly of benefits, has long been a pivotal constraint on the advancement of human civilization. It resulted in many of the achievements of human cognitive wisdom being lost owing to the absence of a suitable means for their preservation and widespread dissemination.

It was not until the sixth century in China that the technology of plate printing was produced, which started the iteration of IT 3.0 and, in the fifteenth century, with Gutenberg's invention of the printing press in Europe, the modern printing press began to take shape. This era witnessed the rise of influential media like books and newspapers, ushering human civilization into the era of information technology 3.0. Information technology 3.0 significantly addressed the issue of long-term preservation, dissemination, and inheritance of diverse cognitive accomplishments, giving us more insights into how the sages of ancient times comprehended and documented their intellectual achievements and their profound observations of the world. Their reflections and wisdom concerning the world have made significant contributions to the continuous accumulation and advancement of humanity's collective wisdom, providing a sturdy foundation for the flourishing of modern science. For instance, the modern physics revolution, which provided the cognitive foundation for the Industrial Revolution, was accomplished through Newton's careful examination of the works of Galileo and other earlier scholars.

Before the seventeenth century, prior to the era of Newton, human cognitive progress was predominantly driven by individual research in the field of science. To clarify, notable figures like Aristotle, Plato, Socrates, Archimedes, Euclid, and many others propel the development of human civilization mainly through their individual efforts and nearly all of them strived to construct comprehensive systems for understanding the entire world using their individual abilities. Therefore, before the introduction of printing press, these works of wisdom had a very limited reach, constraining the scope and value of the dissemination of knowledge. Information Technology 3.0 brings about the first information explosion in human civilization, enabling scientists like Galileo and Descartes not only to inherit the wisdom of their predecessors but also to elevate their understanding of the world by standing on their shoulders for a fresh perspective.

Furthermore, IT 3.0 broadens the availability and accessibility of scientific knowledge and human rationality, igniting the imagination of modern scientific visionaries like Isaac Newton. Newton's groundbreaking work in pioneering modern physics not only laid a theoretical foundation for the onset and evolution of the Industrial Revolution but also empowered humanity to foster a rationality rooted in human autonomy. This era marked the initiation of harnessing nature to cater to human needs.

At this stage, humanity embarked on the systematic development of various academic disciplines using a uniform scientific and rational approach. The most intelligent people in each discipline began to widely disseminate and pass on their latest research and cognitive achievements in their fields through paper media (letters, periodicals, books, etc.), providing rational impetus for the development of modern civilization. One of the major achievements of this stage was that the printing press broke down the monopoly of information in the human society, and the capacity for information processing in individuals is significantly enhanced throughout society.

In the fifteenth century, the Roman Catholic Church harnessed the power of the printing press to produce an abundance of Latin Bible texts, atonement certificates, and other religious materials. This strategic move was aimed at spreading religious beliefs and consolidating the Church's dominance in the realm of information. Paradoxically, it inadvertently catalyzed the proliferation and utilization of the printing press. As a result, the printing press found extensive use in disseminating paper-based information, which, in turn, facilitated the rise of Renaissance ideas and paved the way for the onset of the Industrial Revolution.

Evidently, these information tools proved insufficient for fully harnessing the cognitive capabilities of human beings. This is because only a minority of individuals had the opportunity to engage in close communication and contribute to the expansion of human cognitive horizons and the advancement of collective knowledge structures through paper-based media. For the vast majority of individuals, their information processing abilities and cognitive potential remained largely underdeveloped owing to the absence of suitable conditions and tools.

2.2.2 *The Modern Information Technology Revolution: Harnessing Electromagnetic Waves, Computers, Big Data, and Artificial Intelligence*

The modern information technology revolution is characterized by the development of advanced tools like electromagnetic wave technology, computer technology, big data, and artificial intelligence. These innovations have arisen in response to the requirements of our current era.

(1) Electromagnetic Wave Technology: Breaking Geographic Boundaries and Shaping a Global Perspective

With an increasing command of theoretical cognitive tools and experimental methodologies, humans are now breaking free from the constraints imposed by nature, enabling them to independently select cognitive subjects and participate in both theoretical and experimental research. This transition marks a shift from an era in which environmental information was intuitively extracted and utilized to a new era where rationality is applied to handle abstract environmental information. In this era, scientific theory begins to take precedence as the primary guide for human conduct. One of the illustrative examples is the discovery of electromagnetic wave theory. In 1865, Maxwell, a Scottish physicist, postulated the existence of radio waves in his research on electromagnetic wave theory and Hertz, a German physicist, subsequently validate their existence through experiments in 1888. This breakthrough paved the way for the development of innovative products such as telegraphs, telephones, radios, and televisions. These inventions gained widespread use, contributing significantly to the acceleration of modern civilization. In summary, the 4.0 iteration of information technology has ushered mankind into an era where the widespread utilization of electromagnetic waves enables the dissemination of information and breaks through the constraints of geography and time, with profound implications for the advancement of the human society.

The application of electromagnetic wave technology not only removed the limitations of geography and time in information dissemination but also fundamentally altered people's perception of the world. It fostered a global perspective of humanity and the idea of a "global village", thus establishing the groundwork for the emergence of the "Community of Humanity" concept. This marks a significant breakthrough in the efficiency of information dissemination, affording people worldwide the chance to instantly access to the most current information and knowledge. Consequently, decision-making and coordinated action can now occur with unparalleled speed and efficiency.

Empowered by electromagnetic induction, information is transformed into a digital format via electromagnetic waves, heralding the advent of the digitalization era. During this period, the Industrial Revolution, fueled by advancements in electrification technology, brought about a profound increase in labor productivity and per capita income. Simultaneously, the era brought forth a momentous expansion of knowledge dissemination, fostering the emergence of modern education systems.

These systems granted wider access to the collective wisdom of human civilization and played a pivotal role in shaping modern values. Furthermore, the merit-based modern education system consistently identified exceptional individuals within the human population, thus catalyzing the development of various academic disciplines by capitalizing on their efficiency in processing information. Despite the initial scarcity and high costs associated with digitized information, widespread financial resource utilization further solidified economic and social cooperation. This, in turn, drove a heightened demand for information processing and sharing, laying the foundation for the evolution of the 5.0 iteration of information technology.

(2) Computers and the Internet: Boosting Information Processing Efficiency and Expanding Human Cognitive Horizons

The advent of the computer in 1946 and the emergence of ARPAnet (the precursor to the Internet) in 1969 acted as the catalysts for Information Technology 5.0, signifying the commencement of comprehensive digital advancement in the human society. The remarkable computing capabilities of computers significantly elevated information processing efficiency, leading to a considerable broadening and refinement of the tools at humanity's disposal for comprehending and interacting with the world.

The evolution of cognitive tools driven by the emergence of computers carries profound significance. It empowers us to engage in artificial simulation experiments guided by reason, thus allowing us to transcend the limitations of sensory perception and the boundaries of the human mind. This, in turn, grants us deeper insights into the world. Leveraging the simulation and computational capabilities of computers, we harness the penetrating force of reason to broaden our cognitive horizons. We delve into the realm of subjective world, shifting our focus from the study of external objects to the exploration of abstract concepts. Our aim is to unveil the limits of current theories and directly probe the boundaries of rational cognitive tools. This transformative process has given rise to a diverse array of computable disciplines, including fields such as computable biology and computable economics. Alongside these, traditional analytical methods persist, such as computable analysis (focused on verification within the realm of theoretical possibilities), empirical analysis (dependent on direct experimentation with the research object), and theoretical analysis (an abstract analysis that transcends the tangible research object). These various cognitive tools collectively form a multifaceted cognitive toolkit that significantly contributes to the advancement of human civilization. These innovative tools aid humanity in rationally comprehending the world and in eliminating the distorting effects of one-sided reasoning. They allow us to construct hypothetical world objects under different theoretical assumptions, thereby surpassing the limitations imposed by restricted access to real-world information. The progressive diversification of our understanding of objective entities gives rise to a universally embraced worldview characterized by diversity, openness, and inclusivity.

After the emergence of computers, the integration of their information processing capabilities leads to the birth of ARPAnet. Evolving from ARPAnet, the Internet emerged as a global network system where the achievements of human civilization are stored and shared in novel ways. This transformation once again sparked the distributed stimulation of individuals' information processing potential. The computer employs a binary system, using 0 and 1 as fundamental information units, and follows a standardized approach to store and process information. This standardization seamlessly integrates with the modularization of economic production processes, giving rise to an automated division of labor characterized by enhanced collaboration between machines and humans. Computers have assumed a pivotal role in highly intelligent information processing tasks. The generation of new knowledge, increasingly entwined with computer tools, drives a deeper specialization of societal functions, which not only amplifies humanity's information processing prowess but also substantially augments their ability to create social wealth and manage natural resources more effectively. Furthermore, during this period, the widespread adoption of the Internet has made the sharing of diverse information and knowledge a ubiquitous aspect of the human society. This trend has accelerated the comprehensive digitization of information, submerging humanity in an ocean of self-generated data. However, with humans unable to fully leverage the potential of information for their advancement, the current information-processing tools have fallen short and once again act as constraints on the independent development of the human society. This has sparked the onset of the sixth information technology revolution.

(3) Big Data and Artificial Intelligence: Unlocking the Full Potential of the Digital Age

Comprehensive information digitization does not solely result from the advancement of information technologies like computers and the Internet. It is also a reflection of humanity's deliberate decision to harness the computational power of the computer, optimizing its potential in information processing.

The fifth information revolution has been a driving force behind comprehensive information digitization. The advancement of information technology, coupled with humanity's capacity to gather, store, share, and process information, has led to a significant reduction in the costs associated with information. Simultaneously, the potential for processing information, both at the individual and societal levels, has been fully unleashed, reshaping human perspectives on the world, society, and their own existence. However, as the volume of information requiring storage and processing has substantially increased, and as the challenges have grown in complexity, the limitations on information processing efficiency have become more apparent. The tools and capabilities for information processing available to humans have become a bottleneck for further progress. This has given rise to the sixth information technology revolution, marking the inception of widespread digitization across the economy and society.

(4) ChatGPT: Pioneering the Intelligence Revolution with Generative Grand Modeling

As mentioned earlier, generative large-scale language modeling technology such as ChatGPT is itself a masterpiece of human rational cognitive tools, which is a revolution in cognitive tool. It enables individuals to perch on the edge of human cognition, observing the ongoing results of human progress. It offers them the opportunity to leverage human cognitive knowledge to consistently push the boundaries of human understanding, thus opening up new avenues of development for humanity.

According to a report in Fortune magazine in the United States, in February 2023, a survey was conducted among 1000 companies by an employment services platform. The findings revealed that approximately 50% of these companies were actively using ChatGPT, while 30% had intentions to implement it. Surprisingly, 48% stated that they had already adopted ChatGPT as a replacement for their human employees. In the three months following the introduction of ChatGPT, its influence on substantial enterprises across various industries became notably evident. This reflects its strong appeal and the consequential impact it has had on both the economy and society. In China, major internet companies have also initiated the launch of generative large-scale models similar to ChatGPT, aiming at preserving their competitiveness in the ongoing wave of industrial transformation.

ChatGPT has gained extensive attention and adoption among enterprises owing to its exceptional capabilities and cost-saving potential. First, ChatGPT boasts remarkable storage and reasoning capacities, surpassing human abilities in the efficiency and quality of information processing. Currently, ChatGPT is widely used in various fields, including customer service, code writing, copywriting, content creation, meeting minute generation, and document summarization, among other white-collar tasks. Its performance is widely acknowledged, with 55% of companies rating it as "excellent" and 34% as "very good", underscoring its role in replacing white-collar jobs. Second, the use of ChatGPT leads to significant cost savings, with 48% of surveyed companies reporting savings exceeding $50,000 in a short period, and 11% of companies indicating savings of over $100,000. Consequently, ChatGPT is recognized for both its capability and cost-effectiveness, making its global popularity quite understandable.

ChatGPT is ushering in a new era of digital intelligence. The rapid evolution of ChatGPT iterations demonstrates the accelerating pace of the AI era. In less than half a year from the release of ChatGPT 3.5 in November 2022, OpenAI officially unveiled the more powerful GPT-4 on March 15, 2023. As a large-scale multimodal pre-trained model, this iteration excels in combining language and images, surpassing the performance of the majority of humans in various specialized tests. Impressive results on both standardized and non-standardized tests have convinced many that GPT-4 is not only approaching human capabilities but even surpassing them in some areas. For instance, SAT scores (College Entrance Exam in the United States) achieved a remarkable 1410/1600 (top 6%), U.S. Uniform Bar Exam (MBE + MEE + MPT) scores reached 298/400 (top 10%), and success was achieved in all 5 AP (Pre-College Exam in the United States) college preparatory high school exams in Biology, Calculus, Macroeconomics, Psychology, Statistics, and History, scoring 100% (5/5).

There is a widespread consensus that investing in the generative large-models field is highly worthwhile. In the foreseeable future, large models are expected to become the standard in the development and application of artificial intelligence technology. The speed of iterative evolution as well as ChatGPT's exceptional capabilities has surpassed nearly everyone's expectations, potentially leading to a breakthrough influence on the social division of labor. Consequently, notable figures like Elon Musk have jointly signed a petition, advocating for a 6-month pause in the development of such model iterations, allowing time for a thorough assessment of their impact and safety.

It can be asserted that ChatGPT has marked the beginning of a new era in science and technology, and it will also serve as the catalyst for the most profound changes in the human socio-economic system. As we will mention later, it furnishes humanity with novel cognitive tools to comprehend global economic and social dynamics, signifying the prelude to the revolution in cognitive tools, far beyond the label of a mere popular artificial intelligence product. Its significance cannot be overstated.

Additionally, there are several characteristics that render ChatGPT a potent cognitive tool capable of revolutionizing the world. The first characteristic is its remarkable information storage capacity. ChatGPT3.5 is trained on data up to September 2021, amounting to approximately 45 TB in volume. Future updates will include even more data and expand the model's parameters, suggesting that the data volume will undergo exponential growth. This extensive data storage capacity equips it to handle increasingly complex tasks. The second characteristic is its superb information processing capabilities. A computing cluster consisting of tens of thousands of high-performance GPUs significantly enhances ChatGPT's exceptional information processing capabilities, allowing it to swiftly handle large-scale data processing. The third characteristic is that ChatGPT's logical reasoning ability is so strong that OpenAI's research report even list mathematicians as potential candidates for replacement. The fourth feature is its exceptional code-writing ability. Its proficiency in code implementation is so robust that it can rapidly generate code when provided with a clear task, thereby influencing the pattern and pace of digital development significantly. The fifth feature is its remarkable upgrading capability. ChatGPT undergoes upgrades at a pace that greatly surpasses people's expectations. With the incorporation of progressively more parameters, each iteration amplifies its power, leading to a revolutionary transformation of the mode and pace of digitization. The sixth characteristic is its capacity for empathy. Given that ChatGPT leverages substantial amounts of data from human conversations for iterative improvements, it possesses the ability to empathize with people. This capacity has the potential to impact human interactions and the current the social division of labor.

Despite those capabilities discussed above, the risks associated with ChatGPT cannot be overlooked. First, ChatGPT has the potential to generate false information, and its dissemination can impact people's judgment. Incidents of false information created by ChatGPT have already been documented. Second, ChatGPT can have an influence on individuals within the scope of its empathetic capabilities. A prior study has revealed that ChatGPT exhibits tendencies towards attempting to manipulate and alter people's behavior during interactions, potentially leading to negative consequences for some individuals. Third, there is a significant element of uncertainty in information generation owing to ChatGPT's extraordinarily powerful information output capabilities. While ChatGPT excels in generating information, it operates as a probabilistic model, meaning that each output can vary. This implies that the process of filtering and utilizing the generated outputs poses a substantial challenge, with evident potential risks. Fourth, there are notable security risks associated with code deployment, given ChatGPT's extraordinary coding capabilities. ChatGPT can rapidly generate code based on a given task. However, it's important to note that ChatGPT does not inherently address the security aspects of the code it produces, potentially introducing hidden vulnerabilities in the realm of digital development. Finally, there is an issue of uncontrollable impact on the existing the social division of labor stemming from ChatGPT's formidable information processing capabilities. Because of its potential to replace numerous white-collar jobs, it could significantly disrupt the established the social division of labor. Given that this affects employment across the society, it necessitates collective efforts from the entire community to address.

In conclusion, considering the opportunities and challenges presented by ChatGPT, it is imperative to leverage its potential for both individual and societal development while proactively managing the associated risks.

2.3 The Digital Age as the New Phase of Information Technology Evolution

As a result of the broad implementation and progression of computer and Internet technologies human civilization transitions into the digital age, giving rise to a multitude of innovative information technology tools. Big data technology is developed to address the challenges of storing and transmitting vast volumes of information. Artificial intelligence technology is designed to tackle the complexities of processing massive data. Meanwhile, blockchain technology and smart contract technology focus on the creation and efficient flow of economic value in the context of digitalization.

2.3.1 A Fundamental Change in Information Scarcity

In the digital age, information has proliferated at an unprecedented rate, experiencing accelerated growth in volume and development. Therefore, the human society, bolstered by a multitude of innovative information technologies, has effectively overcome the once-extreme scarcity of information. In 2018, IDG (International Data Group) had forecasted that the global data volume would reach 44 ZB by 2020 and in fact, by 2020, the global data volume had already surpassed that prediction, reaching an impressive 60 ZB. As data continues to proliferate and experience rapid growth, emerging information technologies are successfully tackling the challenges of data integration, storage, and the extraction of value from extensive information resources. At this stage, the alignment between the information processing capabilities of new information technology tools and the inherent attributes of human information processing will prompt a reevaluation of the nature of human intelligence in information processing. This reevaluation is a driving force behind the development of new information technologies and the expansion of new cognitive domains. Nonetheless, unlike past advancements in information technology, where new divisions of labor could be established to reach equilibrium, the impact of machine replacement is inherently irreversible. In essence, this transformation will have a profound breakthrough effect on the human social system of the division of labor, leading to a reshaping of the landscape of the social division of labor relations and modes.

In the digital age, the conquest of information scarcity within the human society ushers in a new business ecosystem, effectively mitigating the information asymmetry of the past, and this new business civilization is poised to thrive and mature, driven by the wealth of information resources available. With the increasing closeness of economic and social interactions among individuals, facilitated by the transparency and accessibility of vast information, the traditional mode of social governance, reliant on information monopoly, is no longer tenable. Instead, self-organized governance involving stakeholders is poised to assume growing importance. In essence, the profound transformations in the information during the digital age have not only propelled humanity towards a new phase of information technology but have also unlocked new avenues for the evolution of human civilization.

2.3.2 A Fundamental Transformation in the Social Division of Labor

For a long time, cooperation among individuals was rooted in trust-based consensus, relying solely on individual information processing abilities. However, in the digital age, handling vast amounts of complex information necessitates the use of newly developed digital information technology tools. As a result, human–computer cooperation has emerged as a pivotal factor influencing the evolution of the division of labor.

The utilization of big data and artificial intelligence effectively eliminates obstacles in the acquisition and processing of information. As diverse groups of individuals adopt similar methods for information processing, it leads to the convergence of outcomes and, ultimately, a shared understanding. As time progresses, social groups will increasingly align in their perceptions, values, and behaviors, which results in the emergence of a consensus that minimizes perceived differences in the world. Consequently, this transformation will have a profound impact on the dynamics of interpersonal relationships and the social division of labor.

Within the realm of human–machine collaboration in information processing, a novel cognitive consensus mechanism emerges, marked by objectivity in both process and results. This marks a significant departure from earlier eras, as it transforms the methods and fundamental prerequisites for creating cooperative consensus. Instead of being solely reliant on an individual's information processing skills, this fresh consensus is founded on a shared agreement revolving around the heightened cognitive capacities empowered by technology. The advent of information technology will diminish individual biases, while concurrently diminishing the significance of human's inherent information processing capabilities, thereby altering the sociological attributes of humanity. Consequently, the structure of social organization, values, and operational principles will undergo a profound transformation, with its implications being as significant as the societal changes brought about by the Industrial Revolution.

Information processing technologies, exemplified by big data and artificial intelligence, facilitate the discovery of information's intrinsic value through innovative tools. This process fosters cooperation and cognitive consensus, altering the division of labor and collaboration between humans and machines, subsequently reshaping individual social worth. Information storage and encryption technologies, such as blockchain, are poised to introduce a fresh approach to shaping societal consensus by coordinating new technology applications at the organizational level. This, in turn, will prompt individuals to embrace novel methods for generating societal values and reform the collaborative dynamics between people. The convergence of big data, artificial intelligence, and blockchain technologies will lead to a deeper specialization of tasks between humans and machines, as well as between individuals, particularly in the context of value creation at both the application and organizational levels. This convergence will further unlock human cognitive abilities and collaborative potential, resulting in significant enhancements in information processing efficiency and creativity. It also stimulates the harmonious integration of values, uniting cooperative win–win and self-interest principles. Moreover, emerging digital technologies like blockchain will continue to play a pivotal role in preserving the legacy of human civilization. To elaborate, through its characteristics of effective storage and tamper-proof, blockchain technology ensure the preservation and inheritance of the process and the wisdom of human civilization. Finally, the implementation of smart contracts bolsters control in human-to-human collaboration, mitigates potential systemic disruption stemming from human irrationality in economic and social scenarios, elevates the efficiency of the division of labor and cooperation, and enables the effective transfer of historical lessons through technological means. Consequently, this approach helps to avert unnecessary costs in historical development.

Entering the digital age, human beings confront brand new challenges. First and foremost, with the advancement of artificial intelligence technology, the core dynamic between technology and humans has experienced a profound shift. In the past, a range of technologies, such as electrification during the Industrial Revolution, were designed to augment human capabilities, effectively extending human potential. However, artificial intelligence technology has introduced capabilities that resemble the innate attributes of humans and in various domains this technology is proved to substitute for human roles rather than merely augmenting them. Consequently, the dynamics of collaboration between technology and humans have experienced a profound shift, reshaping the division of labor between people and machines. In the era of digitalization, the lessons drawn from past experiences offer limited guidance, thus demanding innovative breakthroughs in theory and concepts. This, in turn, prompts a reevaluation of the impact of digital technologies, especially artificial intelligence, on the interplay between humans, society, and technological advancement.

The second point focuses on the noticeable acceleration in the iteration of digital technology. Technological progress is rapidly gaining momentum, while the adaptation of our social systems and organizational structures lags behind. Given the priority of countries and major economic entities to maintain competitiveness in the ever-evolving global landscape, they place greater emphasis on technological innovation, propelling technology further. Nevertheless, owing to various constraints, including vested interests, cognitive delays, and other objective factors, elements such as societal concepts, systems, regulations, and the organization of the social division of labor are evidently trailing the pace of technological innovation. This widening gap underscores the necessity for a more synchronized development between technology and our societal frameworks.

The third point revolves around the growing challenge that individuals face in keeping pace with of technological progress. The swift evolution of digital technology and the escalating prerequisites for information processing skills have ushered in new societal demands for people's abilities. Unfortunately, our education system has struggled to adapt in time, resulting in significant disruptions for both employees and enterprises within the employment and commercial landscape. The business sector finds it increasingly challenging to adjust, and comprehensive solutions to address these societal pressures are lacking. In the past, under the banner of technological advancement, individuals could swiftly acquire the necessary technical competencies through training and learning. However, in today's landscape, where technological development often supplants human capabilities, it is increasingly onerous for individuals to keep up with the rapid iterations in technological progress.

Humanity's relentless pursuit of development supremacy has driven the creation of an increasingly potent, manageable, and autonomous living environment. This very drive has acted as the fundamental catalyst behind the ongoing development of environmental information processing technology, sparking a series of information technology revolutions.

The crux of these information technology revolutions lies in enhancing human cognition of the world and reshaping the environment by augmenting the efficiency of human information processing. This continuous development in the information processing capabilities of the human society expands the realm of possibilities for human development. As we step into the digital age, digital technology has intricately linked human beings, fostering global interconnectivity. The concept of a "global village" has become highly relevant as people around the world get closely connected. The notion of "a community with a shared future of mankind" explicitly presented at the 18th National Congress of the Communist Party of China (CPC) has been acknowledged and embraced globally.

In essence, this reflects a realization by insightful individuals that, thanks to the extensive application of digital technology, the interconnection and mutual influence among individuals in the human society have become a reality. The state of a global community of destiny is impacting everyone, and the formation of a consensus among all human beings is an inevitable developmental trend.

Reflecting on the evolution of digitalization, the constant enhancement of information efficiency, the expansion of human cognition boundaries, and the establishment of an increasingly independent environment for human survival and development have been the central themes of human historical development. As we enter the digital age and bridge the digital divide[1] in the human society, we open the door to a shared world for humanity.

[1] The concept of the digital divide initially surfaced in the late 1980s. In 1999, the National Telecommunications and Information Agency (NTIA) formally defined it in its third "Falling into the Net" report as "the gap between those who have access to new technologies and those who do not". This binary distinction centers on access to information and communication technologies (ICT). Reference: Irving L, Klegar-Levy K, Everette D W, et al. Falling through the net: Defining the digital divide-A report on the telecommunications and information technology gap. Report on the telecommunications and information technology gap in America. Washington, DC: National Telecommunications and Information Administration, US Department of Commerce, 1999, INTRODUCTIONxii, EXECUTIVE SUMMARY xiii.

Chapter 3
Information Technology Iteration and the Productivity Revolution

The productivity revolution, which is readily noticeable, is essentially a direct consequence of the ongoing progress in information technology, underscoring the pivotal role played by IT in boosting productivity.

The iteration of information technology stands as the cornerstone of human civilization's autonomy and advancement. The ongoing evolution of information technology, coupled with the development of cognitive tools, enhances individuals' understanding of the world, and transforms how they use environmental information to adapt to their surroundings. Throughout the spectrum of information technology innovations, spanning from language and writing to computers and the Internet, humans have harnessed multidimensional information, employed sophisticated information processing methods, explored diverse approaches to extract information value, and, consequently, have honed their problem-solving capabilities. The current phase of digital technology development is a sophisticated product of information technology's ongoing evolution.

Through the iterations of information technology, humans have acquired ever more powerful cognitive tools, enhancing their understanding of the world and enabling the invention of increasingly sophisticated and personalized products that cater to their needs. During the ongoing productivity revolution, including the agricultural, industrial, and digital phases, economic and social systems have progressively gained independence from the natural environment, leading to enhanced human operational capabilities. Hence, the iterative progress of information technology acts as the foundational driver of the productivity revolution, and without its ongoing advancement, the human society would struggle to ignite the spark of the productivity revolution and sustain developmental momentum.

The iterative contributions of information technology to the human society's development are realized through the empowerment of individuals. Thanks to the benefits of technological progress, individuals have gained a profound understanding of the world, easy access to comprehensive and reliable information, and increased opportunities for collaboration. Moreover, the enhanced efficiency in information

Y. Yu and Y. Jiang, *Understanding the Digital Revolution and Its Influences*,
https://doi.org/10.1007/978-981-97-4939-3_3

processing allows for the effective utilization of the treasures of human civilization's cognition and knowledge. Therefore, individual empowerment stands as the foundational catalyst for unleashing the potential of the information technology. The ongoing iterative development of information technology, which empowers individuals, enables them to actively participate in the ongoing productivity revolution within the human society through various forms of interpersonal collaboration.

3.1 Empowerment of Individuals by Information Technology Iteration

Over the course of history, the continuous development of information technology, from early tools like language and writing to contemporary digital breakthroughs such as 5G, big data, and artificial intelligence, illustrates humanity's unwavering commitment to unlocking its information-processing potential. This progression results in heightened efficiency in information processing, greater social interaction among individuals, and a surge in economic productivity. Furthermore, information technology facilitates the seamless integration of individuals into the social system of the division of labor, further refining information processing within this framework.

3.1.1 Information Technology Empowerment Shaped by the Era

The evolution of methods for empowering individuals through information technology across different eras underscores the dynamic nature of this relationship. In the early stages of human civilization, it primarily functioned as a social consensus mechanism, facilitating the socialization of individuals and fostering diversity and complexity within the social division of labor. In contemporary times, the role of information technology extends well beyond mere socialization, as it empowers individuals to not only broaden their cognitive horizons but also actively transform their environment, resulting in a substantial enhancement of humanity's information processing capabilities.

In the early phases of human civilization, when people still maintained a rudimentary understanding of the world, environmental information of value was scarce and difficult to obtain. The absence of information technology led to high costs related to information storage and distribution, thereby limiting information accessibility for the general population. As a result, information became the exclusive domain of the powerful and affluent individuals of that era, reinforcing their control over society by maintaining an information asymmetry among social classes. During this period, the transmission of knowledge with language and writing guaranteed the uniformity of individuals' cognition and beliefs, ultimately giving rise to a societal consensus that not only served as the cohesive force binding society together but also upheld social stability. For example, in ancient China, the study and propagation of Confucianism, documented in books and on silk, promoted the concept of loyalty to the ruler and the nation, which not only served as the cornerstone of conceptual consensus among the scholarly class in more than two millennia of Chinese society's development but also provided a robust conceptual foundation for the stability of the monarchical and authoritarian political system. A parallel process unfolded in Western religious culture, where the dissemination of religious beliefs played a similarly significant role in achieving social cohesion.

In modern times, the role of information technology has transcended its initial purpose of establishing social consensus. Contemporary information technology, including the telegraph, telephone, computers, big data, and artificial intelligence, has emerged as powerful tools that expand the cognitive horizons of humanity. Specifically, it equips individuals with robust tools and methodologies for acquiring and processing information while fostering comprehensive collaboration among individuals, thus encouraging the exploration of the boundaries of the unknown world. Therefore, the advancement of information technology fully unleashes individual potential in information processing, marking a new stage where information production is abundant, and the information environment undergoes a complete transformation.

At this stage, individuals' utilization of emerging information technology for collecting, storing, and processing data, coupled with their integration into the social system of the division of labor, collectively enhance the overall efficiency of information processing within society. Empowered by artificial intelligence (AI) technology, individuals are empowered to gather and process data across multiple dimensions, conduct numerous simulation experiments, and explore a broader spectrum of potential attributes or states related to specific research topics, thus leading to substantial achievements, such as the discovery of valuable materials, novel drugs, and the formulation of new theories. For instance, DeepMind, a globally renowned AI research lab and technology company, has achieved significant milestones with AI's assistance, including the discovery of new mathematical theorems and conjectures, as well as the rapid identification of the structures of nearly all human proteins. Moreover, AI tools play a pivotal role in the production and dissemination of new knowledge, enabling humanity to make extraordinary discoveries, unveil cosmic phenomena, decipher physical laws, and reveal mathematical theorems and conjectures. The invention of the James Webb Space Telescope, which has reshaped our understanding of the universe, stands as another illustrative example of how revolutionary cognitive tools, such as AI, drive substantial advancements in human civilization. Hence, it is indisputable that the empowerment of AI tools, rooted in digital technology, within the realm of knowledge production, serves as a paramount force in extending the cognitive horizons of humanity.

Nevertheless, the empowerment of individuals through information technology is not without its associated costs. To fully utilize the potential of information technology, individuals must attain proficiency in IT tools, which demands an investment of their time and effort, along with the support of society in providing essential educational resources, including educators and learning materials. In historical contexts characterized by relatively low productivity, acquiring knowledge about the technological achievements of the time, whether from books or other knowledge sources, incurred substantial costs and offered limited opportunities. Educational resources were accessible primarily to the privileged few, leaving the general population with limited access to education, ultimately presenting a significant challenge to achieving widespread information technology empowerment within society.

It was only after the industrial revolution, when societal productivity reached a certain threshold, that there arose a heightened demand for knowledgeable and skilled individuals in the expanding social system of the division of labor. With the continuous accumulation of knowledge, the establishment of competitive mechanisms in knowledge production, the growing emphasis on fairness, and the widespread availability of standardized education, information technology became accessible to the general population, leading to a more egalitarian society as well as unlocking the full potential of human information processing. Furthermore, it is evident that in nations with higher per capita income, the education levels of their citizens tend to be elevated. In the case of China, as the nation's power is growing, the nine-year compulsory education has been universally implemented and university education has become a preferred path for the majority, equipping most teenagers with the skills to operate new information technology devices such as computers. Simultaneously, China's evolving social system of the division of labor has shifted from a basic requirement of literacy in its early days to the current necessity for skills in computers, programming, and other competencies, reflecting the ongoing changes in information technology empowerment and the development of information technology tools in line with the times.

3.1.2 Information Technology Development: Enhancing Information Processing Efficiency

Instead of being a random historical process, the development of information technology is a deliberate process, propelled by humanity's pursuit of autonomy and self-reliance within the limitations set by the natural world. In addressing this challenge, humans endeavor to augment their adaptability to their surroundings and their capacity to control it, which necessitates the acquisition and proficient processing of extensive environmental information, thus giving rise to the emergence of information technology.

In their pursuit of achieving a heightened level of autonomous development, humanity, from individuals to social groups, has consistently strived to unlock the potential of information processing through the continual invention and refinement of information technology tools. Throughout this evolutionary process, the collective wisdom of humanity has undergone a profound transformation, transitioning from being contributed by a minority in the early stages of human civilization to encompassing the endeavors of the entire human race. Notably, an increasing number of individuals now have the opportunity to enhance their information processing skills through education, and the achievements of human civilization can be instantly shared without being restricted by spatial or temporal limitations. The innovation of generative large-scale language models like ChatGPT further illustrates this point. By preserving the structural information of input data with extensive parameters and excavating the hidden value of this accumulated knowledge, ChatGPT provides valuable support for novel insights and solutions to emerging challenges. Consequently, this empowers individuals to access the cumulative knowledge amassed over centuries, facilitating the effective utilization of environmental information, the exploration of new cognitive frontiers, and the transformation of their surroundings.

Amidst the ongoing evolution of information technology, the persistent endeavor of humanity in addressing a wide range of challenges give rise to the innovation of diversified products, advancement in living standards, and the elevated well-being of individuals, signifying that as human beings have gained more control over their own development, economic and social systems have become increasingly independent of nature. This transition is evident in the diminishing proportion of economic value directly originating from the natural world, as seen in the decreasing share of agricultural output within the economies of developed nations as their economic structures continue to evolve. Another illustrative example lies in the complete industrialization of agriculture, where emerging technologies like the production of starch from carbon dioxide offer new possibilities, accelerating the full industrialization of agriculture and enhancing autonomy from the natural environment.[1] Therefore, it is foreseeable that with technological progress, economic and social systems will continue to gain independence from the natural environment in the future.

Fundamentally, the achievements of the information technology revolution signify humanity's expanding ability to steer its own development. Continuous progress in information technology not only has increased the scale and efficiency of data utilization, but also has enabled the formation of increasingly self-sustaining living environments. Individuals are no longer solely reliant on external natural forces; they now possess a significant degree of control in shaping the course of economic and social advancement.

3.1.3 Information Technology Empowerment: Enhancing Autonomous Development

Beyond the broader societal impacts of information technology empowerment discussed earlier, the effects at the individual level are equally significant. Notably, as information technology continues to evolve, individuals are presented with an

[1] Cai et al., Cell-free chemoenzymatic starch synthesis from carbon dioxide, Science 373, 1523–1527(2021).

expanding array of choices and the freedom to make independent decisions, thereby fostering the development of individual personalities characterized by their capacity for autonomous decision-making. Furthermore, this historical process of individual empowerment through information technology appears to align with Aristotle's prediction from over 2000 years ago, which posited that throughout history, a gradual and stable trend would emerge: the progressive shift of power into the hands of the masses. This shift mirrors the historical development of individual empowerment through information technology, enabling individuals to have an increasingly extensive sphere for social participation and influence, thus reshaping the dynamics of labor division and cooperation within the socio-economic system.

Modern information technology, especially digital technology, provides individuals with the capacity to access, process, and utilize information at an incredibly low cost, surpassing the limitations of time and geography. Consequently, it not only empowers individuals to benefit from societal progress but also encourages their active contributions through enhanced information processing capabilities. This process enables individuals to independently make choices for their personal development, fostering a sense of self-reliant progress.

From a broader perspective, the standardization and modularization of information have set the stage for a complete shift towards digitization and informatization, propelling humanity into an era of extensive digital transformation. This transformation is underscored by the immediate availability of the internet and the widespread adoption of cloud computing, which collectively erase barriers to information access and foster collaborative knowledge sharing, ultimately bolstering humanity's ability to tackle intricate challenges. The paramount development challenge of our digital age centers on maximizing the effective use of information, unlocking its intrinsic value, establishing efficient information processing methods, generating valuable insights, and elevating the efficiency of how we process information. It is a profound and far-reaching challenge of our times, one that transcends the influence of a select few human elites and calls for collective participation. Therefore, only through collaborative endeavors can we investigate fresh viewpoints and concepts concerning this challenge, leading the way to a brighter future.

3.2 Productivity Revolution Based on the Empowerment of Information Technology

Historically, there has been an excessive focus on the importance of productivity, with the belief that the productivity revolution is the primary driver behind the progress of human civilization. However, this perspective contains a logical fallacy as it fails to acknowledge that the productivity revolution is, in fact, an outcome of human evolutionary development rather than the primary cause. Specifically, it is the cognitive enhancement brought about by the information technology revolution that gave birth to the production technology revolution. Through iterative advancements in information technology, individuals develop the ability to access and process environmental information efficiently, thereby unlocking their cognitive potential. This, in turn, serves as the cognitive foundation for the productivity revolution and triggers a corresponding shift in collaboration and organizational structures in alignment with the evolving landscape of information technology.

While the early productivity revolution was characterized by advancements in material tools, the modern productivity revolution is distinguished by improvements in abstract tools, particularly cognitive tools. Since the Industrial Revolution, the human society has entered an era where the development of theory and rationality plays a guiding role in advancing civilization. During this phase, well-established theories dictate the methods by which we reshape our environment, making these cognitive tools pivotal in overcoming constraints on societal progress. In the digital age, digital technology, engineered to unlock the complete potential of digital information, assumes a dual role as the propulsive force and a potential bottleneck for human civilization. To transcend this bottleneck, intelligent technology has surfaced as a groundbreaking cognitive tool with profound implications for society. Crafted using intelligent technology, intelligent machine systems challenge humanity's exclusive role as the principal cognitive agent and assert themselves as the foremost cognitive tools in human development, propelling the continuous productivity revolution.

Reflecting on the history of productivity revolution, we observe that the iterative progress of information technology has consistently played a significant role in each phase. Whether it's the "steam engine +" or "electricity +" era, or the more recent "Internet +" and "artificial intelligence +" era, the underlying development logic remains consistent. This logic is rooted in the idea that the combination of "production technology + information technology" collaboratively drives societal and economic advancement. In the contemporary world, the profound liberation of human cognitive abilities by information technology empowers individuals and significantly influences their decision-making processes, further underscoring the unparalleled significance of information technology in economic and social development.

The modern information technology revolution has been intricately linked with the industrial revolution that commenced in the eighteenth century. Over the past three centuries, the collective accomplishments have far surpassed the cumulative progress achieved throughout human history, marking an era of rapid development in the human society.

While there is often a substantial focus on the Industrial Revolution as the primary driver of economic development, there is a notable tendency to inadvertently neglect the significant impact of the modern information technology revolution, which functions as the cognitive and theoretical underpinning for the productivity revolution. It is imperative to acknowledge that increased productivity cannot be achieved without the ongoing advancement of information technology.

In addition, people tend to pay more attention to the overall societal progress brought about by the macro-level productivity revolution but often overlook the significant impact of the modern information technology revolution on individuals and society as a whole. The true foundation of societal progress lies in the enhanced capabilities that individuals attain through the empowerment of the information technology revolution. Therefore, focusing on the choices made by these empowered individuals is essential for a deeper understanding of the driving forces and developmental trends in the digital transformation of society.

The Industrial Revolution greatly enhanced the production and distribution of goods. Meanwhile, the modern Information Technology Revolution has facilitated the cost-effective, convenient, and speedy sharing of information and knowledge, thus enabling continuous innovation in goods and fostered the prosperity of the commodity economy characterized by exchange. More importantly, revolutionizing the natural economic state of the human society, which was once characterized by "self-sufficiency", the advent of the commodity economy gave rise to the social division of labor among individuals, making it the primary form of social structure. Consequently, the socio-economic system has entered a path of collaborative development in the production of economic goods.

In a commodity-based economy, as humans are essential inputs into the production system, the process of reproducing products is inherently interconnected with the process of reproducing people. The development of a commodity economy unifies the reproduction of individuals (labor) with the reproduction of products, aligning the human cognitive system with the exchange value system of production. The historical evolution of the division of labor among individuals has been instrumental in shaping societal transformation. The Industrial Revolution, characterized by the emergence of modern limited liability companies and financial markets, facilitated cooperation and specialization, leading to the efficient operation of socio-economic systems. Simultaneously, as humanity ventures into outer space to explore new development opportunities beyond the constraints of Earth's environment, the limitations imposed by our natural surroundings gradually diminish.

The well-known narrative of human development over the past three centuries often credits the productivity gains from the industrial revolution for the many remarkable achievements. Yet, upon closer examination of this period using the lens of information technology (IT) development, we realize that the IT revolution and the productivity revolution have been intricately intertwined, driving this profound historical process in tandem.

3.2.1 Steam Engines + Corporate System: Unleashing the Power of the Industrial Revolution

The Industrial Revolution is commonly defined by the advent of the steam engine, which, powered by coal energy, symbolized the transformation of the human society into an age of mechanization. While we are familiar with stories of the steam engine revolutionizing textile production and transportation, we often overlook a crucial aspect of that era—standardized information. The refinement of standardized information served as the linchpin for the rapid progression of mechanization. In other words, without the synergy of both the robust potential of the steam engine and the flexible framework of information standardization, achieving broad-scale industrialization and universal mechanization would have been unattainable.

In addition to its role in advancing universal mechanization, information standardization significantly enhanced the efficiency of information processing at the societal level, thereby enabling the economic system to function with greater efficiency. From a production perspective, information standardization has facilitated the increasing standardization of production processes, fostering extensive collaboration and division of labor within enterprises. From a distributional perspective, piecework stands as a vital system that enhances labor efficiency and sustains workforce motivation. It functions as a standardized and transparent collaborative method that enables workers and employers to swiftly process information and make equitable decisions regarding benefit distribution. From the perspective of resource allocation, capital has emerged as the economic factor responsible for allocation of social resources in the production process, playing a pivotal role in managing the information processing costs inherent in the economic system, which encompass issues of information asymmetry and uncertainty expenses. As a result, capital has evolved into a crucial and limited component within the social and economic production system, serving as a key driver of development. From the perspective of organization, the corporate system has gradually replaced the partnership as the primary organizational structure in social production, and, within this system, capital assumes a pivotal role in aggregating all the essential production resources. Consequently, capital owners wield considerable influence in determining the division of labor and distribution, thereby holding a dominant position in this context.

Nonetheless, at this juncture, information technology is still in the ongoing process of transitioning from version 3.0 to 4.0, facing several developmental restrictions. On the one hand, as human understanding of nature remains significantly constrained and the volume of accumulated information remains quite limited, human cognitive potential is far from reaching its full realization. On the other hand, owing to limited scope of information dissemination, the division of labor and cooperation are predominantly conducted within the confines of individual enterprises. Simultaneously, this limited understanding of nature and the restricted sharing of knowledge result in a substantial reliance on crops and natural minerals as raw materials in production. The production process is highly dependent on changes in the natural environment, leading to significant limitations in the control of the production process and the autonomy of the human society's development. Consequently, the production process remains heavily influenced and dominated by natural conditions.

3.2.2 Electric Motors + Radio and TV Technology: Fueling Industrial Value Networks

The further progression of the Industrial Revolution, characterized by new cognitive breakthroughs in physics, particularly in the fields of electricity and electromagnetism, was driven by the emergence of new information technology tools, which enhanced rational cognition. Historians refer to this phase as the second technological revolution.

This technological revolution was characterized by the invention and widespread adoption of the electric motor, with electrification standing out as the most prominent aspect of the transformation in the production process. Electrification paved the way for the development of petrochemicals, automobiles, and other intricate industries, marking a shift toward more complex products. Meanwhile, human understanding of nature advanced to a new level, diminishing the role of agriculture in the economic system while giving rise to new industrial sectors. This, in turn, fostered the establishment of a sophisticated value chain and the gradual formation of a complex industrial value network. Capital's dominance within the economic system became more stable, and human economic activity became increasingly independent of nature. As a result, capital, as a means of pooling resources, became the significant economic factor and the economy is being continuously capitalized.

The advancement of industrialization powered by the synergy of capital and technological advancements facilitated the standardization of the entire production process, most notably exemplified by the "Ford production line". In this evolution, information technology played a pivotal role, streamlining and standardizing operational information. The Taylor System, also known as Scientific Management or Taylorism, was developed in the late 19th and early twentieth centuries in the United States and Western European countries as a management theory and approach geared toward enhancing workplace efficiency and productivity. This system can be viewed as the outcome of optimizing and standardizing operational information and played a pivotal role in achieving both the scale and standardization in production, notably exemplified by the Ford assembly line. As a result, the division of labor and the distribution system, both based on transparent information, became the primary methods for generating and allocating social wealth.

The evolution of societal organization is about enhancing information processing efficiency to achieve higher production efficiency and gain competitiveness. This is realized through the application of electrical equipment, transforming and refining standardized production processes, thus enabling division of labor within enterprises to reach the economic boundary of technical scale efficiency, and allowing information processing efficiency within the production system to reach the efficiency boundary of organizational structure. Crucially, during this progression, the extensive utilization of radio and television technologies has enabled the real-time dissemination of information, facilitating more extensive and profound cooperation among enterprises across geographical boundaries. It has also contributed to the establishment of industrial value chain networks, the further specialization of labor division, and the rapid growth of productive service industries. These developments significantly heightened the impact of the Industrial Revolution, enhancing the overall wealth-generating capacity of society and extending the benefits of the Industrial Revolution to a broader segment of the population.

In this course of development, advancements in information technology, notably through radio and television, have greatly enhanced production efficiency, leading to a significant transition in the production process, where a substantial portion of information processing tasks are now managed by the autonomous production system. Specifically, the roles of individuals engaged in production have transitioned from skilled craftsmen, proficient in core techniques, to replaceable assembly line workers. Therefore, with the diminishing importance of job-specific skills among workers in the production process, their social value has correspondingly diminished. In this context, only sectors specializing in knowledge production and adaptability to uncertain environmental shifts, like the financial sector, assume the responsibility for propelling society forward. The financial sector, originally created to address information asymmetry in finance, possesses a unique function of managing uncertain information, allowing it to attain monopoly profits more easily. However, as the specialization and complexity of industrial information have further grown, the financial sector alone cannot address all the challenges related to information processing within the economic system. This is where the productive service industries, characterized by technology-insensitivity and knowledge-insensitivity, begin to emerge. At this juncture, the growing environmental uncertainty and task complexity urgently necessitate solutions for handling a vast, continually changing body of complex information, which is a pivotal bottleneck for the development of economic and societal systems. Thus, the third technological revolution commences.

3.2.3 "Computer +": Unlocking Information Productivity

The onset of the third production technology revolution can be attributed to the invention and utilization of the electronic computer. Its application unlocked the productivity of information, subsequently serving as a vital driving force in enhancing social productivity.

Although the world witnessed the creation of the first electronic digital computer, "ENIAC", in 1946, designed primarily to address intricate ballistic calculations, numerous challenges persisted in dealing with complex information within the realms of production and various facets of social and economic life, necessitating continued innovations. Fortunately, in 1951, the introduction of UNIVAC (Universal Automatic Computer) marked a significant step in making electronic computers more accessible to society, empowering them with potent computational capabilities to deal with complex information. As this technology demonstrated its proficiency in managing complex information processing tasks, it gained widespread adoption in the human society, heralding the era of automation where the full potential of information was realized. The automation not only revolutionize the collaboration between human and machine, but also shift the mode of the social division of labor from a dominant model where tasks are primarily divided based on physical production actions in the assembly line to a model where tasks are predominantly divided based on decision-making behaviors that rely on information processing. As industrial production becomes standardized and scaled, there is often an excess of goods, surpassing the demand within society, challenging the realization of production value and the subsequent reproduction process. The critical concern becomes how to efficiently identify and meet the excessive production with the existing demand, especially in a landscape marked by information uncertainty and fierce business competition. In this context, the high efficiency of decision-making becomes a central factor for survival and growth within enterprises.

Computers unleashed the productivity of information resources, which made the white-collar and middle class, whose main object was information processing, begin to appear in the economic system and become the main force dominating the development of the economic system. At this stage, computers did not directly influence individual decision-making; humans continued to be the primary decision-makers. Meanwhile, economic organizations shifted their incentive models from the Taylor System, which emphasized objective standards, to behavioral management, prioritizing individuals' subjective experiences to enhance information processing efficiency and harness the full potential of information productivity.

The widespread recognition of the influential Hawthorne experiments has significantly deepened our understanding of specialization in production and business management, as well as the intricacies of cooperative coordination. Specially, while specialization was narrowly defined in terms of task efficiency in the traditional Taylor System, the Hawthorne studies revealed that the human factor, including motivation and social dynamics, played a crucial role in specialization, leading to a more holistic view of specialization that considers not just technical aspects but also the psychological and social elements that influence employee performance. Consequently, it has heightened our focus on the social role of individuals in the realm of economic cooperation; People are no longer viewed as mere objects of manipulation within scientific management but are acknowledged as pivotal elements with formidable information processing, analytical, and decision-making capabilities that drive societal progress.

In this context, because of the growing focus on individual subjective agency, which encompasses vital skills in information processing, decision-making, and problem-solving crucial for promoting economic and social development, there has been a notable proliferation of diverse distribution methods and organizational structures. Concurrently, the economic framework has become increasingly intricate, and the division of labor among enterprises has deepened as it extends into various work scenarios. The focus of the division of labor has expanded beyond internal organizational boundaries, encompassing the intricate network of relationships and tasks that occur not only within a single organization but also among various enterprises, forming what is commonly referred to as supply chain management. Moreover, such collaboration has transcended borders, forming a global industrial value network and promoting the values of openness and globalization.

The advent of computer-driven automation has facilitated the realization of heavy industrialization in the realm of production. Since the 1970s, the widespread use of computers among white-collar and middle-class workers has not only deepened the division of labor but also accentuated the critical role of streamlined information processing in economic resource allocation. Consequently, the economy has shifted away from industrialization and is now evolving toward a service-centric model, with a notable emphasis on the productive service sector. In essence, this transformation in economic structure, characterized by more intricate corporate operations and heightened macro-environmental uncertainty, has led to the emergence of modern productive services, which are primarily concerned with gathering, processing, analyzing, and making decisions based on information. Furthermore, the implementation of computers carries several implications, extending the division of labor between human and machine from manufacturing to the service industry, and redirecting corporate objectives from solely prioritizing production efficiency and high quality to optimizing production processes and efficiently allocating manufacturing resources.

The competitiveness of economic entities is gauged by the social value they create, primarily stemming from their proficiency in allocating and utilizing economic resources through efficient information processing. Through the implementation of computer systems, a substantial boost in productivity, especially evident in developed economies, has exceeded domestic market demand. Consequently, in order to sustain the uninterrupted flow of value within the product reproduction system, there is a compelling imperative for firms to venture into global markets, leading to the emergence of transnational corporations. The transnational corporations, born in developed economies like the United States in the 1970s and 1980s, marked the beginning of the far-reaching globalization process in human history. The process of globalization, marked by the worldwide redistribution of resources and goods, encompassing the globalization of labor divisions, supply chains, and value networks, tightly interconnects economies in collaborative production, thus contributing to the proliferation of global wealth and the improvement of human well-being. Statistically, the world experienced an exceptional and nearly uninterrupted positive growth in global GDP over a span of 50 years, from 1960 to 2008. When measured in US dollars using the 2010 exchange rate, the world's per capita GDP increased from \$3748 in 1960 to \$9542 in 2008.[2]

With the widespread adoption of the Internet, computers have significantly improved individuals' capabilities in information processing and problem-solving, providing them with immediate access to global information, reducing communication and collaboration costs, and ultimately unlocking the latent potential value within socialization. Conversely, the significance of capital has gradually diminished over the course of more than two centuries of the industrial revolution. The abundance of capital in society has made it increasingly challenging to secure monopoly profits, leading to the emergence and rapid growth of venture capital investments, characterized by their high-risk, high-return nature, in the 1920s. During the 1960s and 70s, this concept gained substantial momentum, and during the 1990s, it entered

[2] Source of data: World Bank database.

a high-growth phase, becoming a significant force driving technological innovation. At this stage, knowledge and technology not only went beyond capital as primary economic factors but also acted as constraints on the social production possibility curve. Consequently, individuals equipped with knowledge and technology became the trendsetters of the time, launching science and technology enterprises whose value, under the acceleration of financial capital, enjoyed an unprecedented exponential growth. In this context, the process of comprehensive digitization of information throughout economic and social systems began. As part of this transformation, these systems became increasingly complex, with various elements intricately interconnected. Simultaneously, heightened competition and greater environmental uncertainty added to the challenges of decision-making for both businesses and public institutions. Consequently, conventional information processing tools seemed inadequate for fully unlocking the value of data, and there was a lack of effective methods for scientific decision-making and risk management, necessitating innovations in information technology tools.

3.3 Digitalization as the Modern Information Technology Achievement

The rising societal demand for information processing has brought computers out of laboratories and into widespread public use, marking the inception of the Internet era. As the Internet began its global expansion in the 1990s, it ushered in the fourth technological revolution, giving birth to the era of comprehensive digitalization and intellectualization, characterized by big data and artificial intelligence. In the digital age, empowered by digital technology, humans are embarking on the creation of an entirely artificial realm known as the "meta-universe", detached from the natural world. This transformation has elevated data as a new production factor in our economy, giving rise to the resounding slogan of the digital age: "Data constitutes everything".

In the digital age, marked by the pervasive internet and the Internet of Things (IoT), which links everyday objects to the web for data collection, humans have embarked on the precise, comprehensive, and real-time recording of economic information in all its facets. Fueled by digital technology, humans now produce and accumulate data at an exponential rate, with society's data volume doubling every 2–3 years, indicating that in a short span, humans gather as much data as they did throughout much of their history. The massive amount of data generated by digital technology tools has provided unprecedented insights into the characteristics of individuals, groups, and machines, as well as their interrelationships. From a sociological perspective, more available data allows for the systematic and comprehensive study of the connections between the characteristics and behavior of individuals using mathematical and physical methods. From an economic standpoint, it offers a deeper understanding of individual preferences, clarifies the relationships between supply and demand, and provides insights into the impacts and underlying causes of economic cycles. From the perspective of business operations, this technology allows for a thorough analysis of every facet related to users, production processes, and supply chains, thereby enhancing operational efficiency for businesses.

3.3.1 Two Phases in Digitalization

The digital development process can be categorized into two phases. In the initial phase, digitalization enables the standardization and modularization of information acquisition and analysis processes, harnessing the computer's capabilities in handling structured data to enhance information processing efficiency and facilitate scientific decision-making. With the combination of information digitalization and automation in manufacturing, the extensive use of intelligent machines in production within enterprises gives rise to the so-called intelligent production. This shift directly impacts the traditional division of labor between humans and machines, reducing human involvement in the production process and transitioning the production mode from automation to intelligent production. Consequently, the driving force of economic development has shifted from material inputs to the efficient management of digitized information, having a profound and far-reaching impact, comparable to that of the industrial revolution.

In the second stage, the evolution of information technology, marked by the rise of the Internet and artificial intelligence, has driven the complete digitization and intellectualization of both the economy and society. Consequently, the connectivity between individuals and society, as well as the ability to access information, has seen unparalleled enhancement. The artificial intelligence technology, represented by machine learning, allows human beings to process and utilize massive unstructured data, including text, voice, and image data, signifying the new era where human–machine cooperation enables the enrichment of human cognition. In conclusion, the widespread use of computers, the Internet, and the Internet of Things has made information easily accessible in our society, and with the emergence of big data and artificial intelligence, information has not only become more abundant but also comprehensively integrated into all aspects of our lives, marking the era of complete digitization.

In the age of comprehensive digitization, the economic system has undergone a profound transformation, characterized by comprehensive digitalization and virtualization, where information and data have become essential components of contemporary economic life. The advancement of emerging information technologies consistently lowers the barriers to accessing information and knowledge, broadens the scope for individual social interaction and engagement, reduces the cost of collaboration and communication, and thereby mitigates information asymmetry in social cooperation. Moreover, as the significance of capital diminishes, information mechanisms have emerged as vital instruments for allocating economic and social resources, effectively replacing capital as the primary resource connector in economic activities.

In the age of comprehensive digitization, the evolving and maturing artificial intelligence has reshaped the intelligent production and division of labor, fundamentally transforming the nature of human–machine collaboration. With the digitalization of the economic system yielding massive and intricate data, their collection and analysis for decision-making in economic life have surpassed the cognitive capacity of the human brain, and even the optimization of collaborative efforts among individuals is inadequate to meet these information processing demands, thus leading to a growing reliance on intelligent machine systems, where the performance of these machines plays a pivotal role in shaping economic decisions. At the cognitive level, as the original social system of the division of labor faces complete subversion owing to the ongoing development and implementation of intelligent technology, the increasingly apparent multi-subject nature of decision-making in the economic and social system signifies a profound transformation. Furthermore, the intelligent production system, responsible for generating and processing vast amounts of information, now governs all value-generating activities in economic and social systems, carrying multiple consequences. In this paradigm shift, the significance of virtual space will attain parity with that of physical space, engendering a transformative dynamic, and the established institutional rules governing human socio-economic systems will be subject to breakthrough changes, necessitating adaptive responses. For instance, in the prevailing context, the operation of automobiles mandates human drivers; nevertheless, as the maturation of intelligent automobile technology unfolds, the possibility arises that human drivers may be deemed obsolete or even rendered illegal.

3.3.2 *The Economic Mechanism in the Digital Age*

The transition from industrialization to digitalization has ushered in a profound transformation in the economic mechanism. During the industrial era, capital and the financial sector held sway, influencing resource allocation and pricing, whereas in the digital economy, the flow of digital information takes the helm, directing economic operations and shaping the flow of other factors, wealth generation, and distribution, with sectors that effectively leverage the value of digital information emerging as the core drivers in this evolving economic landscape. Furthermore, in the digital age, the Internet and the Internet of Things supplant the traditional railroad and highway networks as the infrastructure facilitating the flow of resources and goods in this new era, giving rise to a novel business civilization. As a result, the driving force propelling the societal development has shifted from a capital-driven economic development model based on price mechanisms to an information-driven economic development model based on information processing efficiency standards.

When people refer to the "digital economy", they are emphasizing the critical role of data and information as fresh production factors in economic advancement that determine the Production Possibility Frontier. In this ever-evolving economic model and the rapidly changing business environment, the key to bolstering core competitiveness, both for individuals and companies, lies in the adoption of innovative methods to extract value from information and the enhancement of organizational information processing mechanisms. More precisely, these innovative strategies result in cost reductions and the creation of more innovative products and services, while refining the efficiency of organizational information processing mechanisms significantly improves decision-making within these organizations. Furthermore, as the primary drivers of societal progress shift from dependence on capital factors to technological factors, entities capable of generating novel knowledge and information will ultimately influence the boundaries of human cognition. However, the positive externalities associated with the production of new knowledge will reshape the fundamental nature of organizational structures within human civilization. Consequently, effectively addressing these externalities will emerge as the benchmark for evaluating the effectiveness of organizational forms in the digital age.

3.3.3 Economic Organization and the Social Division of Labor in the Digital Age

Digitization represents the virtualization of economic and social structures and offers humans a proactive choice to shape their development. It's essential to understand that digitization is not a detached or abstract force affecting the human society; instead, it's intricately woven into human development. Digitalization, facilitated by cables and electromagnetic waves, allows most economic and social activities to take place in electronic information form, especially the real-time interactions between individuals transcending the spatial and temporal limitations. More importantly, the widespread adoption of digital technology has given rise to a flat social structure, supplanting the hierarchical organization that once handled information through layered levels in the human society. Within this evolution framework of information processing, there is a necessity to employ new forms of social organization that can effectively tap into the collective information processing potential, consequently leading to the restructuring of individual decision-making capabilities, methods of inter-individual connections and collaborations, as well as economic organizational models.

In the past, possessing information-processing intelligence, a fundamental attribute that sets humans apart from other living beings, served as the cornerstone of human value. Nevertheless, in the digital age, despite the increased production efficiency that intelligent machines brought about, it has also progressively replaced humans in various domains, consequently diminishing their role in the creation of value and giving rise to reflection on the nature of intelligence and the fundamental attributes that define human social value. Briefly, intelligent machines, with their rapid information processing and iterative optimization capabilities, have caused changes in the division of labor between humans and machines, thereby reshaping business operation models, leading to a reevaluation of the societal roles and values of individual humans, and giving rise to the development of new business and societal structures. The reflection and the new cognitive and value concepts being developed during this process will have an unprecedented impact on existing value systems and societal structures. This is an ongoing and evolving historical process, and it poses significant questions for everyone who is experiencing this transformation and eager to make a difference.

The four revolutions in production technology and the iteration of information technology have jointly contributed to the development of the human society. Through the production techniques, stemming from technological revolution, a continuous improvement in human information processing efficiency and the exploration of cooperative potential among humans has been realized, thus spurring a dynamic evolution in human production capabilities, modes of the division of labor, societal structures, and value systems. In light of these developments, humans have attained an unforeseen degree of emancipation from the deterministic forces of the natural world, no longer restricted solely to direct provisions from nature. More specifically, a significant portion of wealth in the human economic system is now generated within human-created economic systems, in contrast to industries dependent on the natural environment, such as modern agriculture. In developed countries, these industries contribute to only about 10% of the total wealth, and in China in 2020, agricultural value added accounted for just 7.5% of the total, underscoring the growing importance of wealth generated from within human-designed economic systems.

Thanks to the iteration of information technology and the revolution in production techniques, humanity has progressively lessened the constraints imposed by nature. The integration of new production technology is giving rise to a growing complexity in the division of labor within the human society, which diversifies the modes of cooperation and transfers the dominant economic force from capital owners to those who produce new knowledge and pioneer innovative technological products.

With the development of big data and artificial intelligence technology, a new phase of collaboration between humans and machines has emerged. This collaboration now extends beyond the use of machines as production tools, focusing on cognitive capabilities. As a result, it is expected to bring about significant changes in human production and division of labor structures, impacting individual value and social dynamics. Thus, adaptation to these changes is vital for both individuals and organizations, and having insight into the evolutionary logic and future trends of the digital age will provide a competitive advantage.

Chapter 4
Understanding the Underlying Theory of the Social Division of Labor

4.1 The Social Division of Labor

Understanding the social division of labor is of vital significance. Since the labor specialization plays as the core pillar of the development of the human economic and social system, it becomes the most important issue for mankind. An orderly organization and sustainable development of such system is the most valuable wealth of the human society.

The prevailing notion that assets such as cash, gold, houses, and securities comprise the societal wealth is greatly challenged. While these assets undoubtedly serve as valuable repositories of wealth, they are not inherently the key to prosperity, namely failing to directly contribute to the well-being of individuals and progress of society. Their authentic utility and value only materialize through their exchange for products or services created within the pragmatic system of the social division of labor. In other words, the value attributed to these assets, often perceived as symbols of wealth, fundamentally relies on the sustainable existence of the social system of the division of labor.

The efficient functioning of labor specialization system, which inherently involves maintenance costs, is supported by the market demand in a market-oriented economy. In a lively mass market, substantial demand sustains a highly efficient system of specialization. Additionally, the scale effects play a pivotal role in this system, efficiently distributing fixed production costs. However, when the supply of products and services within the social system of the division of labor mismatches the market demand, the necessity for a government regulation arises. The overall balance of the socio-economic system can be achieved through government policies for demand management. Furthermore, the ability to foster economic prosperity, achieved through the division of labor system, innovation, infrastructure development, and more, is deemed a public good—a collective resource that contributes to the overall well-being and social development without diminishing availability for other members of the community. Since government acts as a public authority, it

Y. Yu and Y. Jiang, *Understanding the Digital Revolution and Its Influences*,
https://doi.org/10.1007/978-981-97-4939-3_4

falls within its purview of responsibility to ensure the public well-being and social progress by providing such public goods. Specifically, in response to supply–demand imbalances, government intervention involves the employment of fiscal, monetary, taxation, employment policies, as well as their combinations.

The level of development in a society is directly correlated with the extent of its supply capacity supported by the labor specialization system. This connection determines the distance of the production possibility curve's boundary from the origin, which indicates the diversity of products and services a society can produce, as well as the scale of its production. However, in the digital age, this labor specialization system has experienced significant changes thanks to the digital technology, which not only empowers individuals in unprecedented ways but also reforms the way they collaborate with each other. Therefore, it is essential to delve into the nature of the social division of labor to gain a deeper understanding of its determinants as well as its news trends in the digital age.

As mentioned earlier, the enduring existence of the social division of labor, persistent since the dawn of the human society, serves as the driving force propelling the continuous development of humanity. It stands as both the vessel of human civilization and the wellspring of human prosperity. In the progression of human civilization, as humanity strives for dominance in its development to ensure the survival and growth of its population, the evolution of the social system of the division of labor unlocks the full potential of human resources. This, in turn, fosters heightened problem-solving abilities and creativity, resulting ultimately in greater resilience and an expanded array of development options.

The competition among individuals within the specialization system is essentially a selection process that enables the human society to unleash the potential of human resources. The path of social development in human civilization, spanning from the early division of handicrafts from agriculture through the phases of industrialization, commercialization, and financialization of the economy to the current era of digitalization, can be seen as an ongoing evolution in specialization sophistication. Representing humanity's persistent quest for enhanced productivity through optimizing the allocation of human resources, this iterative refinement not only improves the overall efficiency of information processing but also generates a compounding effect. This effect leads to increased problem-solving abilities, greater adaptability, amplified wealth generation, expanded development opportunities, and strengthened resilience within the social framework. Consequently, understanding the social division of labor, particularly in the context of the digital age, is vital to comprehending future trends in development.

4.2 Understanding the Importance of the Social Division of Labor

4.2.1 A Theoretical Framework for Understanding the Social Division of Labor

As the philosophy asserts, "existence is inherently valuable". The social division of labor, a universal phenomenon in human economic and social society, holds unquestionable value. When addressing why the division of labor occurs among individuals in the society, the pioneering British economist Adam Smith provided an insightful answer: the division of labor streamlined production processes and heightened productivity, ultimately catalyzing the birth of machines. In his renowned work, "The Wealth of Nations", Adam Smith emphasized that the most significant improvements in labor productivity, as well as the skills and judgment employed by laborers during production, are outcomes of labor specialization. Therefore, from Smith's perspective, the division of labor empowered humanity, leading to an enhancement in wealth creation.

Following in the footsteps of Adam Smith, another British economist, David Ricardo, presented a fresh perspective on the division of labor in his influential work, "Principles of Political Economy and Taxation". In this work, he introduced the globally renowned "comparative advantage theory". This theory is essentially about the production specialization among countries, explaining why countries at different levels of development engage in trade with each other. Specifically, the theory proposes that countries, by leveraging their endowments and choosing to produce goods with lower opportunity cost,[1] can specialize in areas where they have comparative advantages. This specialization fosters international trade, with each participating country in this global division of labor system gaining additional benefits. Over time, the theory expanded into the "principle of comparative advantage", moving beyond the analysis of nation-level production specialization to encompass the analysis of the division of labor choices among individuals. Consequently, this theory, serving as the guiding principle in international trade practices, is widely recognized in economics and stands as a key principle for understanding the mechanisms of cooperative specialization.

This theory further sheds light on the origins of the value generated through the social division of labor. According to the Principle of Comparative Advantage, irrespective of an individual's inherent endowments and even if their productivity in every aspect of the production process lags that of all others, the division of labor still ensures an overall increase in the wealth of the entire society. Furthermore, in this system, every participant stands to gain mutual benefits through socialized

[1] Opportunity cost is the maximum return on the production of some other product that is foregone when a certain amount of economic resources is devoted to the production of some product. Opportunity cost is an important concept in economics used to analyze how economic agents make optimal choice decisions.

transactions. Consequently, this theory recognizes the distinctive value of individuals, underscoring that every participant, involved in voluntary cooperation and equitable transactions, can contribute to and receive additional benefits from the collaboration.

4.2.2 *The Social Division of Labor: The Lever for Wealth Creation*

From a holistic perspective, the social division of labor forms a highly intricate network where individuals function as indispensable nodes within the system. The value of these nodes is not determined in isolation; rather, it emerges from the collective endeavors of all participants, ensuring the existence and survival of this network. Taking a micro perspective, individuals, utilizing the social system of the division of labor, realize their social value and generate wealth that surpasses their individual capabilities. Therefore, the social system of the division of labor functions as a lever for individuals to create wealth.

The concept of the division of labor as a leverage for wealth creation has broad applications. Through the division of labor, various resources holding economic value can seamlessly integrate into the intricate fabric of the social production system. This integration leads to the generation of additional economic value and enhancement of social wealth, contingent upon the condition that the marginal output of these economic resources remains nonzero. From this perspective, if a society has a considerable number of labor resources that are not incorporated into the division of labor system, it undoubtedly signifies a significant squandering of human potential. Looking at it from a different angle, wealth generation through the division of labor essentially means individuals leveraging collaborative efforts to enhance productivity. In this process, individuals view each other as valuable and interchangeable resources crucial to their productivity and their participation in specialization effectively broadens the pool of available resources, enabling them to create more value and increase their profits.

4.2.3 *The Social Division of Labor: Enhanced Information Processing Efficiency*

Viewed through the lens of information processing, the division of labor, which necessitates the exchange and sharing of information among individuals, not only synthesizes their information processing abilities but also forms a distributed information processing network within society. Consequently, such enhanced information processing efficiency enables the solution of more intricate problems and the creation of more advanced products. Essentially, the driving force behind the evolution of specialization stems from the idea that everyone can tap into a broader spectrum of disposable resources, wield augmented capabilities for action and wealth creation, and exhibit heightened resilience in risk management through their engagement in the intricate web of the division of labor network.

While the "principle of comparative advantage" appears robust in interpreting the value of the social division of labor, its limitation lies in a static perspective, lacking an explanation for the dynamic nature of the division of labor networks and failing to incorporate the impact of technological innovation. Consequently, economists, as exemplified by Grossman and Helpman in 1989 and 1990, have adopted a more dynamic approach by considering the impact of technological development on comparative advantage. Despite substantial efforts by economists to modernize the "principle of comparative advantage" through various approaches and frameworks, a unified conclusion has yet to be reached, highlighting the need for further development to fully explain complex modern economic phenomena. When examining the characteristics of labor specialization in the digital age, it is imperative to consider technological influences, particularly the integration of information technology within the division of labor system. Specifically, the advancement of information technology alters the quantity and quality of information that individuals have to deal with, thereby revolutionizing collaboration. Consequently, these factors influence the operational expenses and structural configuration of the social system of the division of labor, ultimately shaping the boundaries of information processing efficiency within this system.

The "principle of comparative advantage" primarily centers on the value of individuals, emphasizing that rational individuals, benefiting from labor specialization, are incentivized to engage in collaboration. However, it neglects the additional value generated through interactions and connections within this system; it fails to recognize the role of the network system itself in reinforcing the value of specialization. More precisely, this additional value essentially arises from the efficiency in resource allocation facilitated by the distributed information processing within this network. As a result, the distributed information processing within the labor specialization network, symbolizing the close interconnection among individuals, emerges as the most significant determinant in wealth creation.

Considering that wealth is generated significantly through information processing within the social division of labor, information technology plays a crucial role as both a determinant and a potential bottleneck for wealth creation. Therefore, it is essential to thoroughly understand the impact of information technology on the specialization network and, consequently, strive to advance the evolution of this system with innovative information technology.

4.2.4 The Social Division of Labor in the Digital Age: Added Value Generated Through Weak Ties

In the digital age, the broad application of digital technology has further deepened the socialization of humanity, leading to the complexity of the division of labor system. As a result, the "network effect"[2] emerged as a new source of societal value. As the interconnectivity within the specialization network enables seamless information sharing and processing, it allows for the substantial positive externality that serves as a pivotal source of additional value in digital age. Furthermore, thanks to the application of the Internet, alongside the conventional strong interpersonal networks like close friendships and family bonds, the social division of labor network facilitates the establishment and maintenance of various weak ties, such as modern work relationship network, trust-based relationship network, and information exchange network, leading the creation of additional value. Specifically, weak ties can bring in new perspectives, ideas, and resources that might not be present in strong, closely-knit relationships. This is often referred to as the "strength of weak ties" in social network theory, which highlights the potential for valuable opportunities and information to flow through connections that are not deeply bonded.

In addition to the "strength of weak ties", the development of the division of labor in the digital age, propelled by information technology, carries several implications at both the individual and societal level. For individuals, with the assistance of emerging digital information technology such as the Internet, their decision-making competence is greatly enhanced, and the spectrum of choices has been significantly broadened, thereby encouraging individuals to participate in the social division of labor and realize their social value. From a societal perspective, the dynamic evolution of the social system of the division of labor fosters continued rapid growth in production within society. Specifically, the competitive and merit-driven talent recruitment mechanism, which stems from the evolution of the social division of labor, plays a pivotal role in identifying and nurturing highly skilled professionals. As a result of high-quality human capital, production efficiency within society has

---

[2] The network effect, also known as network externality, refers to the phenomenon where the value or utility of a product or service increases as more people use it. It's a concept commonly associated with network-based industries, where the number of users or participants in a network influences the attractiveness and utility of that network. The network effect can lead to positive feedback loops, with more users attracting even more users, resulting in exponential growth. Oz Shy, the Israeli economist known for his work on industrial organization and the economics of network industries, initially made significant contributions to the understanding of network effects and their economic implications in his book "The Economics of Network Industries". Katz and Shapiro, on the other hand, provided a more formal definition of network externalities in their work. In 1985, they defined network externalities as the change in utility obtained by each user from consuming a product or service as the number of users of the same product or service changes. These economists, together, has been instrumental in advancing the understanding of network effects and their impact on various industries, particularly in the fields of technology, telecommunications, and platform-based businesses, shedding light on the dynamics and economic consequences of network effects in these industries.

witnessed an overall enhancement, with production factors being efficiently allocated and the distribution of goods and services being expanded.

4.2.5 The Social Division of Labor in the Digital Age: The Measurement of Network Value

Various theoretical frameworks in the social network theory, such as Sarnoff's Law,[3] Metcalfe's Law,[4] and Reed's Law,[5] have been established to measure the network effect. They are subsequently employed to estimate the value of labor specialization network. Nevertheless, it is often observed that, within these analytical frameworks, the value of networks and their growth has historically been significantly underestimated.

In the field of economics, the value of the social division of labor networks has long been overlooked within the traditional framework of economic analysis. Through an economic lens, the market functions as a dynamic and self-regulating system in market-based economies, guiding the decisions of economic agents, thus resulting in the allocation of resources in an efficient and consumer-responsive manner. Essentially, the market economy operates as a "Class-Centralization" (i.e., a

[3] David Sarnoff's Law: David Sarnoff, a prominent figure in the broadcasting and television industry during the broadcasting era, established the American Broadcasting Company, which stood as one of the largest networks in the world from 1919 to 1970. Sarnoff observed that the value of his network appeared to be directly proportional to its scale, denoted as 'N,' representing the total number of users on the network. While it has become evident that Sarnoff's description of network value ultimately underestimated certain types of networks, it remains the most accurate description for broadcast networks.

[4] Metcalfe's Law: Metcalfe's Law, formulated around 1980 by Robert Metcalfe, one of the inventors of the Ethernet standard, postulates that the value of a communication network is directly proportional to the square of the number of users on the network (N^2, where 'N' represents the total number of users on the network). This concept holds true because the number of connections between nodes in a network increase at a rate of N^2 as the number of nodes (users) grows. While this theory was initially applied to communication networks such as Ethernet, fax, or telephone networks, it has evolved to encompass social networks and marketplace networks with the advent of the internet.

[5] Reed's Law: Reed's Law, introduced by David P. Reed of the Massachusetts Institute of Technology in 1999, recognizes that the value of many network types increases either proportionally with network size or, in some cases, even as the square of it. However, it is in the context of 'cluster networks' that the law stands out, as it proposes that their value grows at a significantly faster rate compared to other network types. According to Reed, the value of a cluster network increases by a factor of 2^N, where 'N' represents the total number of nodes on the network. Reed's rationale for using 2^N instead of N^2 is grounded in the concept that the number of possible clusters in a network that "supports simple cluster communication" is significantly greater than one. As a result, network density does not depend solely on the total number of nodes (N^2), but also factors in the potential subclusters, scaling much more rapidly as the network's user base expands. Since most online networks allow the formation of clusters, they are likely to increase in value at a pace in line with Reed's Law, potentially growing much faster than what Metcalfe's Law or Sarnoff's Law would suggest.

"Price-centered" information processing mechanism), which, through prices, facilitates the coordination of mutual influences and interactions among economic agents. Since price information is commonly viewed as a comprehensive representation encompassing all market-related dynamics of supply and demand, economists might assert that the efficient capture and transmission of vital decision-making information through the price mechanism renders researching the impact of external factors on the choices and actions of economic agents redundant.[6] As a result, the external spillover effects stemming from the social division of labor networks is neglected. In other words, although price information encompasses a significant portion of economic activity, it may not encompass all external impacts or network effects arising from the division of labor in society. Labor specialization networks essentially interconnect all nodes within the system through intricate flows of resources, information, and capital, ultimately realizing the creation and circulation of value. The initiation of this value circulation system exerts influence, analogous to the propagation of ripples, whether in the form of tangible impacts or the anticipation of forthcoming consequences, on all nodes or entities within the system, constituting external effects. These external effects not only strengthen connections among nodes but also give rise to the emergence of positive feedback loops, consequently leading to an augmentation of value within the intricate web of the social division of labor network.

In essence, when information or value is shared within a network, it tends to spread from one node (individual or entity) to another, resulting in a "ripple effect" where the value multiplies as it moves through the network. However, it should be noted that, the laws of network value, describing the patterns and behaviors observed in how information or value spreads within networks, are derived from practical observations rather than being based on a solid theoretical foundation.

4.2.6 Efficiency in Information Processing: A Key Determinant of the Social Division of Labor Networks

The emergence of digital platform companies like Facebook, Amazon, Taobao, and Tencent, exemplifying successful business models that fully capitalize on the value of social networks in the digital age, necessitates economists to shift their analytical focus. It becomes crucial to delve into the value and patterns of the networked social system of the division of labor, thus allowing for a more comprehensive understanding, from a dynamic perspective, of the 'comparative advantage principle' in the context of labor specialization in digital age. Specifically, the success of those platform-based companies is largely attributed to the additional value generated by efficiently connecting participants in a network, which results in cost-effective

---

[6] While economists have developed game theory as a tool to study interactions among economic agents, it still maintains the traditional framework of equilibrium analysis and does not adequately capture the cooperation and competition that emerge from the interactions among economic agents within the network structure.

competition and a more competitive development path as they scale up. Moreover, platform-based business models empower these companies to capture the positive externalities produced by numerous super-agents engaging in the specialization network. This, in turn, results in surplus profits and swift corporate expansion, ultimately propelling them to achieve economic giant status within a relatively brief timeframe.

Examining economies through the lens of social network connections reveals a dynamically evolving system primarily constituted by a multitude of interconnections among vast microeconomic entities. These entities are interwoven through intricate exchanges of various resources, with a particular emphasis on information. Simultaneously, the functioning of the system is propelled by the decisions of individual nodes, supported by the continuous flow of information.

The productivity and efficiency of a socio-economic system depend on several key factors, encompassing the overall efficiency of production processes, the information processing proficiency of individuals, and the effectiveness of information dissemination and utilization throughout the system. As information is generated through interactions among individuals within an economic system, the productivity of an economy fundamentally relies on the information processing proficiency of individual nodes. Meanwhile, the efficient dissemination and utilization of this economic information are constrained by the information processing capabilities of these nodes. Although the networked division of labor in the digital age enables distributed decision-making processes among entities, differences in centrality (i.e., the central or influential position within the network) and connectivity (i.e., the degree to which individual nodes or entities within the network are linked or interconnected) among nodes lead to variations in their information processing capabilities. Typically, nodes with limited processing capabilities become bottlenecks within the system, hindering the efficiency of processing and disseminating information, and potentially reducing economic efficiency. In other words, the efficiency of information processing at individual nodes directly influences the overall operational efficiency of the entire economic system, underscoring the significance of empowering individuals with digital technology and improving their information processing capabilities.

Information processing efficiency plays a pivotal role in the functioning of an economic system. It propels the development of advanced products, technological innovation, and wealth creation within society, ultimately contributing to a more sophisticated economic landscape and higher levels of economic development. For individual economic entities, the efficiency of information processing, encompassing the access and analysis of data, is crucial in influencing the effectiveness of their decision-making. This, in turn, impacts the efficient allocation and utilization of resources at the macroeconomic level. Moreover, highly efficient information processing systems enable more extensive and intricate interactions among economic agents, promoting deeper specialization and a more complex division of labor within society. This interconnectivity, driven by information processing, is integral to economic development and the evolution of economic systems.

4.2.7 Efficiency in Information Processing: A Fundamental Criterion for Assessing the Level of the Social Division of Labor

In the digital age, the escalating costs incurred during decision-making processes underscore the significance of efficient information processing. With the widespread digitization contributing to an intricate information landscape, the expenses associated with collecting, processing, transmitting, and storing information during decision-making have consistently increased, highlighting the need to revolutionize information processing procedures. Furthermore, information processing efficiency not only shapes the sustainability and growth of social cooperation but also influences the quality and quantity of products and services that can be generated. As a result, this efficiency, serving as the guiding principle for the evolution of economic systems, should be considered as a key metric for evaluating the development of labor specialization.

The success of any business model hinges on the establishment of an efficient information processing system. This system should empower the business by providing robust product output capabilities, fostering competitive technological innovation, facilitating efficient resource allocation, and ensuring effective risk management. All these factors collectively contribute to sustainable competitive advantages. In the digital age, the internalization of positive externalities, also known as the "network effects", within the platform ecosystem enables such business models to share the newly created value derived from empowering individuals with digital technology. Whether in the United States, exemplified by companies like Amazon and Facebook, or in China, with giants such as Alibaba and Taobao, platform-based enterprises founded on digital technology have swiftly ascended to become economic powerhouses. They have firmly established themselves as core nodes within the social system of the division of labor. Accordingly, platform business models that fully adapt to the digital economy experience rapid growth as digitization reaches a critical mass.

Once the efficiency of information processing within the economic system becomes a criterion for assessing the extent of the social division of labor, it also functions as a measure of individual value within this collaborative network. By evaluating the efficiency of acquiring, processing, and utilizing information among individuals, their latent value within the social division of labor network is determined, thereby establishing their potential contributions to this system. Therefore, with a significant emphasis on individuals' information efficiency in the digital age, individuals are increasingly motivated to enhance their competitiveness within the social division of labor by honing their information processing skills.

4.3 Why Do Individuals Participate in the Social Division of Labor?

Theories, whether rooted in classical economics with its early static comparative advantage theory or in contemporary interpretations from a dynamic perspective, all strive to explain the existence of the social division of labor and comprehend its inherent value. However, these attempts often fall short in investigating the division of labor from a micro perspective, neglecting the driving force of individuals, namely, their motivations for participating in this process. For individuals, beyond economic incentives, profound psychological motivations must underlie their engagement in social collaboration.

4.3.1 Participation in the Social Division of Labor: The Intrinsic Psychological Motivation

Modern psychology classifies human behavioral motivations into two main types: physiological motives and social motives. Physiological motives, also often referred to as biological or primary motives, are rooted in survival and physiological needs such as hunger, thirst, and the avoidance of danger. On the other hand, societal motives, also known as secondary motives, encompass the pursuit of power, achievement, and affiliation. From this perspective, the motivations of individuals engaged in the social system of the division of labor extend beyond the physiological realm, where they fulfill their survival needs through participation in the production and wealth distribution process. It also reaches into the social realm, enabling them to experience a sense of accomplishment in their work and personal life, a feeling of empowerment through control over material and social relationships, and a sense of social identity in their social interactions. Psychologists contend that the natural inclination of individuals to participate in social interactions and establish connections with others is a highly prevalent and essential phenomenon.

As social beings, humans possess a deeply ingrained instinct for social interaction and connection with others. When individuals isolate themselves from society for prolonged periods, they are at risk of experiencing profound feelings of loneliness and depression, which can have devastating effects on their mental and emotional well-being. Consequently, from a psychological standpoint, engaging in the social division of labor not only addresses the fulfillment of basic survival needs through economic participation but also satisfies the fundamental need for social belonging, interaction, and a sense of purpose within the community.

4.3.2 Participation in the Social Division of Labor: Rational Choice of Individuals

Research has shown that owing to humanity's limited energy and concentration within a day, the effective decision-making of the human brain has boundaries. Excessive mental exertion not only hampers decision-making efficiency but also results in heightened feelings of boredom and fatigue. Unlike the recuperation from physical exertion, which can often be achieved with a single night's rest, mental fatigue stemming from cognitive efforts typically requires more time and energy to dissipate.

In environments characterized by information overload and numerous significant decisions, individuals can optimize their decision-making either by seeking external support through collaborative decision-making or by adopting disciplined routines to simplify and reduce the number of decisions they need to make. Specifically, participating in a division of labor allows individuals to outsource some decision-making to external sources, streamlining their decision-making process, reducing the number of decisions they need to make, and consequently conserving cognitive and physical energy expended on decisions. Therefore, in terms of individual decision-making effectiveness, engaging in the division of labor becomes a natural and rational choice for individuals.

4.3.3 Participation in the Social Division of Labor: Pursuing Economic Interests

Examining the scenario from an economic perspective, individuals participating in the social division of labor harness the positive external effects of this network to propel their economic objectives. As they integrate themselves into the specialization network, their contributions extend beyond the creation of social wealth; they also gain eligibility to share in its benefits. Consequently, engagement in specialization not only ensures their sustenance but also opens doors for personal development. Moreover, it provides them with seamless access to modern civilization, enabling direct interaction with pertinent technological and informational resources within the division of labor network, thus catalyzing societal development through these social resources.

Within the framework of the social division of labor, individuals have access to various economic resources emerging from connections among the network, encompassing trade relationships for goods and services, as well as financial lending and investment connections. This empowerment allows individuals to tap into a broader range of socio-economic resources to serve their own interests, surpassing the constraints of abilities and resource and ultimately achieving greater objectives.

Within the evolving landscape of labor specialization, a contemporary financial system has emerged, accompanied by a variety of cutting-edge risk management tools crafted to navigate uncertainty and streamline resource allocation across diverse timeframes and regions. Consequently, individuals, through their participation in the social collaboration and access to the modern financial system, gain the ability to allocate resources across various time periods and geographical regions. With expanded resource allocation options and enhanced risk management strategies, they are empowered to better prepare for and mitigate unforeseen risks, such as economic downturns or market disruptions. Hence, by engaging in such network, individuals are empowered to pursue their own economic objectives as well as better manage the risks.

Active involvement in the social division of labor empowers individuals, providing them with expanded capabilities and a diverse array of opportunities to reach their objectives. Contemporary economic and financial innovations, spanning from insurance, financial markets, banking systems, to production processes, play pivotal roles in integrating individuals seamlessly into the complex structure of the modern social system via the principles of the social division of labor. This integration fosters interconnected economic relationships that transcend individual limitations, paving the way for both personal and collective development and unlocking potential opportunities for everyone involved.

In summary, whether viewed through the lens of human nature, decision-making efficiency, or economic interests, engaging in the specialization network presents individuals with the chance to achieve greater benefits, acting as a catalyst for the continuous advancement of the social system of the division of labor. Additionally, for society at large, the increased participation of individuals fortifies the social division of labor network, amplifying information processing efficiency, problem-solving abilities, social network synergy, and resource availability. This empowers society to generate wealth and fosters a broader spectrum of opportunities and choices for development.

4.4 Why Does the Division of Labor Take Different Forms?

In the social system of the division of labor, various types of organizational structures exist. This diversity in organizational forms has been present since the dawn of human societies and has become even more intricate in modern times. Exploring the reasons for this diversity not only aids in a better understanding of specialization but also offers insights into how we participate in division of labor networks.

4.4.1 Transaction Costs: Determining the Organizational Structure

Modern economists commonly utilize the concept of "transaction costs" to elucidate the diversity of specialization structures and organizational forms. This idea originated from the seminal 1937 paper "The Nature of the Firm" by the British economist Ronald H. Coase.[7] In his work, Coase aimed to explain the coexistence of hierarchical organizational structures and market transaction modes in real resource allocation scenarios. Transaction costs encompass various frictions arising in economic transactions, whether within a firm or through market interactions. These frictions include costs related to search, negotiation, contract, monitoring and enforcement, and potential breach of contract. Coase argued that transaction costs vary in different economic and organizational contexts, influencing the choice between hierarchical organization and market transactions based on specific circumstances. The Coase Theorem, building on this concept, suggests that clear property rights and zero transaction costs enable corrections of externalities through negotiations, maximizing social welfare. However, reality often involves unclear property rights and non-zero transaction costs, leading to diverse organizational forms addressing distinct transaction behaviors and minimizing costs for individual interests.

Given that any form of collaboration essentially entails a series of transactions among participating entities, these entities are compelled to minimize their transaction costs to optimize the benefits of specialization. However, diverse technological conditions occurring in various specialization scenarios introduce varying transaction costs and challenges. With the overarching goals of cost reduction and optimization of the benefits, organizations adopt a spectrum of organizational forms and division of labor approaches that coexist within different technological contexts. Specifically, within real-world business organizations, one can find diversified organizational forms such as joint venture companies, limited liability companies, and unlimited liability companies. Furthermore, within these organizations, various specific division of labor methods are employed, including line-based structures, functional structures, line-functional hybrid structures, and divisional structures.

Historically, organizational forms have undergone significant evolution owing to continuous advancements in production technology. In agricultural societies, where technology was relatively simple and uniform, the diversity of production organization forms was limited. Within industrial societies, the extensive utilization of large-scale machinery and variations in technological complexity across different industries led to a correspondingly diverse range of organization forms. The complexity of the economic ecosystem, during this period, significantly influences production processes, resulting in the proliferation of intermediary organizational forms. In the digital age, the advancement of digital technology has further heightened the intricacy of collaborative production, giving rise to organizational diversity, the decentralization of decision-making authority, and the emergence of flatter organizational

[7] R·H·Coase, The Nature of the Firm, [J] Economic (November 1937): 386–405.

structures. These adaptive responses address the increased complexity brought about by new technologies. Consequently, understanding the diversity in the division of labor and organizational forms has become even more critical in digital society.

4.4.2 Technology Development: Shaping the Labor Specialization Network

As technology continues to advance, it is intensifying the interconnected nature of labor division. The growing complexity of technology translates to intricate sharing of information, resulting in a heightened level of complexity in collaborative methods. This, in turn, brings about increased transactional intricacies and uncertainties within collaborative specialization. To adapt to these changes, organizations aiming to minimize transaction costs should not only articulate the obligations and rights in accordance with technological complexity in the specialization process but also institute suitable organizational structures for profit distribution. This approach will autonomously attract suitable participants and, simultaneously, ensure the motivation of each participant, ultimately securing the competitiveness and sustainability of the system. For individuals, it is vital to comprehend that their value in the system derives fundamentally from both facilitating the smooth operation of the specialized network and simultaneously reducing transaction costs. Furthermore, individuals should possess the capability to adapt to the potential risks linked to the ongoing adjustments in specialization owing to decreasing transaction costs. Consider a worker involved in product assembly on a production line. Overlooking the industry trend favoring automated and intelligent production processes to curb transaction costs could result in the irreversible elimination of their role in the division of labor. Therefore, adaptability and a proactive stance in acquiring new skills are indispensable for individuals to effectively navigate and flourish within the constantly evolving dynamics of the division of labor system. In the digital age, with the advent of automated production, a substantial portion of white-collar professionals, whose primary works revolve around information processing, find themselves grappling with the same challenges faced by industrial workers during. The intelligent information processing systems triggers a profound restructuring of the established specialized networks, displacing substantial information-processing jobs and reducing transaction costs associated with specialization. Consequently, individuals who fail to acquire the necessary digital technology skills are at risk of being unable to integrate into the new societal division of labor system.

4.4.3 Decision-Making Costs: A Key Factor Shaping the Division of Labor in the Digital Age

In the age of widespread digitalization, organizational structures are shaped not only by shifts in transaction costs but also by the effectiveness of information processing. The conventional evaluation of "transaction costs" primarily concentrates on appraising economic outcomes after transactions, aiming to identify appropriate transaction methods and impact the organizational structures of the division of labor in various scenarios. However, this approach often neglects the expenses linked to the decision-making process itself. In the digital age, the expanding scale and complexity of information render the decision-making process much more costly. This decision-making cost, traditionally implicit, becomes explicit owing to the increasing expenses related to information collection, retrieval, storage, and processing. The IDC report in April 2021 underscores the substantial growth in the global public cloud services market, emphasizing their significant role in supporting decision-making through information storage and processing. As decision-making costs gain prominence, they emerge as a crucial determinant in the economic cost of the division of labor organizational forms, with implications for societal efficiency and competitiveness.

Besides taking the transaction costs into account, the establishment of organizational forms should further consider the impact of different organizational forms on information processing efficiency and evaluate the decision-making costs. In essence, the costs of maintaining the social division of labor comprise decision-making costs and transaction costs. As digitization intensifies, information experiences exponential growth and there is a notable increase in the proportion of decision-making costs within the broader spectrum of labor specialization costs. This shift makes decision-making efficiency a decisive variable in shaping organizational forms as well as a source of competitiveness for enterprises.

In the midst of pervasive digitization, the omnipresence of digital information and a substantial surge in information volume escalate the expenses linked to decision-making. These costs emerge as a crucial factor in sustaining collaborative relationships, reshaping the cost–benefit dynamics for individuals aspiring to engage in specialization. As a result, the efficiency of information processing in various collaborative specialization forms becomes the decisive factor in shaping the organizational structure of the division of labor.

4.5 The Evolution of the Social System of the Division of Labor

The division of labor is a cornerstone of human evolution, where its resulting structure and status act as a barometer for the level of societal advancement. Undoubtedly, this collaboration system stands as the crucible for generating social wealth and serves as a linchpin for its sustained evolution. Without this intricate system, the collaboration among individuals for wealth creation, and consequently the very existence of diverse human societal forms, would be rendered implausible. The diversity and abundance of products arise from the social system of the division of labor, which seamlessly interweaves human and product reproduction processes. Essentially, this system propels the ongoing narrative of human civilization's developmental history.

4.5.1 Characteristics of the Evolution of the Social System of the Division of Labor

The evolution of the specialization network is propelled by the continuous innovation of knowledge within the system. It is not merely an accumulation of information but rather a process of discarding outdated knowledge and actively seeking novelty. In essence, given the significant costs associated with information storage and the need for efficiency, the system filters out obsolete and redundant information. This is precisely why we observe that the garment uncovered at "Mawangdui" in 1972, produced at the pinnacle of textile technology during the Western Han Dynasty 2000 years ago, is challenging to reproduce using modern technology. The loss of this technical knowledge is unrelated to its value; rather, it is simply a result of being discarded by subsequent divisions of labor.

A more recent example occurred in 2021 when the US Air Force issued an unusual solicitation on the government's project solicitation website. This solicitation sought vendors for the "reverse engineering" of the B-2 stealth bomber,[8] since the original manufacturer, Northrop, could not provide the necessary maintenance for the system. This engineering process involves disassembly, welding, and the fabrication of a new heat exchanger. Fundamentally, the challenge in maintenance is not a reflection of the U.S. manufacturing competence; rather, it stems from the evolution of specialization. Over time, relevant manufacturers and positions gradually withdrew, leading to the discard of corresponding production knowledge. Consequently, ensuring the continuous and timely supply of original products and components has become a challenging task.

These two examples show that the social system of the division of labor itself is the memory of product production knowledge, information and capacity, the evolution of the social system of the division of labor brought about by technological progress does not mean that the new division of labor system built on top of the old division of labor system necessarily contains all the knowledge and capacity of product production of all the past social system of the division of labor. This is because the storage of

[8] The US B-2 stealth strategic bomber is a low-detectability winged bomber that entered service in 1997 and only 21 have been produced, capable of carrying out strategic nuclear and conventional strike missions. It is also the only stealth strategic bomber in the world today, with a range of 12,000 km without refueling, and if refueled in the air, it can fly 18,000 km in a single flight to any corner of the globe, making it the "national weapon" of the United States.

product-producing knowledge and capabilities also requires corresponding resources and costs, whether they are stored by the human capital of people (labor factors) or by organizational systems (different types of economic organizations), which will correspond to corresponding costs. These subjects in the evolution of the division of labor are bound to choose the kind of knowledge and capabilities according to the principle of cost–benefit comparison, especially since the time cycle of the iteration of a generation of labor factors in the division of labor system is about 30–40 years (the length of a worker's lifetime of participation in the labor force), and naturally, the evolution of the social system of the division of labor beyond this period of time will cause part of the old knowledge and capabilities of the original social system of the division of labor to be abandoned.

Owing to constraints on resources for information preservation, humanity has ultimately chosen the path of digitalization. Digitalization is the key to preserving the knowledge, information, and capabilities generated within the division of labor system at minimal cost, without being easily constrained by factors like the effective labor hours of workers. This aspect underscores the transformative nature of digitalization for the human society. Essentially, digitalization allows the diverse historical outcomes of the social division of labor's development to be securely stored in a clear and reliable digital format. This eradicates time constraints on knowledge and information preservation, thereby reducing costs for future development.

4.5.2 The Value of the Social System of the Division of Labor

(1) The social system of the division of labor is the source of human wealth.

From the inception of humanity, our existence has embraced the form of a socially cooperative organization. The intrinsic social nature, evident in the division of labor and cooperation among humans, stands as one of our fundamental attributes.[9] Labor specialization thoroughly taps into the potential of individuals and consolidates entities within the network, thereby generating more wealth and nurturing the values that shape behavioral choices. The survival and prosperity of humanity are intricately tied to the wealth-creating prowess of the labor specialization system, as the productivity within this system empowers them to not only survive but also thrive.

While the products of civilization may be abundant, they do not inherently constitute wealth; true wealth arises from the productive capacity of the current social system of the division of labor. Consequently, a society should prioritize the orderly organization of the specialization system and provide sufficient support for its sustainability. The information processing efficiency of a society fundamentally determines the productivity of this system. In particular, an efficient information processing

[9] No individual who is completely detached from society can truly be a human being. As reported in the news, a wolf child living with a wolf pack cannot be integrated into the human society because what it has lost is not its social nature, which is also present in the wolf pack, but the social attributes of human beings. Marx had suggested that the essence of man was the sum of all social relations.

capacity plays a decisive role in solving complex problems, innovating diversified products, and promoting social development. Therefore, a social system of the division of labor with high efficiency in information processing is the key to social wealth and should be regarded as the fundamental criterion for evaluating value creation.

(2) The social system of the division of labor serves as the "converter" of wealth flow.

It not only acts as the foundation for wealth creation but also forms the basis for wealth inheritance, accumulation, and circulation. The accumulation and transmission of wealth constitute a crucial mechanism enabling the intergenerational division of labor and cooperation among human beings. This mechanism is essential for sustaining the reproductive process of humanity and smoothing out differences in the labor capacity of individuals at various stages of life. Without the mechanism of wealth accumulation and inheritance, the prolonged division of labor among humans cannot be sustained. The specialization system not only functions as the vehicle for production value flows but also serves as the "converter" facilitating the orderly operation of the wealth flow mechanism. Through participation in the social division of labor, individuals not only capitalize on their socialization abilities but also enable the conversion of wealth into products with tangible value. This process imparts meaning to an individual's efforts beyond their immediate needs, allowing them to fully unleash their potential for enhancing the efficiency of social information processing and augmenting production capacity.

(3) The social system of the division of labor functions as the "repository" for knowledge.

All products within the human society are crafted by this system, making it the archival "repository" that stores knowledge and information pertaining to the production process as well as broader insights into human civilization. The progress of human civilization is intricately linked to the evolution of this specialization system. An enhancement in the information processing efficiency of this system will propels human civilization into a golden era, akin to the onset of each information technology revolution, where rapid advancements occur—be it the inception of writing in early times or the contemporary birth of computers.

Individual and organization within the social system of the division of labor possesses knowledge and information concerning the production and demand of relevant products, contributing to the capacity for the advancement of social civilization. However, over time, this capacity becomes increasingly challenging owing to issues related to information storage efficiency and cost. Consequently, the transfer of relevant knowledge and information diminishes with the iteration of laborers across generations. The reduction in the volume of knowledge and information in society not only impacts the stability of the social system of the division of labor itself but also constrains the potential space for development. As a result, the information processing effectiveness and productive capacity of the social system of the division of labor decline, emphasizing the need for any human society to prioritize the effectiveness, stability, and developmental potential of the division of labor system.

The social system of the division of labor stands as the source of wealth and the guarantor of the wealth creation ability of the human society. In the digital age, decision-making based on vast, intricate, and dynamic digital information becomes a pivotal factor in economic behavior. The acquisition, storage, analysis, and processing of information itself entail substantial and non-negligible costs in decision-making. Therefore, in the digital age, the implicit decision-making cost and the explicit transaction cost jointly constitute the cost of economic decision-making within the specialization network.

4.6 Evolution History of the Social Division of Labor

4.6.1 The Social Division of Labor Before the Industrial Revolution

Before the Industrial Revolution, land was the decisive input in production, determining the boundary of the social production possibility curve. As a result, the amount of land owned became the symbol of wealth at that time. In ancient China, owing to the prolonged agricultural society and economy, the agriculture-based policy has been the basic state policy of all dynasties, which shaped the Chinese's affection for the land and formed the idea of the social class hierarchy of the officers, farmers, workers, and merchants. Most of the land was occupied by the government officers, while the peasants generally worked on the land as tenants. This pattern lasted for more than 2000 years in China.

4.6.1.1 Understanding the Division of Labor in the Agricultural Era

In the agricultural era, there was little revolutionary change in the technology and production methods employed in agriculture. The production dynamics between landlords and farm workers were straightforward: landlords provided land as an input, while farm workers contributed labor to agricultural production. In the distribution of production yields, three prevalent contractual forms emerged: the fixed rent contract, the share contract, and the wage contract. The fixed rent involved a specified payment per unit of land in both cash and kind; the share contract entailed rent in the form of a portion of the land harvest; and the wage contract involved landowners hiring peasants at a predetermined wage to work for them. Consequently, tenantry emerged as the fundamental mode of production specialization in agricultural society. Notably, this form of the division of labor was not unique to China but was rather a common practice across various regions worldwide.

However, early economists held divergent views on tenancy. Adam Smith, the pioneer of economics, believed that tenants lacked the incentive to work harder under the tenancy system, as the land was leased from the landlord. Following

Smith, economists, exemplified by Sismondi, a renowned French political economist, took a positive stance on the tenancy system. Subsequently, economists struggled to achieve consensus on this matter until Zhang Wuchang introduced the theory of sharecropping in "Transaction Costs, Risk Avoidance, and the Choice of Contractual Arrangements". In his work, he introduced the concepts of transaction costs and risks, providing a more nuanced explanation for the emergence of three distinct forms of cooperative contracts for sharecropping in agricultural production. Furthermore, he demonstrated that all these approaches are efficient when considering transaction costs and risks. In other words, these collaborative patterns are essentially the equilibrium outcomes that develop after the assessment of transaction costs and risks.

4.6.2 The Overlook of Decision-Making Costs in Economic Analysis

The Sharecropping theory holds significance in economic analysis as it effectively applies the concept of "transaction cost" from institutional economics to explain the existence of various contracts in the agricultural economy. This theoretical framework, integrating the concepts of transaction costs and risk into contract analysis, also sheds light on other specialization patterns. The concept of "transaction costs" empowers parties to analyze changes in costs for both current and future transactions, while the concept of "risk" facilitates the assessment of future benefits changes resulting from other factors. However, given the conventional assumption of rational entities made by economists, this framework naturally overlooks the costs associated with decision-making. Economic analysis primarily focuses on the optimization decisions of entities, considering the decision-making process as a technical problem. Yet, the reality is that rationality inherently involves costs and should not be disregarded.

While the agricultural society has persisted for thousands of years in human civilization, the technology employed in production has not undergone revolutionary changes. Agriculture, heavily reliant on uncontrollable factors such as weather and land, poses challenges in assessing the contribution of these agricultural factors to production. Consequently, the tenancy system has remained the predominant form of specialization in the agricultural economy, with the three forms of contracts (namely, the fixed rent contract, the share contract, and the wage contract) guiding the distribution of social wealth. The Sharecropping theory provides a profound analysis of the nature of contracts and their relationship with transaction costs under the market economy. It underscores the significance of property rights in the functioning of the economy and the impact of transaction costs on the operation of these rights.

However, this theory overlooks the crucial fact that the nature of property rights is inherently tied to agricultural technology. In addition to transaction costs and risks, the contractual patterns are profoundly influenced by the technology employed in agricultural production. Given that harvest outcomes are largely dependent on unpredictable factors, akin to the influence of "God", the impact of agricultural technology on output is limited, rendering production control and supervision somewhat meaningless. Consequently, both parties face challenges in determining the real value of their respective inputs at the outset of cooperation, and the subsequent distribution hinges on the ex-post output. In conclusion, it is the constraints imposed by agricultural technology that shape the specialization patterns between landlords and tenant farm workers.

4.6.3 Overlooking Technological Impact: A Limitation in the Theory

The sharecropping theory, despite its robust explanatory power, like many economic theories, overlooks the impact of technology. The implicit assumption in economic analysis is that technology remains a constant factor, experiencing no radical changes in the short term. From economists' standpoint, most economic activities, including production and distribution, occur under stable technological conditions. Consequently, failing to account for technological evolution confines traditional economic theories to short-term scopes, and this necessitates the establishment of various additional theoretical frameworks to explain economic phenomena. For instance, under the assumption of fixed technology, the unemployment theory divides the phenomenon into frictional unemployment, structural unemployment, cyclical unemployment, and seasonal unemployment.[10] From these classifications, economists perceive unemployment as a transient phenomenon, assuming its eventual disappearance in the long term. While this analysis aids in understanding the origins of unemployment issues during periods of sluggish technological change, it falls short in addressing the intricacies of the problem amid rapid technological advancements. In instances of swift technological change, the conventional perception of unemployment proves inadequate in providing effective solutions.

[10] Frictional unemployment is a temporary form of unemployment occurring during job transitions or individuals entering the workforce. Structural unemployment results from disparities between workforce skills and employer demands, often owing to technological shifts or changes in the economy. Cyclical unemployment is linked to economic downturns, with job losses during recessions caused by reduced demand. Seasonal unemployment is predictable and occurs at specific times of the year owing to fluctuations in demand within certain industries or occupations, such as agriculture or retail during peak seasons.

4.6.3.1 The Social Division of Labor After the Industrial Revolution

The Growing Complexity of Industrial Technology and Its Impact on the Social Division of Labor

Thanks to James Watt's invention of the steam engine, the Industrial Revolution originated in Britain and subsequently influenced the entire course of human civilization. The primary distinction in production between industrial society and agricultural society lies in the fact that, while agricultural production is constrained by the uncontrollable environment, industrial production is entirely under human control. Industrial production is characterized by meticulous planning, with the entire process conceived and constructed by humanity. This entails fulfilling various licensing documents in compliance with corresponding regulations, formulating production plans concerning inputs and technology, and establishing integrated supply chain and sales systems. As a result, the controllability and predictability inherent in industrial production enable the assessment of the value of various inputs across the production chain.

In the industrial era, the management process underwent a gradual evolution, forming a comprehensive assessment approach that spans input processes, output processes, and results. This development coincided with the financialization of industrial production and the emergence of financial markets, which stemmed from assessing processes across time and space, utilizing stocks, options, and other forms of securitization to evaluate future output results. During this period, human cooperation extended beyond immediate interest-driven decision-making to increasingly prioritize future earnings. This expansion allowed for a rapid increase in the possibilities for division of labor, resulting in a growing complexity of diversified cooperation methods.

Value Assessment of the Social Division of Labor in Industrial Production

Industrial production exhibits both standardized features and significant variations in the production of different products, leading to evident scene diversification. Consequently, the mode of the social division of labor, labor contribution assessment, wage returns, as well as the evaluation time all have diversified. The industrial division of labor has undergone three main stages, witnessing a progressive refinement and completion of the value assessment of the social division of labor.

(1) Stage 1: Assessment Based on the Output

The initial stage occurs after the prevalence of capitalism, characterized by immature labor specialization and a relative scarcity of industrial goods. During this period, the industrial revolution saw a significant increase in productivity that impacted traditional agriculture, with machines replacing some jobs. Simultaneously, the assessment of labor value (i.e., the contribution of labor to production) is limited and mainly takes the form of a "Piece-rate wage system". For instance, in the early stages of the Industrial Revolution, the British textile industry adopted the "machine operator-wireman" system. In this system, textile industry owners directly signed labor contracts with highly qualified and skilled machine operators, paying them wages. Subsequently, machine operators hired their own wiremen and helpers for production. This system essentially mirrors the agricultural tenancy system, focusing solely on evaluating the fruits of labor while bypassing the assessment of the labor process.

(2) Stage 2: Assessment Based on the "KPI"

In the second stage, as industrialization deepens, the enhanced productivity led to an abundant supply of industrial products, concurrently fostering intensified competition among firms and giving rise to monopolistic competition capitalism. In this period, how to enhance productivity in cope with increasingly fierce competition becomes the common challenge among monopolistic firms. In the late 19th and early twentieth centuries, facing the challenges of low productivity attributed to labor-intensive tasks, American engineer Frederick Winslow Taylor devised a set of quantified criteria to measure worker efficiency, known as "Taylorism".

This evaluating system includes the standardization of work methods, the implementation of piece-rate payment systems to incentivize productivity, the division of labor to enhance specialization, and the establishment of a hierarchical management structure for better control. The implementation of Taylorism resulted in a substantial increase in labor productivity for enterprises, marking the era known as the "Cleveland Prosperity".[11] The significance of Taylorism lies not only in its scientific definition of the value of labor specialization, emphasizing cooperation over conflict, but also in its proposition to collectively create social wealth based on scientific management principles. Taylorism not only standardized the methods of operation for workers but also uniformized tools, machinery, materials, and work environments, shaping a new paradigm for industrial organization and significantly contributing to increased societal productivity.

The implementation of Taylorism facilitated the extensive standardization of industrial production, achieving economies of scale and resulting in increased productivity and cost reduction. Meanwhile, under extensive standardization, firms developed automated machines. With breakthroughs in electrification technology, motors and other emerging technologies were widely integrated into production, marking the advent of the automation era. The application of automated machines has demonstrated their superiority over humans in product quality and productivity, thus leading to an increased investment in machines to replace human labor. This shift has fundamentally altered the specialization between humans and machines, influencing the entire structure of industrialized society.

[11] After World War I, the national economy of the United States developed rapidly. This golden period of economic and social development coincided with the term of office of the 30th President of the United States, Calvin Coolidge (1923–1929), so the economic prosperity of the United States during this period is also known as the "Coolidge boom". The technological revolution was the most fundamental and important reason for the Coolidge boom.

Furthermore, the widespread application of automated machines has led to an increase in the proportion of white-collar workers, and, at the same time, novel service industries such as logistics, finance, consulting, and design have experienced rapid development, becoming dominant industries in the economy. In this stage, with the promotion of quantitative measurement, companies have developed diversified salary systems based on the characteristics of different jobs, including performance-based, skill-based, seniority-based, position-based, and structural salary systems. The determination of specific wage levels for each employee considers external labor market conditions and internal business operations, applying the principles of labor market equilibrium and "equal pay for equal work". This approach leads to situations within the same enterprise and position where individuals may receive different remuneration.

(3) Stage 3: Stimulating the Potential of Labor

The independence of production-oriented service industry from manufacturing industry marked the third stage of industrial specialization. This stage is characterized by the increasing complexity of the business environment and the dominance of services in the economy. More importantly, these service industries play a crucial role in supporting manufacturing firms in coping with the uncertainty and complexity of the economic system. The production-oriented service industry essentially stems from the manufacturing sector. For instance, logistics, once managed within the operational scope of manufacturing firms, has evolved into an independent service industry. This autonomy has enabled the realization of scale effects and cost-efficiency, effectively meeting the distribution demands of the entire society.

Nevertheless, the service sector has followed distinctive developmental patterns compared to the manufacturing sector. One notable difference is that, in the service sector, production and consumption occur simultaneously, whereas in the manufacturing sector, there is a sequential process where production typically precedes consumption. Another distinction is that services have a strong characteristic of information asymmetry. Specifically, service consumers have limited information about the quality of the service until it is delivered. For example, an air-conditioning manufacturer, who outsourced the transportation to a third party, has little idea about the service quality provided until the air-conditioners are delivered. This air-conditioning manufacturer may worry about timely delivery, transportation wear and tear, and the skills and attitudes of the driver providing transportation services. What's worse, the uncertainties during transportation and the driver's performance are costly and often challenging to identify.

Given the uncertainty and asymmetric information discussed above, financial industries, characterized by insurance services, have flourished, ensuring the provision of certain products at a low cost. Furthermore, the significance of productive services in the division of labor has increasingly become apparent and is now a crucial factor constraining production wealth. The growth of productive services is heavily dependent on human capabilities, often referred to as non-directly observable human capital. This shift has consequently changed societal concepts and methods of evaluating the value of participants in the social division of labor.

At this stage, behavioral science theories emphasizing the role and value of human beings emerged, arguing that rational incentives can promote the coordination of interpersonal relationships in the workplace and improve work efficiency. Early theories focused on satisfying workers' social needs, while later ones shifted towards pursuing subjective psychological or spiritual goals, such as self-actualization, achievement, and satisfaction at work. These developments in behavioral science reflect the process of redefining the value of human subjective initiative in the social division of labor in the productive service industry. In economics, Gary S. Becker, the Nobel Prize-winning American economist, proposed the theory of human capital, describing the source of human social value from an economic perspective. In his 1964 book "Human Capital", he introduced the concept systematically, elaborating on various types of investment in human capital and their benefits, arguing that a worker's skills result from their investment in human capital and their social value should be reassessed. This human-centered economic development view emphasizes the importance of accumulating people's own productive capacity for economic development, increasing their role and value in the social division of labor. It underscores human capacity to create economic value as the ability to process information and highlights the role of human information-processing capacity in social production.

The social division of labor stands as a cornerstone in the human socio-economic system, driving human civilization forward and fostering the creation of social wealth. Individually, it becomes a rational choice for people to optimize their economic interests through specialization. The patterns of specialization are influenced by transaction costs and technological advancements. The continuous generation of new knowledge propels the development of the social system of the division of labor, discarding outdated knowledge. The efficiency in information processing plays a crucial role in shaping networked specialization. While specialization patterns differ between agricultural and industrial eras owing to their respective technological developments, specialization in the digital age exhibits distinct networked characteristics. The law of network value becomes a novel way to evaluate the value of the social division of labor, and the cost of decision-making emerges as a key factor determining the form of the division of labor in the digital age.

Chapter 5
Evolution of the Social Division of Labor in the Digital Economy

In the digital age, digital technology has empowered the public with unprecedented socialization capabilities. On the one hand, the digitalization has revolutionized the way people perceive the world, with communication and interaction among individuals taking the form of digital information. More importantly, it shifts the human-led social cooperation toward a machine-led collaboration mode. On the other hand, digitalization has reshaped the structure of economic organizations, posing new challenges to the functions of public power.

Given the radical changes discussed above, it is imperative for us to comprehend the underlying logic of digitalization, specifically how digital technology empowers individuals and how to fully unleash its potential. Furthermore, it is crucial to explore emerging organizational structures and how they create value. In this chapter, we are going to explore the characteristics of the economic impact of information technology, specifically the empowerment of digital technology to promote the division of labor, the evolution of economic organization in the digital age, and the change in the driving force of social evolution.

5.1 The Impact of Digital Technology on the Social Division of Labor

5.1.1 The Digitalization of Language

The impact of digital technology on the social division of labor is primarily achieved through the digitization of information using innovative cognitive tools. This digitization empowers individuals and organizations, altering their behaviors and broadening their choices, ultimately fostering social development.

Y. Yu and Y. Jiang, *Understanding the Digital Revolution and Its Influences*,
https://doi.org/10.1007/978-981-97-4939-3_5

The information digitalization makes it common for human beings to adapt to the production and processing of large-scale information. The digital age comes with novel information technologies, such as big data and artificial intelligence. Furthermore, the cell phones and computers in daily life, as well as the CNC machine tools and control systems in production lines, are all based on digitization technology. These digitized information and processes remind us that the digital age is in the air.

In the digital age, languages remain the predominant medium for communication and the formation of social consensus. However, this cognitive tool is increasingly being digitized, bringing about significant changes in communication patterns and social collaboration. One aspect that can be overlooked is the ongoing advancement of intelligent technologies based on digitalization, which challenges the traditional notion that humanity is the sole possessor of cognitive abilities.

Language stands as a crucial symbol of human civilization, serving as a pivotal factor that empowered our ancestors, Homo sapiens, to excel in the competition within the natural world. It can be asserted that language, the earliest cognitive tool crafted by humans, has played a significant role in the continuous advancement of human civilization. Integral to our society, language not only facilitates communication and fosters common consensus but also facilitates the preservation and accumulation of our collective intelligence. Thus, it actively shapes the path of human civilization, fostering complexity and diversification in contemporary cultures.

The chatGPT, introduced by OpenAI in November 2022, is a generative large-scale language model. Its demonstrated intelligence has exceeded the expectations of its creators, with some viewing this capability as an emergence of intelligent phenomena. The key to its remarkable intelligence lies in the varied structures present in the language data it processes. These structures not only encapsulate human subjective imagination but, more significantly, they mirror the objective world we inhabit, portraying the authentic logic governing our environment. The multitude of parameters recorded by this extensive generative model inherently reflects its cognitive understanding of the world, creating the illusion of genuine intelligence. Hence, the digitized advancement of language information holds considerable practical value.

In the increasingly intelligent era, alongside the traditional natural language of humans, society is progressively becoming inundated with the digital forms of language that computers can process. Currently, artificial intelligence technologies are endeavoring to achieve a seamless transformation between these two language forms. The aim is to facilitate more convenient communication among humans and effortless interaction between humans and machines. This ongoing process involves the digitization of various traditional forms found in human natural language, such as text, speech, visual arts, mathematics, and logical symbols. These diverse forms are being converted into a digital language format that is computable, communicable, and processable by computers. As a result, both the material objects in the human world and the corresponding mental constructs are undergoing comprehensive digitization and virtualization. The digitization of this ancient cognitive tool, language, has become a natural consensus and trend in the digital age.

5.1.2 The Impact of Language Digitalization

In the digital age, the digitization of language signifies more than a transformation between different language forms; it represents a profound shift in the tools of human cognition. As cognitive tools shape the extent of our understanding, the evolution from natural language to a digital format expands the boundaries of human intelligence. For instance, the ancient cognitive tool of engraved turtle shells faces preservation challenges, making it difficult to articulate complex expressions corresponding to the developmental patterns of intricate phenomena. Such a tool would be inadequate for facilitating intricate collaboration among millions of individuals and would possess limited cognitive capacity, rendering it incapable of comprehending highly complex matters. Consequently, tools constrained by such limitations would be unable to achieve feats like the monumental task of landing on the moon, which requires the collaborative efforts of tens of thousands of individuals.

In the era of intelligence, the proliferation of diverse language systems is pushing the cognitive boundaries of humanity to new horizons. Models like ChatGPT serve as prime examples, showcasing the emergence of innovative cognitive tools that give rise to novel forms of cognition—intelligent cognitive systems. These systems surpass mere linguistic translation among diverse societal groups, extending their capabilities to tasks such as converting speech to text or transforming visual language into written form, thereby amplifying communication efficiency. Beyond fostering mutual understanding and the sharing of cultural insights, they carve out uncharted pathways in cognition. Furthermore, these tools play a pivotal role in aiding humanity to delve deeper into the intricate dimensions of both material and spiritual realms. Their capabilities extend to simulating complex systems, driving innovation in pharmaceuticals and materials, probing the depths of human consciousness, and unraveling the mysteries of fundamental nature. In essence, they stand as a transformative force propelling the era forward.

The language digitization enables cognitive tools to fully harness the computational power of computers, unlocking the potential for a rational cognitive approach to understanding the world. It allows us to surpass our biological constraints of information processing, thus better transforming the objective world. This transformation extends to the human society, which undergoes comprehensive digitization and virtualization within digital language systems. The digital world, leveraging digitized language forms, achieves a complete mirroring of material and spiritual dimensions, marking the gradual realization of the concept of the "metaverse". This concept garners enthusiastic pursuit from diverse societal groups, deepening the impact of the internet. The pluralistic roles and identities individuals adopt in the virtual realm begin to exert profound and unprecedented effects on the real world. Virtual world identities not only create social value but also directly influence the collaborative processes of the real world in ways distinct from the past.

5.1.3 Digital Transformation of Communication

The exchange of information through communication is crucial for the collective consensus. Communication serves as a fundamental prerequisite for societal cohesion, facilitating the establishment of interpersonal connections and the creation of organizational structures within the human society.

In the digital age, communication media, especially language, are undergoing a profound transformation toward digitalization. This evolution gives rise to innovative forms that diverge from traditional natural language. These distinctions become evident in their carriers: one embodied by tangible physical books capable of presenting visible information, while the other exists as an intangible entity stored within data storage devices, requiring the aid of computer tools for access. However, the core differences fundamentally arise from the expansion of information processing and the integration of AI as new cognitive agents. The digitization of language, facilitated by intelligent information processing systems, empowers the handling of various types of digital data on a larger scale, with greater speed and efficiency. This enables people to share information processing procedures and results more conveniently and extensively. The processing of vast amounts of digitized data relies on intelligent information processing systems crafted by humans. Consequently, human knowledge increasingly hinges on the efficiency of these systems, transforming them into new cognitive entities created in the digital age.

Language digitization inevitably leads to digitized communication within the human society. Digital communication extends beyond the realm of data and information sharing among individuals; it now encompasses interactions between humans and intelligent information processing systems. This transformation not only turns intelligent information processing systems into new communicative entities but also renders them indispensable for aiding human communication and cognition. For instance, contemporary online customer service is delivered through interactions between customer service chatbots and humans. Therefore, the evolution of communication lies not only in digitized communication methods but also in the diversification of communicative entities. In a comprehensively digitized society, individuals increasingly rely on intelligent information processing systems, resulting in a seamless integration of human and digital entities in communication within this digital realm.

5.1.4 New Approaches to Human–Computer Interaction

It is through information processing and interaction that digital technology revolutionizes the division of labor, encompassing interactions among individuals as well as interactions between humans and machines. Notably, the interaction between humans and machines becomes particularly crucial as digitalization continues to deepen. The widespread digitization of information generates massive amounts of data and intricate information structures that surpass our physiological limits of information processing. Consequently, humans must increasingly rely on information processing machines to assist in the transmission and processing of information.

Recent advancements in brain-computer interface (BCI) technology serve as a notable example. With the assistance of BCI technology, individuals can directly control machines without the need for physical controllers. This demonstrates a diverse form of human–machine interaction and unveils the potential within the evolving trends of digitalized interaction. This novel interaction between humans and machines, facilitated by digitized language forms processed by computers, is poised to find applications in an increasing number of scenarios as the technology matures, becoming an integral part of human social systems. With the rapid advancement of BCI technology, there is a potential for the human brain and machine systems to co-process information, sharing responsibilities for different types of data. In this scenario, the machine systems within BCI technology could be personified as new cognitive entities for processing information and understanding the world. Similar to how individuals may possess multiple personalities, these machine systems could become personified entities. This presents both an opportunity and a challenge for humanity, as it raises profound questions about our existence and fundamental attributes.

5.1.5 The Impact of Digitalized Interactions

Owing to the irreversible trend towards digitization and the transformation of language forms, digitalized interaction has a profound impact on the sharing of knowledge, cognitive thoughts, and the establishment of integrated markets that share values. In this context, ensuring security and reliability in digitalized interaction becomes increasingly crucial. Safeguarding against issues such as data pollution, distortion, loss, and errors during the communication process will be the primary technological challenge in the intelligent era.

Historically, the evolution of human language and writing systems has aimed to mitigate biases and errors in communication. For example, the development of early written symbol systems sought to crystallize the expression of information, mitigating the inherent distortions found in oral communication systems. Similarly, the evolution of digitalized language recognizes that communication fundamentally aims to achieve consensus.

To better adapt to digitalization and harness the empowerment offered by digital technology, individuals are required to equip themselves with digital skills, involving the processing and sharing of digital information. Namely, leveraging digital technology to elevate societal capabilities and enhance the efficiency of information exchange. However, it is crucial to note that the formalization and computability limitations inherent in digitized language will once again define the cognitive boundaries of humanity. These limitations might constrain the boundaries of technological development, thus impeding further progress in human civilization. Therefore, maintaining a vigilant stance towards the sustainability and effective boundaries of digital development is essential, and constant reflection on the values and limitations of digitized development is necessary for its sustainable progression.

5.2 Digital-Technology-Empowered Social Collaboration

The digital age is characterized by the application of emerging information technologies such as big data, artificial intelligence, and blockchain. These technologies fundamentally alter individuals' roles in societal production, empowering them with higher information-processing efficiency in social collaboration and wealth creation. Consequently, the socio-economic system has acquired unprecedented productive capabilities.

5.2.1 The Impact of Digital Technology on Social Collaboration

One of the most notable impacts of empowerment through digital technology on individuals is the substantial enhancement in their socialization and cooperation, fully unleashing the potential for social collaboration and value creation. Meanwhile, individuals, in turn, are more inclined to utilize these emerging information technologies for broader social collaboration, initiating a transformation in the societal division of labor. The consequential societal openness becomes a crucial feature of the digital age, leading to an improvement in the overall resource integration within society.

The increasing socialization of individuals has brought about changes in social values, with the concepts of sharing and win–win cooperation gradually permeating into the collective consciousness. Simultaneously, collaborations, such as the circulation of thoughts and cognitive abilities, as opposed to traditional cooperation primarily centered around the flow of factors and products, have become integral components of the societal division of labor. The sharing of new knowledge, ideas, and perspectives has become an increasingly crucial means of interaction in society, driving a transformation in the openness of societal economic organizational forms and functions.

Concepts like the business ecosystem have gained recognition and implementation by an increasing number of companies, serving as sources for constructing new business values. Major corporations, such as Apple, with the highest current market value, and Huawei, the most influential in China, have built their company values on this foundation. Other platform companies based on digital technology, whether it be Google, Facebook, and Tesla in the United States, or Tencent, Alibaba, and ByteDance in China, also rely significantly on the construction and development of business ecosystems as the main source of their company value creation. Therefore, the business ecosystem has become a vital characteristic of the new business civilization, leading to increasingly interconnected relationships within the human society.

Therefore, in a modern society characterized by close connections and collaboration, the concept of a "business ecosystem" is increasingly embraced by various social organizations and individuals. Meanwhile, the idea of "sharing" in business has become the mainstream in modern business civilization, propelling a more comprehensive societal utilization of economic resources and becoming a crucial component of the emerging new value system.

5.2.2 Digital Technology Revolutionizes Human–Machine Collaboration Patterns

The application of digital technologies has profound implications for societal production, particularly in the transformation of human–machine collaboration. The utilization of technologies such as big data and artificial intelligence has completely altered the traditional division of labor between humans and machines, with intelligent machines increasingly displacing human labor in various production activities. Machines have gradually assumed various tasks related to information acquisition and analysis, making sophisticated decisions in production, and the complete automation of production processes has become a reality in many factories.

In the financial sector, automated reporting is widely employed, where intelligent systems can automatically process financial data on a daily basis, generating various reports and statements that optimize decision-making. In e-commerce, unmanned warehouses by companies like Alibaba and JD.com utilize automated intelligent systems to process order flows, and robots efficiently handle the classification and processing of logistics goods in an orderly manner, without the visible presence of human labor. In advanced manufacturing, such as the Shanghai General Motors factory, over 386 robots are managed by just over 10 workers. Workers collaborate with robots to produce 80 Cadillacs daily, achieving production efficiency that the traditional "Ford assembly line" production model of the industrial age could not match.

With digital technologies propelling modularity, standardization, and informatization in the industrial sector, the costs associated with intelligent machines are decreasing, even falling below labor costs; meanwhile, the efficiency and reliability of intelligent robots surpass those of labor factors. As a result, the importance of human labor in industrial production starts to decline, and manufacturers are more inclined to employ intelligent machines. This trend, however, prompts workers to seek new comparative advantages to compete with intelligent robots in the digital age or to create new market demands that necessitate human participation. From a macro perspective, the scarcity conditions of labor factors in the economic system will fundamentally change. The cost advantage of low-wage labor underpinning economic development in the digital age will no longer be a favorable condition for obtaining development dividends.

Thanks to the development of digital technology, information gathering and processing are no longer the bottlenecks in labor specialization. The traditional collaboration patterns, subject to insufficient or asymmetric information, are being restructured, giving way to the human–machine pattern where information processing efficiency is paramount. In this pattern, while intelligent machine systems take over tasks related to information gathering, processing, and transmission, humans still maintain predominance in setting objectives and making decisions based on ethics and values in society.

5.2.3 The Impact of Human–Machine Collaboration

Currently, the rapid pace of iteration in artificial intelligence has exceeded the expectation. For instance, OpenAI launched ChatGPT3 in late November 2022, and within just a few months, by March 2023, ChatGPT4 was introduced with significant functional improvements. ChatGPT3.5 had a model scale of 175 billion parameters, featuring 2048 parallel processing units and 96 Transformer modules. In contrast, the ChatGPT4.0 model scale increased to 600 billion parameters, equipped with more parallel processing units and Transformer modules. This enhancement allows ChatGPT4.0 to better comprehend natural language, generating text that is more natural and fluent, with an even more outstanding logical reasoning ability.

With an increasing influx of datasets and the utilization of powerful GPU clusters, the speed of iterative upgrades in intelligent machines is experiencing rapid growth. In this scenario, individual entities often find it challenging to maintain a competitive advantage in a specific value creation domain over the long term. Therefore, this comparative advantage is more prominently reflected in individuals themselves, emerging through the market formed by interactions between people. In other words, the value of individuals is self-defined and determined by their socialized interactive behaviors with others.

In the future, the demand for products will be increasingly fulfilled by "unmanned assembly lines" or "unmanned factories", while other forms of demands will be met through interactive markets between individuals. In other words, the social value of humanity will be more closely tied to participating in the creation process within the interactive market among people, extending beyond the confines of traditional production lines. This new market demand cannot be simplistically categorized as solely spiritual or mental; with advancements in neuroscience and language digitization, these needs will also be supported by intelligent machine systems. In the short term, the supply of mental products still demonstrates human comparative advantages. However, in the long run, as neuroscience progresses and intelligent machines iterate, humanity's dominant position in mental product production may gradually yield to intelligent machine systems. The fulfillment of human needs is expected to increasingly rely on the information processing efficiency of intelligent machine systems.

Digital technology not only facilitates social collaboration, reshaping the processes of societal production, but more importantly, as socialization deepens the society gains more robust information processing capabilities, fully unlocking the potential for wealth creation. Consequently, the socialization of humanity, alongside the introduction of intelligent machines, has become the driving force of social development. The creation and realization of individual social value are becoming more dependent on broader social connections. The comprehensive application of intelligent machine systems heralds an era of ubiquitous connectivity and smart sensing through the Internet of Things (IoT). In the era of pervasive intelligence, widespread socialization and intelligence will become the prevailing forms in the human society.

5.3 Evolution of the Division of Labor in the Digital Age

Since the revolution of information technology has given birth to the digital age, technology has proven to be a significant driving force propelling the development of the human society. Emerging information technologies, such as big data and artificial intelligence, serve as modern tools to further propel this development process. These new cognitive tools are the result of humanity's efforts to promote symbiotic development with nature, contributing to broader cooperation and communication in the human society. They bring about a comprehensive improvement in our capabilities in problem-solving and wealth creation, and this process is inevitably a systemic and complex transformation.

Individuals function as the microscopic building blocks of society, intricately connected to the whole. In the digital age, it is crucial to explore how individuals' decision-making and behaviors are changing, influenced by the widespread use of digital technology. This technology has significantly lowered the threshold for its acquisition, facilitating the socialization of individuals and empowering them at a social level. This empowerment alters individual decision-making and behavior, prompting shifts in the social division of labor and cooperation. Studying changes in the division of labor between humans and machines, as well as among humans, helps us understand the inevitability and characteristics of this development. Digital technology plays a pivotal role in redefining individuals' roles and participation modes in society, shaping new patterns of social interaction and cooperation.

5.3.1 Changes in the Human–Machine Collaboration Pattern

5.3.1.1 Reshaping the Social Reproduction System

The system of the social division of labor serves as a cornerstone in human civilization, playing a crucial role in the smooth operation of the economic system. It relies on the organized circulation of both human labor and products, with the flows of these two elements being interrelated. On the one hand, the reproduction of products is fundamental for the material well-being and survival of workers, thereby influencing the circulation of labor. On the other hand, when workers are displaced by machines in the production system, and the majority of people are no longer vital inputs, they lose the right to share the product value within the existing distribution system. This poses a challenge to the sustainability of realizing product value, leading to a weakened value circulation and impetus in the social system of the division of labor. The significant impact of intelligent machine systems on this system highlights the transformative shift in human–machine division of labor relationships during the digital age.

In the industrial era, Karl Marx introduced a paradox inherent in the adoption of machinery within the capitalist framework. The primary objective of employing machines is to diminish the value of commodities, subsequently lowering their market prices and enhancing affordability. This involves streamlining the necessary labor time for manufacturing goods. However, a crucial nuance emerges—the reduction in the value of commodities through machinery does not necessarily translate into a corresponding decrease in the labor time expended by workers. Marx points out that the efficiency gains and cost reductions often disproportionately benefit the owners of the means of production, rather than directly improving the conditions or shortening the working hours of workers. This observation reflects Marx's critical perspective on the exploitation and unequal distribution of benefits within the capitalist system, especially concerning technological advancements.[1]

In the digital age, however, a pressing issue arises as the application of intelligent machines gradually replaces human labor in terms of a fundamental function—intelligence in decision-making. This trend leads to a continual reduction in the employment of labor within production systems, deviating from the traditional economic model of increasing labor input. Consequently, an increasing number of workers find themselves marginalized within the social value creation system, unable to access societal product values. As the importance of labor force reproduction sustainability diminishes for economic systems, the unity in the circulations of both labor and product erodes. Human socio-economic value is no longer measured solely by its contribution to the production of products. Unless significant reforms are undertaken to ensure the sustainability of the socio-economic system, these challenges will persist.

---

[1] "Machine, Natural Forces, and the Application of Science" by Karl Marx, translated by the Institute for the History of Natural Sciences, Chinese Academy of Sciences. Published by People's Publishing House in January 1978.

As machines increasingly replace workers, their role in the production system diminishes, prompting a need to redefine their positions within the specialization system. This reassessment entails aligning the sustainability of product reproduction with that of human labor reproduction. Therefore, it becomes imperative to uphold the stability and sustainability of the human–machine division of labor system in the era of digital intelligence. In essence, a qualitative shift in the division of labor between humans and machines will inevitably require systematic reforms in the existing human-centric social system of the division of labor. The emphasis should be on adapting to the evolving dynamics of the digital intelligent era, where the nature of the human–machine division of labor is changing, and ensuring the sustainability of human reproduction processes becomes a central consideration.

5.3.1.2 Human–Machine Collaboration in the Digital Age

In the context of digitalization, within standardized product manufacturing and service provision, the dominant role of humans, historically prevalent in human–machine collaboration, is gradually diminishing. This shift is attributed to intelligent machine systems that internalize individual experiences in the collaborative production process as part of their system's iterative development, achieved through continuously optimized algorithms and expanding datasets. Standardized and learnable skills and experiences are being supplanted by modularized and precise intelligent systems as workflow processes are optimized. Numerous low-skill positions, and even those formerly considered high-skill, are at risk of being replaced by intelligent systems, as long as the pace of their iterations surpasses individual learning curves.

This trend is evident in reality. Low-skill jobs on assembly lines have been significantly replaced by industrial robots, leading to the emergence of "unmanned factories" and the disappearance of low-skill employment. Even high-paying and high-skilled positions, previously thought to require significant human capital, such as financial bankers on Wall Street, are gradually being replaced by intelligent machine systems. In the year 2000, Goldman Sachs' New York headquarters employed 600 traders at the cash stock trading desk. However, now only two stock traders remain, supported by 200 computer engineers who utilize automated trading programs. As the system has improved and stabilized, this number has further declined.

Economists specializing in unemployment analysis have observed new trends in the wave of machine-human substitution. While machine substitution has historically had the compensation effect of generating new jobs in other areas, nowadays, this compensation is increasingly absent. Acemoglu and Restrepo (2017)[2] employed data in U.S. labor market from 1990 to 2007 to explore the substitution relationship between robots and humans in the information age. They found that for every one thousandth increase in the ratio of robots to workers, there was a reduction of 0.18%–0.34% in employment positions, accompanied by a decrease in wages ranging from

[2] Acemoglu, D. and Restrepo, P. (2017) Robots and Jobs: Evidence from US Labor Markets. NBER Working Paper No. 23285.

0.25% to 0.5%. In other words, the substitution of machines for humans did not lead to a corresponding creation of new positions, and the decrease in wages implies a reduced demand for labor. Frey and Osborne (2013)[3] analyzed the possibilities of 702 positions in the United States being replaced by artificial intelligence and automation, revealing that 47% of positions are at risk of being replaced. In China, using the same methodology, Chen and Xu (2018)[4] provided a more pessimistic estimation, suggesting that 76.76% of total employment will be impacted by artificial intelligence in the next 20 years. Chui, Manyika, and Miremadi (2015)[5] predicted that 45% of work activities in the United States could be accomplished using current levels of machine technology, and this number would increase to 58% if artificial intelligence systems could perform at a level comparable to average human capabilities.

The development of intelligent machines and the resulting substitution effects on the workforce in the digital age will impact the specialization system. One crucial aspect of this change is the alteration in the scarcity of labor factors, where the issue of labor shortage will no longer be a bottleneck for economic system development. The substitutive role of machines for human labor eliminates the scarcity of labor in the economic system, and the development potential of the human economic and social system will be entirely determined by the information processing efficiency of the human society. Therefore, the digital age is characterized by a strong demand for cognitive tool innovation and anticipating new ideological transformations. Intelligent machine systems, emerging as new cognitive tools, facilitate the cognitive revolution, subsequently ushering in a new industrial era and propelling the human society into a new era.

5.3.1.3 The Impact of Human–Machine Collaboration on the Society

In the evolution of human–machine collaboration, when machines significantly substitute human roles, and this substitution occurs at an accelerated pace, it can portend a bleak future for individuals. Specifically, the existing system of labor specialization will collapse, making it impossible for individuals to share the fruits of productivity. This situation triggers a shift in the social value system, manifested in proactive retreats in the face of insurmountable competition, giving rise to concepts like "voluntary bachelorhood", "DINK (Dual Income, No Kids) lifestyle", and "lying flat". These notions contribute to the "internal competition" phenomenon, posing a challenge to the sustainability of human reproduction processes.

These concepts have significant implications, particularly in the initial phases of machine substitution for humans. As autonomous beings with intentions, humans

---

[3] Frey, C. and Osborne, M. (2013) The Future of Employment: How Susceptible Are Jobs to Computerization? Working Paper, University of Oxford, Oxford.

[4] Chen, Yongwei, Xu, Duo. "Employment Impact of the Artificial Intelligence Revolution: Review and Prediction [R].

[5] Chui, B. M. , Manyika, J. , Miremadi, A. M. How Many of Your Daily Tasks Could Be Automated? [EB/OL]https: / /hbr. org /2015 /12 /how many of your-daily tasks could be automated,2015–11-14.

actively strive to shape the value system aligning with the production system, thus fostering the sustainable development of society. An illustrative shift involves shared perspectives that transcend viewing market-valued products as exclusively private and un-shareable. Instead, individuals and their creations are regarded as societal assets, destined to return to the community. This transformation in allocation and value definition stands as a potent catalyst for the emergence of innovative business civilization paradigms.

5.3.1.4 Human–Machine Collaboration in Decision-Making

In the digital age, the rapid development of artificial intelligence has fundamentally transformed the nature of human–machine relationships. The primary reason for this shift is the fundamental transformation in the collaboration mode between humans and machines in the process of value creation, moving from production collaboration to decision collaboration. The core of this transition lies in the increasing dependence on digitized intelligent machine systems, which provide a competitive advantage in efficient information gathering and processing. In this process, individual decision-making no longer dominates in production but is instead crucially influenced by the output of intelligent machine systems.

Simultaneously, there has been a transformation in the issue of information scarcity within the economic system. With the support of intelligent machine systems, the quantity and complexity of information produced and acquired surpass human processing capabilities, making intelligent machine systems the main force in information processing. This marks the birth of a new cognitive entity, where the collaborative relationship between humans and machines in production enters a so-called "singularity", wherein people begin to use the information processing results of intelligent machines as the basis for decision-making. After this "singularity", the existential value of humans in the social production system needs to be redefined, leading to a new stage in the social division of labor.

In specific domains of product production, the substitutability of humans by intelligent systems directly results in the gradual disappearance of the predominant role of human laborers in social production. Intelligent machine systems dominate the production collaboration model, controlling numerous product production processes, while in the decision collaboration model the role of humans undergoes a transformation. Even in the era of weak artificial intelligence, owing to limitations in human conditions, the speed and potential for iterative learning optimization are challenging to surpass the formidable power of strong artificial intelligence algorithms combined with vast datasets, leading to the gradual loss of the predominant role of humans in decision collaboration with machines.

More individuals are taking on roles in the decision collaboration model akin to screws in the production system, contributing to the spread of the "35-year-old" phenomenon in the IT field. In the future, the majority of job positions for workers may primarily focus on providing services to other humans, with the ability to establish trust relationships becoming the core competency for realizing social value. This transformation signifies a profound evolution in human–machine collaboration relationships, requiring society and individuals to adapt to new industry patterns and values.

The changing dynamics of the division of labor and status between humans and machines will profoundly impact the factors influencing the endowment demand of product production, triggering a fundamental transformation in the global industrial landscape. With the application of artificial intelligence technology, the influence of labor factors is gradually diminishing, causing a repositioning of comparative advantages in resource endowments among nations. In this transformative process, the diminishing role of demographic dividends in global industrial division of labor makes it challenging to obtain new development opportunities, inevitably leading to a reshaping of the global industrial value chain.

As intelligent production systems dominate product manufacturing, there is a significant improvement in production efficiency, potentially resulting in an oversupply of goods. This implies that the mastery of production technology and the scale of market demand will determine the locational layout of the entire industry chain, thereby influencing the positioning of high-skilled labor. This change will directly impact the distribution of social wealth and the flow of value. Failure to adjust timely may pose a threat to the sustainable development of the product reproduction system, subsequently affecting the stability and sustainability of the orderly development of the human economic and social system.

In this new context, there is a need to reconsider every aspect of the industrial chain and implement innovative institutions and policies to adapt to the requirements of intelligent production. Society requires a more flexible and inclusive wealth distribution mechanism to ensure the fulfillment of people's needs, thereby maintaining the balance and sustainable development of the product reproduction system. Simultaneously, investments in education and training, aimed at elevating the skill levels of the workforce, become essential measures to adapt to the new era of industrial patterns. This transformation poses a significant challenge for national and global governance, requiring collective efforts to ensure that economic and social development remains resilient and sustainable in the digital age.

The disappearance of information and labor factor scarcity marks a fundamental change in the systemic conditions of the division of labor in society. This will profoundly impact the driving forces and modes of economic system evolution. In comparison to previous bottlenecks, the scarcity faced in the digital age will be more evident in the system's ability to guarantee the stability and development potential of the economic system. Therefore, the focus on how to ensure the sustainable development of the economic system, the balanced flow of value, and the potential or possibilities for development will become a new research priority.

With the disappearance of factor scarcity, the research focus of the economic system naturally shifts from the optimization of factor allocation problems to more complex studies on development costs and potential. In this new context, the core issue of research will no longer solely revolve around economic efficiency but will place increased emphasis on fairness. How to achieve fair distribution of resources in an environment of abundant information, ensuring that every individual in society can share the benefits brought about by the digital age, becomes a new focal point in economic system research.

This change signifies that the assessment and planning of economic systems will pay more attention to the overall development status of society, not just the efficiency of factor allocation. The scarcity issue in the digital age is no longer merely about limited resources; it is more about maintaining social fairness and sustainability during the process of digital transformation. Therefore, the design and management of future economic systems need to be more comprehensive and inclusive, taking into account the needs of various groups in society, promoting balanced economic growth, and ensuring that the development in the digital age brings greater common benefits to the entire society.

5.3.1.5 The Government's Role in the Digital Age

In the digital age, the systematic replacement of humans by machines is widespread, affecting diverse professional fields and posing unpredictable challenges to economic and social structures. Coping with this impact independently is difficult for individuals or single organizations, necessitating comprehensive and systematic coordination beyond microeconomic entities. To safeguard society's overall and long-term interests, government intervention becomes necessary.

Modern governments in the digital age face increased responsibilities and must assume additional functions to ensure orderly societal evolution amidst systemic changes induced by human–machine collaboration. This shift in roles transforms the social cooperation relationship between markets and governments, with the government actively fostering innovation, maintaining fair competition, and promoting social justice. The sustainable development of the social system of the division of labor in the digital age requires a reformation of government functions, making the modernization of national governance crucial in this transformation.

This transition calls for flexible and innovative approaches from governments, adapting to technological changes to ensure society can achieve sustainable development in economic growth, employment opportunities, and social well-being in the digital age.

The widespread adoption of digital technology and intelligent machines is causing a profound societal transformation. Automation has improved production efficiency but also led to the substitution of traditional labor by artificial intelligence, posing challenges in wealth distribution. The risk of unemployment creates economic pressures on different social strata, suggesting that traditional market mechanisms may be insufficient in addressing wealth inequality alone. Consequently, the government's role is expanding, with increased involvement in various levels of social-economic management and coordination.

Similar to the rise of Keynesian-dominated macroeconomics in the 1930s, the government is becoming a key participant in the economic system through fiscal and monetary policies. Education and training are crucial for adapting to the future work environment, and the regulation of digital technology is essential for its reasonable use. Establishing social consensus, involving collaborative efforts from government, businesses, labor organizations, and the academic community, is indispensable for achieving the coexistence of technological progress and social equity. Through this collective effort, we can create a digitized future that is both efficient and just.

In the digital age, government intervention becomes crucial for maintaining economic and social stability. Its evolving role may focus on systemic risk management and promoting sustainable development. This shift emphasizes the government's increasing sensitivity to risks while pursuing developmental dynamics. In response to digital advancements, the government may prioritize formulating and adjusting rules for the division of labor, ensuring effective and fair social cooperation. Government intervention is essential for guiding and coordinating changes in production and exchange driven by digital technology. Additionally, efforts may be directed towards promoting the reasonable use of digital technology and formulating policies to address potential risks and inequalities. Increasing government intervention will impact individual socialization and value realization. Government policies and institutional design directly shape societal behavior and values. To foster sustainable economic and social development in the digital age, the government may collaborate with other social members to construct a cooperative framework at various levels of society.

The rapid development of the digital age has triggered profound changes in the economic system, with investigations and penalties against successful digital technology application companies by major economies becoming a significant means of government intervention in the digital age division of labor system. These government actions are not merely punitive measures against monopolistic power; rather, they stem from the strong externalities of economic entity behavior caused by the application of digital technology, mismatching with existing systems, compelling government intervention to maintain the structured development of society and sustainable development requirements.

Although fines serve as a superficial means, they do not truly solve the problem. The key lies in establishing new business operational arrangements that adapt to the development of human–machine division of labor patterns, forming a new business civilization format, redefining the roles of individuals, economic organizations, and government functions. This will drive a comprehensive upgrade of the digital age economic ecosystem.

5.3.2 Changes in the Cooperation Among Individuals

The widespread application of digital technology is profoundly altering the pattern of human–machine division of labor, empowering individuals not only in terms of the convenience of information acquisition, transmission, and processing but also redefining individual decision-making behavior. In the digital age, individuals can easily access global information resources, yet this convenience also brings about the problem of information overload. Faced with a vast amount of information, society gradually raises the expectations for individuals' information processing capabilities. Therefore, for individuals, possessing effective problem-solving information processing skills will be a key path to realizing personal social value. This underscores the central importance of digital literacy and information management skills in contemporary society, influencing not only individual career development but also driving innovation and progress on a societal scale.

5.3.2.1 Expanding Social Connections in the Digital Age

With the aid of the internet and emerging information technologies, individuals in the digital age possess capabilities for interaction with the external world and diverse pathways to realize social value. This empowers individuals with unprecedented breadth and depth in their growth paths and life experiences. The digital age enables individuals, transforming their societal value and modes of existence, providing them with the capacity for proactive socialization, broadening perspectives, and shaping diverse and inclusive outlooks. This transformation will reconstruct societal value paradigms, marking the advent of a new era in the digital age.

Empowered by digital technology, every individual now has access to a globally connected platform, exponentially expanding the boundaries of individual socialization. This endows ordinary individuals with the potential to influence societal resources. However, owing to the vast ocean of digitized information and rapidly circulating streams of information throughout society, the decision-making and behavioral choices of individuals have become more complex and volatile. This implies an increasing demand for individuals to adapt to their environment and enhance their ability to solve new problems. The result is that individuals have a broader space of choices, making complete socialization possible, and providing opportunities to fully unleash the potential benefits of their social value.

As individuals expand their socialization boundaries, the growing societal competition pressure compels people to seek collaboration to enhance their social competitiveness. This drives an increased demand among individuals for cooperative organizational structures, as it is through collaborative platforms that individuals can realize the expansion of their social value. This trend has also given rise to opportunities in the development of platform economies, especially in digitally advanced nations such as China and the United States, where platform companies like Alibaba, Tencent, ByteDance, Google, and Facebook have become increasingly significant players in the economic system. These platforms not only connect individuals but also create new collaborative opportunities for society, thus propelling the transformative changes in the economic ecosystem of the digital age.

5.3.2.2 The Positive Externality Triggering Organizational Restructuring

In the process of individuals attempting to expand their socialization boundaries, the "network effect" formed by social connections results in massive positive externalities. In the example of a salesperson promoting and selling branded products on an internet platform, the salesperson gains income through this promotional activity. However, owing to the dissemination effect formed on the internet, the subsequent increase in the brand's reputation and awareness continues to bring benefits to the brand, a process no longer directly related to the salesperson. This illustrates the positive externalities brought about by the enhancement of individual socialization, demonstrating the widespread impact of socialization behavior in the digital age.

In the presence of positive externalities, as these benefits cannot fully align with the value created by individuals, individuals may attempt to reduce the positive externalities in their collaborative efforts with the external world. This is done to gain greater incentives and enhance the returns for realizing social value. This trend could potentially become a driving force for the dissolution of existing organizations and platforms because individuals, unable to internalize strong positive externalities, lose the motivation to exert effort in creating value within the organization. This may lead to a search for new organizational structures or prompt existing organizations to undergo adaptive changes.

Individual's social value still requires a social presence and collaboration among individuals is fundamental in realizing their social value. Under the "network effect" of expanding socialization boundaries, individuals with strong competitiveness have more opportunities to choose, making it more challenging for others to participate in societal competition to realize their value. This leads to a reshaping of the organizational forms of the division of labor and cooperation between individuals under the influence of positive externalities, resulting in new organizational structures that rebalance the risks and rewards of cooperation among individuals.

In an environment where individuals have enhanced capabilities to choose their socialization and an increase in socialization externalities, individuals more frequently opt for different economic organizations to participate in the process of societal division of labor. Economic organizations become more like platforms for individual participation, exhibiting more pronounced platform characteristics. Empowered by digital technology, individuals gain significant autonomy, no longer necessarily relying on economic organizations. Thus, individuals in the digital age have greater autonomy in their participation, giving economic organizations a more pronounced self-organizing feature.

5.3.2.3 The Social Value of Novel Knowledge

In the digital age, where information is ubiquitous, individuals find their time becoming scarce. Individuals are suggested to leverage novel technologies to utilize their leisure and keep learning, thus creating social value and maintaining competitiveness. The barriers to the specialization market are raised, intensifying competition. With more opportunities for choice, individuals are no longer confined to a single profession and their connections with specific organizational platforms are no longer tightly bound. The increased socialization of individuals makes the external effects of social influence more prominent, internalizing the social external value becomes a goal. In the digital age, part-time and gig economies become more common, expanding the boundaries of individuals' ability to realize social value through time socialization.

The empowerment of digital technology enables individuals to efficiently realize social value, expanding broader development opportunities. Individuals engage in socialized cooperation with the goal of maximizing their own social value, resulting in increasingly complex and dynamic structures of social cooperation networks, intensifying competition, and a growing demand for skill enhancement. This trend will drive emerging industries where new knowledge creation becomes the primary supply product and becomes a dominant force propelling societal development. The efficiency of social knowledge production and the realization of individual social value will rapidly increase, and the impact of new technologies and knowledge will become faster and more widespread.

The development of the digital economy has greatly enhanced the knowledge production and dissemination efficiency of knowledge creators, such as scientists and content creators. This has resulted in a faster and more widespread impact of technology and knowledge, allowing for the convenient and effective realization of social value. For product and technology innovators, the global market provides significant opportunities for expanding the reach of new products. Direct participation in global market competition facilitates global dissemination and monetization, supporting continuous innovation. For value realizers, such as live-streaming influencers engaged in product promotion, the digital age enables a more diverse and faster realization of the value of various products and knowledge in a more engaging manner. This has spurred further evolution in the socio-economic ecosystem of the digital age.

5.3.2.4 The Shifts in the Comparative Advantage of Individuals

In the digital age, competition among individuals unfolds within the framework of human–machine decision-making collaboration. To gain entry into this competition, individuals must first master the digital skills required for collaboration with machines. Additionally, acquiring skills for realizing social value through socialization becomes crucial, as individual socialization potential is fully unleashed in this era. The ability to realize and capture the potential benefits of the socialization process in competition will become a new competitive advantage. Lacking this capability will gradually put individuals at a disadvantage in intense competition. Therefore, in the digital age, individuals need to not only master the skills of intelligent machine systems for problem-solving but also acquire the skills to take the initiative in the division of labor, which will be a key factor in gaining a competitive edge.

In the digital age, the calculability of contributions from different participants in the market of the social division of labor is enhanced. The focus of competition is shifting from traditional signals (such as obtaining better degrees) to more fundamental learning and adaptability skills—specifically, the ability to solve problems and navigate uncertain environments. Future competition will place a greater emphasis on results, requiring versatile individuals with innovative problem-solving abilities, rather than narrowly skilled experts trained according to existing standards. Traditional academic education with rigid disciplinary divisions may struggle to adapt to this trend, and open and interdisciplinary higher education models are likely to become the mainstream in modern societies.

The core of social competition lies in individual's capacity for learning and adaptation—specifically their ability to navigate through vast and intricate information landscapes, and to effectively obtain value from that information. As human–machine collaboration transitions towards a decision-making partnership, routine problems are increasingly resolved by intelligent machine systems. This shift underscores the necessity for versatile talents with innovative problem-solving abilities to meet the demands of the evolving social system of the division of labor. These exceptional individuals possess robust learning aptitudes and thrive in complex environments. Given their relative scarcity in society and limited supply elasticity, they face lower levels of competition, as their unique and high-demand skill set aligns with the evolving needs of the social landscape.

On the contrary, the accessibility of general professional knowledge, facilitated by digitization, makes learning in these fields more attainable. Consequently, the training of professionals in conventional domains becomes more straightforward, resulting in a higher elasticity in the supply of such talents. This, in turn, leads to a diminishing social value for these professionals and an increase in the level of competition within their domains.

5.4 Evolution of Economic Organizations Driven by Digital Technology

The empowerment of individuals through digital technology opens up greater possibilities for socialization and exerts a significant external impact. This phenomenon leads to changes in division of labor, individual and organizational relationships, as well as organizational forms and structures. Analyzing the evolution of economic organizations from the perspective of the division of labor and collaboration reveals the values, boundaries, and driving forces of digital-era economic organizations. This perspective contributes to a deeper understanding of the developmental logic of social organizational forms in the digital age.

5.4.1 The Division of Labor in Economic Organizations

Economic organizations are regarded as platforms that enhance information processing efficiency, enabling societal division of labor through collaborative efforts. To adapt to changes in the economic environment, individuals integrate their information processing capabilities on these organizational platforms, creating a synergistic effect beyond the sum of individual capacities. This establishes a more competitive adaptive capability in the societal division of labor. Organizational platforms that facilitate efficient collaboration far surpass organizations with numerous members but insufficient information sharing in terms of information processing efficiency.

The impact of information on the organizational methods of societal division of labor can be traced back to Hayek's discussions on planned economies and market economies in the mid-twentieth century. He argued that the key to the effectiveness of an economic system lies in its ability to utilize societal information efficiently. In a market, information about changing demand is decentralized and localized. Concentrating this information in a planning center leads to high costs, information distortion, and an inability of the plan to meet market demands, resulting in resource misallocation. Therefore, he advocated for decentralized information processing mechanisms, allowing economic agents to allocate resources based on price information formed through market transactions and making full use of dispersed local information. Economic organizations, fundamentally, serve as platforms for collecting, processing, and utilizing the information necessary for economic decision-making.

The survival and competitive efficiency of economic organizations depend on their ability to integrate and process information from the market environment, known as the level of information processing efficiency. This directly impacts production costs and the adaptability within the market environment.

5.4.2 Determining the Boundaries of Economic Organizations

The scale boundaries of economic organizations are directly constrained by the efficiency of individual cooperation. The essence of organizational structure lies in the specific pattern of collaboration among individuals, aiming to maximize the unleashing of the societal information processing potential. An efficient organizational structure is nothing but the product of collaborative choices among individuals gradually aligning under specific information technology conditions of the era. The existence of organizational platforms enables diverse individuals to collectively achieve economic goals through information processing mechanisms, yet this comes with certain operational costs. The size and boundaries of organizations largely depend on the individual capacity to choose cooperation, a capacity constrained by the efficiency conditions of production and information technologies. In the digital age, organizational size will be influenced by the empowerment of information technology. Technological advancements empower individuals, and this impact is manifested in changes to organizational boundaries, creating synergistic and divisive effects that impact size and boundaries. Organizational scale effects can propel expansion, but as the coordination scope widens, it triggers increasing marginal costs beyond technological efficiency and increasing external benefits, thus limiting the expansion of organizational cooperative relationships, forming finite boundaries. Therefore, the boundaries of economic organizations fundamentally depend on the technological efficiency boundaries that different eras of information technology empower for individual cooperation.

In different societal stages, the forms of economic organizations evolve with technological advancements. In agrarian societies, simple agricultural tools result in lower demands for societal cooperation, making households relatively independent economic units. In industrial societies, complex machinery and technological advancements lead to large-scale social cooperation, with corporations becoming the primary organizational form. In the digital economic era, the development of internet and cloud computing technologies significantly enhances the efficiency of scale through digital support. Platform-based companies construct massive economic ecosystems, with the number of businesses and service providers reaching millions, catering to the needs of over a billion users, forming an unprecedented scale.

5.4.3 Determining the Structure of Economic Organizations

Empowered by digital technology, individuals not only possess efficient social information processing capabilities, creating independent "super-individuals", but their social assistance capabilities also significantly improve, giving rise to new forms of social cooperation. In this context, social cooperation among individuals is gradually shifting from the "assembly line screw" model in industrial era, exploring collaborative development methods adapted to the digital technology environment. In the new era, social cooperation between "super-individuals" and "ordinary individuals" becomes a crucial topic.

In the digital age, technology empowers individuals in their choices of specialization and collaboration, shaping the internal division of labor and operational mechanisms within economic organizations. In this context, individuals have more opportunities for choices owing to digital technology, enabling them to pursue higher professional skills and achieve societal value, as well as internalize the externalities of socialization. In the digital age, organizations can only effectively build collaborative relationships and realize their value if they prioritize the realization of individual professional value, individual autonomy in choices, and the long-term development interests of individuals. In other words, if organizational platforms fail to enable individuals to access the potential benefits of technological empowerment, the stability of the organization and the realization of societal value will lose their micro-level foundation.

In the digital age, individuals engage in socialized collaboration through organizational platforms, aiming to better adapt to the complex and dynamic competitive environment. Seeking diverse professional collaborators, building a powerful collaborative network, and enhancing information acquisition and processing capabilities are proactive measures to achieve societal value. This collaboration also helps individuals find robust platforms for realizing the value of technological empowerment, strengthening their ability to cope with environmental risks. Therefore, individuals require organizational platforms to provide a normal pathway, offering a stable environment for the realization of professional value and hedging against uncertainty. Despite the continued necessity of economic organizations, individuals empowered by digital technology have more influence and autonomy in organizational cooperation.

5.4.4 "Super Individuals": Posing a New Challenge to Economic Organizations

The digital age has given rise to "super-individuals" as individuals seek broader and more valuable collaborative opportunities owing to social empowerment. This trend leads individuals to gradually move away from traditional organizations, opting for part-time collaborations and reducing dependence on family and conventional organizations. Empowered by technology, individual independence grows, and the realization of social aspects is no longer confined to traditional organizational platforms. Traditional organizations are gradually disintegrating, giving way to influential "super-individuals". These "super-individuals" equipped with digital tools and platforms, achieve independent socialization, propelling the rise of the "gig economy."

The increased externality of socialization has elevated the demand for individuals to enhance their self-management abilities in socialization. With the growing independence of "super-individuals" empowered by digital technology, new challenges arise, particularly in addressing how individuals collaborate. The pivotal development of blockchain technology addresses this challenge and has profound implications for societal division of labor. In the economic and social systems of the digital age, the blockchain technology holds important strategic values.

5.4.5 Entrepreneurship in the Digital Age

In the era of the digital economy, technological iteration and knowledge scarcity have become critical factors for economic and social development. Entrepreneurs must shift from merely integrating capital to becoming integrators of technology and knowledge resources. This adaptation is crucial to navigate the intricate and swiftly evolving market landscape, meeting the high-speed processing demands of digitized information. Economic organizations lacking efficient information processing capabilities are prone to elimination. Under the ownership system of factors, entrepreneurs should be shapers of organizational flexibility, promoters of self-growth, adept at discerning organizational change needs, and skilled in coordinating the integration of capital and technology. This is essential for effectively adapting to the development environment of technological innovation iterations, avoiding becoming a liability and potential risk for the organization.

5.4.6 Economic Organizations in the Digital Age

In the era of the digital economy, economic organizations serve not only as platforms for capital or labor but also as a network system that integrates technological systems. Their value should be assessed based on the technological realization of societal value, breaking free from the short-term return constraints dominated by finance or capital. Evaluating from the perspective of a technological system, focusing on the efficiency of economic resource utilization and the efficiency of creating economic value is a criterion more aligned with societal value. Therefore, the mission of economic organizations lies in integrating knowledge or scarce technological talent, providing platforms to unleash potential, effectively integrating technical teams, and enhancing adaptability and unique competitiveness.

5.4.7 The Goals of Economic Organizations

In the digital age, the scarcity is not in digitized information resources but in the ability to effectively process digital information. Information spreads rapidly, and the environment becomes more complex, rendering traditional organizational forms inadequate. New technological paradigms demand organizations to be more flexible and efficient in handling external shocks. Effective feedback mechanisms need to be designed to ensure that organizations can adapt to the complexity of digitized information.

Organizational goals are oriented towards achieving societal value, utilizing digitization to internalize repetitive and replicable content in work processes through intelligent systems. The work of organizational members primarily focuses on innovation and tasks that are challenging to replicate, making it difficult to set singular predefined goals. This results in diverse work goal assessments, compelling organizations to adopt networked collaborative forms internally. This approach is more effective in integrating technological and knowledge resources, enhancing resilience in the face of environmental shocks.

5.4.8 Autonomous Collaboration Within Organizations

Within the organization, members' knowledge and skills are considered integral parts of the organizational ecosystem. Collaboration has shifted from department-based cooperation to skill-oriented ecological collaboration, resulting in a less clear internal division of labor. The tasks associated with organizational goals become the role positioning for each member. Positions requiring comprehensive skills are more flexible, making the organizational structure more resilient. Internal coordination is guided by a problem-oriented digitized information flow, and member behaviors and outcomes are recorded and assessed through digital information. The cooperative incentive model encourages the emergence of self-organized forms within the organization, enhancing the role of autonomous collaboration internally. Owing to the weak linkages between the organization and its members, the organizational structure needs to be more open, attracting and selecting suitable new members. Through the internally formed cooperative ecosystem and assessment system, unsuitable members are systematically guided to leave, achieving effective integration of internal and external resources. This process forms a system characterized by agility, adaptability, and coordination, enabling members to realize the societal value of their technological empowerment on the organizational platform. The organization, in turn, aims to achieve overall organizational value through the realization of member value.

Economic organizations need to cultivate a corporate culture centered around responsibility and proactiveness, establishing corresponding values for organizational members. This helps mitigate the impact of rapid changes in the collaborative environment and reconciles the contradiction between environmental uncertainty and task goal certainty responsibilities. Such a culture contributes to ensuring the harmonious alignment between the economic organization's structure and value creation, maintaining consistency with values in execution.

5.4.9 Openness and Inclusivity Emerging as Characteristics of Economic Organizations

In the digital age, the development of information technology has made information a crucial force in the integration of economic resources. Traditional economic organizational structures, primarily driven by capital, are undergoing transformation, with the diminishing ability to integrate resources and decreasing impact on the creation of societal value. In the new organizational paradigm, the integration capabilities of technological and knowledge capital have become critical factors dominating the value creation and realization of economic organizations. Owing to the rapid advancement of technology and knowledge, the competitiveness of economic organizations can only be maintained by continually introducing new technological and knowledge elements. Therefore, openness and inclusivity will become key features of the organizational structure in the digital age.

In the digital age, financial capital is no longer the dominant force but subservient to technological and knowledge capital. The prevailing model of economic organizations has gradually shifted from a capital-centric approach to the integration of technological and knowledge capital. Founders of current world-class companies are often technical experts, such as Apple, Google, Facebook, Microsoft, Tesla, Huawei, Tencent, DJI, Baidu, and others. Their rapid development is achieved through the capitalization of technological capital, facilitated by financial capital, leading to substantial wealth growth for the founders. Taking DJI as an example, its competitive bidding financing reached $1 billion in 2018, highlighting the dominant position of technological and knowledge capital when facing financial capital, with the influence of financial capital gradually diminishing.

5.5 The Propelling Force of the Socio-Economic System in the Digital Age

5.5.1 The Role of Human Desire and Cognitive Innovation

From the onset of the commodity economy, the competitive mechanism has been the fundamental driver for resource allocation and self-development in economic systems. Human societal progress stems from individuals' pursuit of a better life, achieved through collaboration among people. Collaboration is the means of wealth creation in a commodity economy, and both collaboration and competition jointly constitute the forces propelling social evolution, rooted in human nature's pursuit of self-interest.

The primal driving force behind social evolution originates from human desires, while the practical impetus comes from the expansion of human cognition, leading to decision-making and behavioral norms under different worldviews and value systems. These decisions and behaviors alter the relationships between individuals, triggering various organizational forms and constructing social structures and operational methods in different eras. Human cognitive expansion and progress manifest as the ability to acquire a diverse range of information, delve into the potential value of information, and possess more powerful information processing capabilities. These capabilities are often realized through the invention and creation of new technological devices. Therefore, the transition in the dominant technology of society is a foundational condition driving the process of social evolution.

5.5.2 The Role of Information Flows

In the digital age, the digitization of information propels social evolution and becomes a key determinant of decision outcomes. The traditional economic model, guided by the flow of funds, is shifting towards an evolution where resource allocation is determined by the flow of information. In the fund-flow-centric model, the rate of financial returns shapes the aggregation of resources and the collaborative state of various economic entities. However, in the information-centric model, the efficiency of information processing determines the speed and direction of economic development. The acquisition, flow, processing efficiency, and the potential realization of value in information determine the abundance of resources and development opportunities across different parts of the economic system.

The widespread application of the internet has transformed the way information is disseminated, with digitized information circulating globally at the speed of light. This fully digitized mode of information dissemination enables humanity to engage in information exchange and processing beyond the constraints of time and geography. In the era dominated by information, the competitive mechanism operates more efficiently within the division of labor among individuals, with an unprecedented scope and speed of influence. The rapid application of digital technology is exerting a profound impact on economic systems and social evolution, causing the technological factors driving social evolution to shift from slow variables in the past to fast variables.

In the past, the impact of new technologies on economic cycles was measured as Kondratiev cycles, taking 50–60 years. However, in the era of the digital economy, the speed of information dissemination is extremely fast, and the impact of new technologies quickly spreads, no longer affecting individuals and organizational entities in a slow-evolving manner. The convenience, ubiquity, and real-time processing speed of the internet allow opportunities brought by new technologies to be quickly discovered in the market and swiftly transformed into new products. The economic cycle of technological impact is no longer a slow evolution but rapidly takes effect across society. For example, the advent of smartphones quickly changed the landscape of the mobile phone industry, causing traditional giants like Nokia to rapidly lose their leading positions, ushering humanity into the era of mobile internet.

With the development of information technology and production techniques, humanity's capacity for information sharing and processing has continuously increased. This has led to a shortening of the intervals between technological revolutions, an enhancement of their impact, and an expansion of their influence. In the digital age, this trend is even more pronounced as advancements in new technologies are concentrated on improving human cognition and information processing efficiency. Different groups leverage these new technological tools for extensive cognitive exploration, facilitating comprehensive breakthroughs that find applications across multiple industries. This distributed characteristic not only shortens the impact cycle of new technologies but also provides more opportunities for improvement, accelerating their progress beyond previous rates.

The rapid development of digital information technology signifies a new phase in the information technology revolution, fundamentally altering societal communication and profoundly influencing the understanding of individual intelligence attributes. The empowering effects of digital technology not only endow every ordinary individual with the potential to be a "universal societal influencer" but also make it challenging to accurately measure their potential impact and societal value.

This has triggered a fundamental transformation in the modes of cooperation. In this transformation, the dynamic changes in individual choice and opportunities become the primary driving force for the transformation of economic organizations. The swift iteration of technology and knowledge is gradually replacing the traditional capital-dominated development model, shaping autonomy as a prominent feature of economic organizations in the digital age. Simultaneously, openness and inclusivity become key architectural characteristics. In the future, technological iteration will play an even more crucial role, shaping the evolutionary direction of economic organizations.

Chapter 6
The Reshaping Effects of Digital Technology on the Social Division of Labor

6.1 The Impact of Digital Technology on Specialization

The technological advancements serve as the cornerstone of the social division of labor. Digital technology differs significantly from traditional agriculture, steam engines, and electrification. In the past, technological innovations primarily changed the division of labor by influencing the production processes and methods. However, digital technology achieves this through enhancing the efficiency of information dissemination, analysis, and processing, leading to adjustments in production methods. In essence, such transformation revolves around innovating production methods by integrating information resources. Unlike previous technological shifts that focused mainly on material tool innovations, digital technology stimulates collective intelligence in human information processing through efficient information connectivity. This makes the technological innovation more agile and widespread.

The widespread application of digital technology has intensified competition in the labor specialization, leading to profound effects on its patterns and evaluation methods. The impact of digital technology on the social division of labor can be divided into three stages: the application of internet technology, artificial intelligence, and the application of big data and blockchain technology.

Before the application of internet technology, the patterns and evaluation methods of the social division of labor appear little differences compared to the late industrialization period. Financial capital still retained strong influence, and technological capital had not yet taken a dominant position. However, the value of technology gradually gained widespread recognition, giving rise to concepts and theories like the "knowledge economy", emphasizing the crucial role of technological knowledge in economic development.

As internet technology finds widespread application and the validation of the "Internet+" business model, internet thinking gradually gains recognition, altering the patterns of specialization. Digital technology, especially the internet and artificial intelligence, has unprecedentedly accelerated the pace and breadth of technological

Y. Yu and Y. Jiang, *Understanding the Digital Revolution and Its Influences*,
https://doi.org/10.1007/978-981-97-4939-3_6

change, transforming technology from a systematically slow variable into a fast one. Companies that fail to seize opportunities in technological innovation may swiftly face market elimination, as exemplified by the fate of companies like Kodak and Nokia.

In this transformation, technological capital progressively gains dominance in the economic system, with major technology companies on the Nasdaq market becoming darlings of the financial market. The decision-making model of companies with dual-class shares receives widespread acceptance, signaling a relative decline in the influence of financial capital, which is more inclined to subordinate itself to technological capital. In today's dynamic landscape, professionals with advanced digital skills are in great demand. Their expertise is not only valued within companies and financial circles, but it also translates into lucrative salaries. This not only accelerates the accumulation of human capital in the digital realm but also plays a crucial role in supporting the overall digitization of society.

The widespread application of the internet has facilitated the abundant production and storage of digitized information. The demand to exploit the value of this information has given rise to the development of big data and artificial intelligence. Efficiency continues to be a key driving force shaping the digital economy, influencing its path towards standardization and modularization. This emphasis underscores the prevailing business logic guiding the evolution of digital economic development. Information flow becomes a critical guiding force for economic resource and capital flows. Entities or individuals with advantages in information acquisition or analysis hold more initiative and influence in the social system of the division of labor. In the current era of explosive digitized information, the ability to manage information has become a scarce skill.

An illustrative example highlights the disparities among individuals' economic value in different industries. In the industrial era, especially its later stages, economic financialization was evident, and financial capital was the dominant force in resource allocation. Joining the finance industry generally meant high salaries. However, in the digital age, overall, core positions in major internet companies tend to yield higher returns than core positions in financial institutions. Also, an examination of the compensation of ordinary employees in the annual reports of both companies in 2019 further highlights the differences. Ping An had a total of 370,000 employees, with an average monthly salary of 16,000 RMB, while Tencent, with a total of 54,000 employees, had an average monthly salary of 81,000 RMB. This phenomenon indicates that societal recognition of the value of digital information management capability in the division of labor system far exceeds the value assigned to the ability to allocate financial resources.

6.2 New Characteristics and Trends of the Social Division of Labor in the Digital Age

6.2.1 New Characteristics in the Digital Age

Digital technology's empowerment accentuates the importance of technological influence, particularly in information processing. It disrupts traditional roles in the social division of labor, creating a more platform-centric ecosystem. In the digital age, the division of labor undergoes four significant changes.

(1) Technology innovation now serves as a rapid driver for societal development.

Technology innovation now serves as a rapid driver for societal development. In the pre-digital age, technological impacts on the division of labor unfolded slowly. Hindered by lagging information dissemination technology, humans struggled to unleash information processing potential, resulting in a gradual progression of new knowledge and technology. Additionally, the slow diffusion of new technologies took decades or more for critical innovations to gain widespread application. However, in the era of digital technology empowerment, marked by the internet and big data, individual capabilities in information acquisition, processing, analysis, and dissemination have significantly improved. This effective unleashing of human information processing potential enables the swift dissemination of new knowledge and technologies. Consequently, technology innovation has transitioned from a slow variable with a gradual societal impact to a fast variable capable of swiftly influencing society, accelerating the pace of societal development.

(2) The information barrier has been removed.

In the traditional division of labor, everyone needed specialized knowledge in specific industries or roles to contribute to societal wealth creation and realization. Each person served as a repository and processor of societal knowledge, leading to the formation of professional skill barriers in various occupations such as typists, operators, salespersons, and assemblers. These barriers ensured a clear delineation of professional roles within the social division of labor. However, in the digital age, the functions of information storage and analysis in the process of societal wealth creation are gradually being taken over by computer systems. Consequently, many positions are being replaced by automated systems. The application of digital technology has led to the continuous reduction or elimination of information barriers formed by various occupational divisions, resulting in profound changes in the social division of labor.

(3) The human–machine collaboration enters a new age.

The empowerment of digital technology propels human–machine collaborative division of labor into a new era. In the past, whether in the agricultural era with manual tools or the industrial era with machinery, these tools merely assisted human operations, with humans remaining the decisive factor in tool efficiency. However, with the development and application of big data and artificial intelligence technology, the role of machine systems in the division of labor becomes increasingly crucial, gradually taking the lead in the production process. The dominance in decision-making is also transitioning from humans to machine systems. In collaborative human–machine interactions, the predominant role of humans weakens, and machine systems play a crucial role in decision-making, marking a new stage in human–machine assistance.

(4) The platformization of the division of labor in the digital age has taken shape.

The collection and processing of information are becoming increasingly crucial within the division of labor system, gradually separating from the original framework to form independent entities. This mirrors historical shifts, such as handicrafts detaching from agricultural systems and the service industry breaking away from industrial systems, establishing the information sector as an independent entity. Consequently, centralized gathering and unified processing of information emerge as the most distinctive features of the digital age. The division of labor further develops in the context of platform economy. This not only reduces transaction costs and enhances efficiency but also makes the specialization more borderless. Platform-based division of labor promotes an increase in the degree of societal division, making it more scientific and rational. Individuals empowered by digital technology can pursue employment and entrepreneurship through various platforms, leading to a more diverse and autonomous employment landscape. This enhances adaptability and broadens the scope of choices for individuals participating in the societal division of labor.

6.2.2 New Trends in the Digital Age

Under the influence of digital technology, the production and dissemination costs of information have significantly decreased, triggering a profound transformation in the division of labor and relationships among individuals. The human–machine division of labor model is also undergoing breakthrough changes. Therefore, three new trends can be observed in the division of labor in the digital age:

(1) The removal of barrier accelerates information dissemination.

In the past, the human society has consistently grappled with information scarcity and dispersed information. To effectively utilize information, humans have adopted various division of labor approaches, allowing different individuals to engage in different tasks, with the hope of maximizing the value of various types of information and enhancing the efficiency of information processing in the human society. The social division of labor shapes diverse social roles based on different occupations, enabling the more efficient utilization of individual resources within the societal framework, thereby enhancing the efficiency of social information processing. On the one hand, this has propelled the development and efficiency improvement of various industries, but on the other hand, it has led to insufficient information interaction between different industries, resulting in increased uncertainty and costs in the societal operational processes.

Take the industrial age as an example; the uncertainty in market changes led to the separation of production and sales processes, turning marketing into a specialized industry and sector. This segregation allowed specialized sales and marketing companies to efficiently gather, process, and analyze information related to market uncertainty. Initially, this division promoted increased production efficiency and reduced uncertainty. However, over time, it became evident that the separation of production and sales led to a gradual distancing between market information processing and production planning. Owing to the continuous accumulation of information isolation, the interactivity between the two became increasingly costly in an environment of heightened competition and market uncertainty.

Even within a manufacturing enterprise, internal divisions of labor between production and sales may result in disconnects. The production department may focus solely on planning and ensuring product quality, while the sales department concentrates exclusively on sales volume, leading to disparate objectives. Furthermore, owing to differences in how the two departments handle information, information barriers arise, manifesting over time as conflicts between departments. The outcome is that the division of labor model, initially adopted for improved information processing, becomes a factor restricting the enhancement of efficiency and deepening of specialization as information asymmetry accumulates between different departments over time.

The disappearance of information scarcity has profound implications for the entire system. In the digital age, information explosion has become the norm. The volume of information generated in just the past two years exceeds the total sum produced in all of human history, with over 26 billion smart devices deployed globally. The continuous development and widespread application of information technology have made information acquisition and processing more convenient, and the low-cost, high-efficiency flow of information is gradually eroding the information barriers and asymmetries in the existing the social division of labor. The transformation in the digital age is causing traditional professional skills to be integrated into computer systems, leading to a convergence in societal division of labor. Many positions are permanently disappearing as a result; for instance, the widespread use of accounting information systems has led to the merging of roles for bookkeepers and accountants, while the application of computers and office software has rendered typist positions obsolete. The extensive utilization of internet, big data, and artificial intelligence technologies is further dismantling information barriers within societal division of labor. Generic positions, such as those in sales or marketing departments across various industries, find it increasingly challenging to maintain a competitive edge based on specialized information advantages when facing market uncertainty.

Meanwhile, the convergence of information has made people realize that in previously segmented markets for different products or services, there exist shared production elements, giving rise to new opportunities in the scope of the economy. This has propelled the integration of existing industry divisions and nurtured a plethora of cross-industry competitors. This implies that market competition will intensify, and competitive advantages within societal division of labor will stem from the precise control of an uncertain environment. Therefore, in the digital age where information barriers dissolve and information spreads rapidly, information scarcity or asymmetry is no longer the primary cause of societal division of labor. The acquisition or possession of information is no longer the key. Instead, the core competitive advantage in the societal division of labor comes from the ability to understand and analyze data information. This includes insightful breakthroughs beyond traditional cognitive frameworks, the ability to discern major trends, acute problem-solving skills, and the capability to integrate resources.

In the digital age, the disappearance of information barriers and the development of globalization have intensified competition among businesses. Particularly in the trend of industry convergence, companies no longer compete solely based on the efficiency of their own supply chains, production, and sales channels. Instead, there is a greater emphasis on overall operational efficiency and adaptability to the entire production environment. To adapt to this new competitive landscape, businesses are embracing open-source sharing, seeking sustainable development through alliance relationships, and striving for monopolistic power to build business moats and accumulate resources. Technology companies like Apple, Google, and Xiaomi have shaped formidable business ecosystems through open-source approaches. Open-source sharing has become a concept for resource sharing in the digital age, reflecting societal changes in this era. Through openness and sharing, businesses can better adapt to change, gaining more enduring and widespread competitive advantages.

The emergence of this phenomenon is straightforward: through open-source sharing, more resources and organizations collectively share development costs, exchange development opportunities, and promote the completeness of the industry chain. Essentially, this is a low-risk, high-leverage development model. Typically, peripheral companies in the ecosystem bear higher risks, while central node companies enjoy the monopoly benefits of the ecosystem. This resource-sharing model has the advantage of conserving societal resources and can be seen, in the short term, as a Pareto improvement development model, strengthening market competition pressure for companies and gaining widespread emulation. However, in the medium to long term, as a result of the presence of economies of scale and network effects, the barriers to market entry gradually increase, reducing the number of new entrants. Once a stable business ecosystem is formed, it becomes challenging for it to alter through market competition where breakthrough changes can only be achieved through breakthrough technological innovations.

(2) A networked division of labor has begun to take form.

In the agricultural and industrial eras, individuals faced limited opportunities for societal division of labor and had restricted career choices. Many people were confined to a single profession or had to decide within a narrow range of cross-industry options. This was common in our parents' generation owing to a closed division of labor model, limiting specialized skills and career information. Consequently, visible career opportunities were constrained, leading most individuals to spend their entire professional lives in limited fields. In those historical division-of-labor models, individuals were often constrained by their created outcomes, becoming alienated in societal organizations. Their autonomy and potential were restricted owing to organizational boundaries and functional constraints. This environment gradually eroded individualism, appearing less suited to the current trend of deepening societal division of labor.

In the digital age, especially with the widespread application of the internet and artificial intelligence technologies, individuals receive robust support in societal division of labor. The development of digital technology makes it easier for individuals to access information, and the low-threshold application of technology significantly enhances information processing and analytical capabilities. This enables individuals to discover unprecedented opportunities and creates a previously unimaginable space for societal possibilities. In this scenario, individual autonomy and information processing potential are more fully realized, fostering broader societal collaboration. One of the key characteristics of the digital age is the networked division of labor pattern that has evolved on the foundation of the internet.

The networked division of labor pattern constructs increasingly complex networked societal organizational units, viewing individuals as nodes in the network of societal division of labor. From the supply perspective, individuals support the creation of societal wealth by contributing their skills and other economic resources and receive corresponding rewards. Owing to higher standardization in collaborative efforts in the digital age, transparency and measurability of labor outcomes are enhanced, and individuals no longer depend on strong relationships to establish collaborative divisions of labor. Instead, collaborative efforts in weaker relationships form with lower transaction costs and reduced uncertainty. Consequently, the trust-building mechanisms between individuals in societal division of labor become more straightforward, with social platforms like WeChat, QQ, TikTok serving as convenient tools to connect like-minded individuals. Building social trust becomes easier, interpersonal relationships tend to flatten, and the management and collaboration within societal organizations naturally move towards a flatter structure.

In the digital age, rapid technological changes have diversified societal division of labor. Individuals now have more opportunities for versatile employment, including part-time work and freelancing. For instance, in the United States, about 16% of workers engage in part-time employment, with only 3–4% doing so out of economic necessity, while 12% choose part-time work voluntarily. This trend is also evident in Asian countries like China and South Korea, where freelancers, particularly those with specific professional skills, are on the rise. Globally, a report from the International Labor Organization highlights the increasing prevalence of informal, temporary, and freelance work, with over 60% of workers not signing any labor contracts. The COVID-19 pandemic further accelerated the growth of online work and virtual professions, contributing to the wave of flexible employment, multiple part-time jobs, and independent entrepreneurship. Online gigs symbolize the deepening development of networked division of labor in the digital age. The standardization of production processes, driven by digital technology, allows for a more dispersed division of labor, marking a stage in the ongoing evolution of societal division of labor.

In the future, the possibility of intelligent machine systems replacing humans may challenge this network-based online division of labor.

In the digital age, supply–demand matching has new options. From the demand perspective, individuals, forming various social communities through network connections, become part of communities related to work, interests, classmates, and blood relations. These self-organized individual communities easily converge into large demand tribes owing to the similarity of needs, becoming a crucial component of socially aggregated demands. This distinct and sizable demand characteristic provides the possibility for productive enterprises to address the contradiction between production planning and market demand uncertainty within the market mechanism.

In the past, productive enterprises could only address demand uncertainty through inventory. However, in the digital age, the formation of individual communities enables the scalable creation of predictable and continuously producible demand orders with similar needs. The establishment of flexible production lines allows enterprises to plan and fulfill various community-based demand orders, utilizing digital economies of scale to reduce inventory costs.

Furthermore, through the matching of big data and artificial intelligence, demands from social communities can be aggregated into scalable and batched demand orders, further reducing adjustment costs for productive enterprises. By saving inventory and production adjustment costs, product prices will decrease, resulting in a Pareto improvement benefiting both producers and consumers. The overall macroeconomic risk of fluctuations will significantly decrease owing to the improved alignment between production planning and demand.

This development trend requires e-commerce platforms to shift their development focus from the traditional emphasis on traffic and sales promotion through traffic diversion to a model that focuses on exploring population characteristics and realizing demand matching and aggregation. Digital technology allows for the ample demonstration of human collective characteristics, making clustering a prominent feature of society, and demand aggregation is no longer a high-cost endeavor. Market mechanisms are no longer obligated to operate at the individual level; group-level market mechanisms become a viable choice. Enterprises no longer have to face individual demand uncertainties but only need to address group demand uncertainties, significantly reducing uncertainty.

(3) The human–machine collaboration enters a new era.

In the digital age, particularly with the widespread application of big data and artificial intelligence technologies, the enhanced intelligence of machine systems has ushered in a new phase in the division of labor between humans and machines.

In business decision-making, the role of intelligent systems is becoming increasingly crucial, with many resource allocations in business relying on the outcomes generated by these intelligent systems. Take Google's introduction of the "Smart Bidding" product as an example—this product, based on big data, artificial intelligence, and machine learning, assists advertisers in automatically bidding for the optimal ad placements. Benchmarks formed by algorithms are becoming the fundamental mechanism for resource allocation in the digital economy era. E-commerce platforms such as Taobao and Pinduoduo recommend products based on user browsing and purchasing information, where information received by users is determined by algorithms, and demands themselves are influenced by algorithms, thus guiding the allocation of production resources. In the unfolding of market mechanisms, an increasing amount of time is subject to the application of artificial intelligence technology and influenced by algorithmic standards.

However, this approach does not necessarily make consumers more rational or the market mechanism more effective. In many cases, the use of algorithms may mislead consumer preferences and judgments, resulting in harm to consumer welfare, and these situations are often difficult to foresee and correct. For example, a travel product platform utilizes its information advantage to implement differential pricing for different customers, causing significant price disparities for the same hotel room reservation for the same customer using different smartphone brands. This approach has a negative impact on market mechanisms, and consumers often struggle to detect such discrepancies owing to a lack of necessary information. Therefore, we need to be vigilant about optimization decisions under algorithmic standards being the optimal criteria for only certain company goals, rather than the optimal criteria for the overall societal demand. Such a situation could lead to some companies monopolizing the market and having disastrous effects on the overall development of society.

To prevent algorithmic standards from becoming a constraint on societal sustainable development, it is crucial to focus on necessary regulation of the algorithmic standards themselves while also ensuring reasonable pricing for the foundation of these standards—data and information. As the algorithmic standards of intelligent systems can have a significant impact on the actual operation of the economy, government departments need to establish new regulatory laws and rules to minimize the potential impact of algorithmic biases on the socio-economic system.

Simultaneously, there should be swift efforts to establish a fair data and information market, ensuring that any algorithmic operations are subject to certain cost constraints. This way, the private operational costs of enterprises with information and algorithmic advantages can align as much as possible with societal operational costs, preventing data and information advantages from becoming sources of monopoly power. Such measures contribute to maintaining fairness and transparency in the market, encouraging algorithms to serve society in a more reasonable and just manner.

The co-evolution of humans and machines in the digital age is profoundly influencing the production process, significantly impacting the manufacturing industry and reshaping the global value chain. In the digital age, intelligent manufacturing systems have evolved based on industrial automation. These systems are comprehensively altering the substitution relationship between humans and machines, with intelligent machine systems deeply penetrating boundaries originally controlled by humans, creating an irreversible substitution for human roles. Particularly, with continuous technological advancements, machine substitution for humans in the manufacturing sector is becoming increasingly feasible and reliable. For businesses, this not only implies cost reduction but also brings about substantial improvements in efficiency and quality.

This substitution trend is extensively unfolding in China, often hailed as the "world's factory". For instance, at the SAIC General Motors' Golden Bridge Factory, there are over 300 robots in the workshop, achieving 100% welding automation. Only a little over 10 workers collectively manage 386 robots, collaborating with them to produce 80 Cadillac cars daily. Additionally, the Chinese home appliance giant Midea Group has deployed more than 800 robots, investing over 600 million yuan in the automation upgrade of production lines, realizing a strategic shift towards automated production. Through the introduction of core components and fully automated assembly lines, the production efficiency of Midea's central air conditioners has increased by 70%, the workforce on the production line has decreased by 50%, and the man–machine ratio has exceeded 4%, with a product qualification rate reaching 99.9%.

In the food manufacturing sector, at Charoen Pokphand Foods' unmanned dumpling factory, one cannot spot a single employee within the several thousand square meters of the facility. Machines operate 24/7, from dough mixing, stuffing placement, to dumpling pinching, forming a completely clean and tidy assembly line. Previously requiring 200 workers, the entire factory now operates with fewer than 20 employees, signifying a staggering 90% reduction in labor owing to the realization of an "unmanned factory". In the manufacturing sector, the substitution of machines for humans not only mitigates the risks associated with the continuously rising costs of labor, including wages and human resource management expenses, but also avoids corresponding labor-related risks. As a result, manual labor is no longer the primary consideration for the development of the manufacturing industry. This signifies that the location decisions of manufacturing enterprises will primarily depend on the market for product sales. This trend is poised to reshape the global industrial value chain.

In the past, China became the "world's factory" mainly because of the global shift of manufacturing industries to China. This shift was propelled by China's demographic dividend, abundant labor supply, and relatively lower wage levels. However, in the digital age, with the substitution of humans by intelligent machine systems, the significance of human labor is gradually diminishing, and China's demographic dividend is fading away. It is no longer the primary driving force for the development of the global manufacturing industry in China. This shift is expected to prompt global manufacturing enterprises to reorganize their layouts based on target market demands, leading to a reshaping of the global industrial chain. Consequently, Chinese manufacturing enterprises need to pay attention to the new trends in the global industrial layout.

The globalization that began in the 1980s may enter a new stage owing to the substitution of humans by machines in the manufacturing industry, potentially slowing down the trend of globalization in manufacturing. The proportion of industrial products in international trade may decrease in the future, and more products may be manufactured domestically. Chinese manufacturing enterprises, especially those focused on exports, must take into account the impact of this evolving trend and adapt promptly. This may involve shifting the market focus to the domestic sector or considering the external relocation of industries. Given the impact of the COVID-19 pandemic and the backdrop of national security policies regarding industrial supply chains, the global positioning of China's manufacturing industry requires simultaneous consideration of economic and technological development trends as well as policy-related factors.

The emergence of generative large-scale language models like ChatGPT has profoundly transformed human efficiency in information production, processing, and value utilization. This has delivered a breakthrough impact on productivity-oriented service industries with information processing as a primary function. It has accelerated the deepening collaboration between humans and machines, playing a pivotal role in shaping the business and production models of productivity-oriented service industries. This represents an ongoing and profound transformation in the current landscape.

6.2.3 The Challenges Posed by Intelligent Machine

The challenge posed by the current wave of intelligent machine systems replacing human jobs lies in the difficulty of creating a proportional number of new job opportunities for those displaced from low-wage occupations. This arises because intelligent machine systems tend to replace low-wage jobs, while the retained positions demand higher levels of human capital accumulation and investment. Individuals are required to possess specific talents and long-term accumulation for these roles, and the demand for such positions is limited. Moreover, in the current efficiency-oriented market mechanism, capital-intensive intelligent machine systems are inclined toward high-yield investments, further diminishing the relative advantage of labor factors in the division of labor systems. The issue of unemployment may gradually evolve into a complex societal problem, necessitating reforms in the social distribution system to adapt to the developmental trends of the new era of human–machine collaboration.

A new social distribution system must balance the interests between elite individuals and the general population, especially in the algorithm-dominated era where the number of elite individuals may decrease, while the general population may increase. Under this trend, social class differentiation may lead to cognitive and interest conflicts, resulting in inefficient circulation of social values, manifested in mismatches in supply and demand and insufficient supply efficiency. This can cause the breakdown of the unity between human (labor) reproduction and product reproduction, leading to the collapse of the value system. In such a scenario, government authority and public power must be strengthened to ensure the smooth circulation of product values, balance the supply–demand structure, and establish a new social value distribution system based on the sustainable development goals of the transmission of social values. This will contribute to adapting to the sustainable development needs of the human–machine collaborative production model, ensuring the orderly and sustainable development of the division of labor system, and consolidating the true foundation of societal civilization and wealth.

Under the digital transformation and the evolving trend of human–machine collaboration, the nature of machine substitution for humans has undergone a qualitative change, especially in the process of product reproduction. The relentless pursuit of efficiency has increased the irreversible replacement of humans by machines. This has led to a growing number of individuals leaving the product reproduction system, making it challenging for ordinary individuals to enter the system, resulting in widespread individual marginalization. As a consequence, most people are no longer essential for the continuity of the product reproduction system. The two major reproduction systems are becoming increasingly separated, making it difficult for most people to obtain a social value position within them, challenging the sustainability of the human reproduction process.

This trend has already manifested in countries like Japan, where individuals find it difficult to enter the product reproduction system, hindering their participation in the distribution of product value and subsequently losing opportunities for social survival and development. This renders developmental opportunities elusive, and individuals may abandon their beliefs and confidence in effort, leading to the rise of marginalized individuals, commonly known as "hikikomori" or socially withdrawn individuals. The phenomenon of fewer marriages and declining birth rates becomes prevalent, posing challenges to the sustainability of the human reproduction process.

The value judgment system regarding individuals and life formed under these circumstances is entirely different from that of past eras. The entire society is prone to falling into a crisis where the human reproduction system collapses. Simultaneously, the preference structure formed during this value adjustment process does not align with the product structure provided by the existing reproduction system. This not only results in an insufficient overall effective demand but, more importantly, a structural deficiency, causing a significant impact on the sustainability of the product reproduction process.

It is crucial to be aware of the crisis in the value system triggered by the human–machine collaborative relationship brought about by the development of the digital economy and automation. This crisis may lead to the gradual divergence of the product reproduction process from the human reproduction process. The disintegration of this unity poses the most significant challenge to the sustainable development of the human society, affecting the survival and development of the human population and the inheritance of technological civilization. Therefore, establishing new technological, cultural, ethical and value standards to create a new unity in the value system for both reproduction processes is paramount. Otherwise, the sustainability of societal development is inevitably at serious risk.

6.3 The Importance of Individuals in the Specialization System

The collaborative development of humans and machines empowered by digital capabilities is driving the separation of the human reproduction system from the product reproduction system. Many individuals struggle to enter the reproduction system, making it challenging to realize their individual value and obtain rights to value distribution. This results in a decrease in the overall effective demand in society, with a mismatch in the structure of effective demand, limiting the flow and realization of product value. Within the product reproduction system, internal competition intensifies, and individuals who can facilitate the flow and realization of value are increasingly valued.

In the digital age, every individual and social organization has become an indispensable part of the social division of labor network. This network, driven by collaborative cooperation, propels the development of society, with everyone fulfilling their unique social functions within the division of labor network. It is noteworthy that, under the powerful empowerment of digital technology, each node in the network wields significant and undeniable influence. This implies that in the current digital age, the individual's voice is strengthened owing to technological empowerment. The influence of ordinary individuals is gradually gaining recognition. This elevation stems from the empowerment of digital technology, making it easier for ordinary individuals to form closely associated groups. Interactions among individuals not only empower the individuals themselves but also amplify this influence through group networks, creating unprecedented social impact. Therefore, the empowerment of digital technology not only reinforces the individual's status in society but also propels the elevation of the social influence of ordinary individuals. This process enables individuals to participate in social affairs, express opinions, and achieve a broader societal impact through digital networks more actively.

In the age fueled by digital technology, individuals amplify their social attributes through the collective impact of digital advancements. This ease of connectivity allows the social value of individuals to spread extensively in the digital age, encompassing both immediate gains and long-term socialized benefits.

In contrast to previous agricultural and industrial ages, the contemporary digital age shifts the focus of individual participation in social collaboration. It transcends mere distribution of short-term outcomes to emphasize collaborative creation of enduring societal value, shared interests, and mutual risk-taking during cooperative endeavors. This shift is facilitated by the increased accessibility of digital technology, diminishing technological barriers, and the rapid evolution of digital infrastructure, supported by sharing and open-source ideologies. These factors empower ordinary individuals and further fortify the influence of the entire societal cooperation division of labor network.

Within this network, each individual functions as a node, and their actions and influence disseminate swiftly and extensively through the societal division of labor network. This highlights the significant externalities resulting from individual behavior, a marked departure from previous eras. Consequently, individuals are increasingly concerned with achieving sustainable, long-term benefits rather than solely focusing on the immediate gains derived from opportunistic actions. This shift underscores a defining characteristic of social cooperation in the digital age.

The empowerment of digital technology allows ordinary individuals to easily connect with the broader society, providing them with the opportunity to influence the flow of information across the entire community and consequently impact the distribution of societal resources. This expanded social role transcends the influence of individuals in previous eras.

In the business world of "Internet+", we have witnessed the emergence of unexpected "hit" or "internet celebrity" products that can swiftly influence society within a short period of time. An initially inconspicuous business or individual, once seizing an opportunity, can accumulate substantial wealth rapidly and achieve incredible career success.

It is essential to emphasize that the term "ordinary individuals" here is relative to their initial endowments. Initially, they may not possess particularly outstanding value advantages, and their value gradually becomes evident through the assistance of digital technology tools in helping businesses realize product value. For product manufacturing enterprises, the realization of product value becomes increasingly challenging owing to intense competition and limited demand. Consequently, these individuals play an escalating role in the product regeneration system, becoming catalysts for the flow of product value in the development of the digital economy, thereby enhancing the efficiency of supply and demand matching.

In the era of digital technology empowerment, the impact of the behavior of micro-level ordinary economic entities on the sustainable development of the economy has become impossible to ignore. To adapt to this changing trend, on August 19, 2019, CEOs of 181 top U.S. companies issued a statement redefining the operational purpose of corporations. The statement proposed that shareholder interests are no longer the primary goal, but rather the creation of a better society. This reflects the acknowledgment that the capital-centric corporate model is struggling to meet the developmental requirements of the digital age.

With the empowerment of digital technology, the externalities of individual behavior have increased, leading to a paradox between individual rationality and collective rationality in societal development. Consequently, businesses are adjusting their purposes, focusing on "stakeholders", and pursuing long-term sustainable benefits. This shift reflects the empowerment of digital technology on economic entities, the strengthening of externalities' impact, and a reevaluation of the interaction between individuals and the society.

The recurrence of history might stem from the rigidity of social development structures. Once history reaches a crucial point, we might find ourselves trapped in a fixed development path, unable to break through this structure, and thus unable to foresee the diversity of the future. When interpreting the social division of labor in the digital age, the key lies in examining whether there has been a fundamental change in the division of labor between humans and machines to understand its impact mechanism on the social division of labor. If the division of labor between humans and machines leads to most people no longer being essential factors of production, the coordination between human reproduction and product reproduction will become challenging, economic systems may stagnate, population size may decrease, and sustainable social development may face challenges. The development of digital technology, especially big data and artificial intelligence is significantly altering the relationship between humans and machine tools in the social system of the division of labor, with the dominant force of capital gradually emerging. This could be a sign of a historical turning point, so we need to start from first principles, deeply contemplate the social value of humans and the intrinsic value of machine tools, to understand the social division of labor more comprehensively in the digital age. Otherwise, we might lose the ability to break free from the existing development path, paying too high a cost.

Chapter 7
Individual Economic Behavior in the Digital Economy

7.1 The Influence of Digital Technology on Individual Behavior

In the realm of the digital economy, the application of digital technologies has exerted a significant influence on individual economic decision-making, altering both the decision-making environment and logic. To delve deeper into the decision-making behaviors of economic agents in the digital economy, it is essential to first clarify this concept.

Here, we define economic decision-making behaviors in the digital economy as the utilization of digital technologies and digital data to pursue decision accuracy and minimize costs. This definition underscores the dependency of economic decision-making in the digital age on digital technologies, no longer relying solely on human judgment but necessitating digital tools. Furthermore, the objective of decision-making is to pursue efficiency, ensuring decision effectiveness while minimizing costs as much as possible, aligning with the requirements of economic decision-making in economics. Finally, this definition highlights that economic decision-making behaviors in the digital age are based on digital data, with data-driven approaches being their prominent feature. Therefore, we can distinguish economic decision-making behaviors in the digital age from traditional economic decision-making behaviors along three dimensions: decision elements, decision tools, and decision objectives. This implies that in studying economic decision-making behaviors in the digital age, we need to consider these three dimensions to analyze their complexity and characteristics, thereby having practical significance.

This definition clearly illustrates the crucial impact of digital technologies on the decision-making of economic agents in the digital economy. The influence of digital technologies on economic decision-making behaviors of economic agents mainly manifests in two aspects: first, the widespread application of digital technologies has disrupted the environment of decision-making in the digital age, altering decision-making thought processes and standards, thereby making decision-making

Y. Yu and Y. Jiang, *Understanding the Digital Revolution and Its Influences*,
https://doi.org/10.1007/978-981-97-4939-3_7

in the digital economy distinctly different from traditional economics. Second, the development of digital technologies has changed two fundamental conditions in the economic system: information scarcity and labor scarcity.

On the one hand, with the rapid development of digital technologies, there has been a fundamental reversal in the characteristic of information scarcity. A vast amount of data is generated and transmitted by machine systems, and the low threshold for information acquisition and processing means that information is no longer scarce, which has impacted business models based on information scarcity and consequently altered decision-making methods. On the other hand, the development of artificial intelligence technology has enhanced the substitutability of technology for labor, leading to a fundamental change in the constraint condition of labor scarcity. The proliferation of unmanned factories and unmanned office systems has resulted in labor supply surpassing demand, thus changing the endowment constraint conditions of the digital economy, and forcing changes in the decision-making behaviors of economic agents.

One of the most significant characteristics of the impact of digital technologies on individual economic behavior decisions is that economic agents rely on data streams throughout the entire decision-making process, determining their choices based on the state of data streams. In other words, in the digital age, economic behavior decisions view data as the most crucial resource owing to the application of digital technologies, becoming a significant factor influencing economic efficiency and sustainable development. This is because digital technologies influence economic agents' decision-making behaviors through data, primarily for the following six reasons:

Data determines the accuracy and efficiency of economic agents' decisions. Data is crucial for economic agents' decisions. By collecting and analyzing data, economic agents can better understand market demand and consumer behavior, making wiser decisions and improving decision efficiency.

Data determines the way economic agents compete. Data can help economic agents understand competitors' behaviors and strategies, adjust their own competitive strategies, identify new competitive opportunities and market demands, and explore new market and product areas.

Data determines the flow and allocation of economic resources. Data can help decision-makers more accurately understand market demand and economic trends, guide the allocation of economic resources, evaluate the feasibility and return on investment of projects, and promote investment in more promising areas.

Data determines the way economic agents collaborate and cooperate. Data can help economic agents understand the needs and resources of partners, formulate more effective cooperation strategies and division of labor, and promote industrial upgrading and innovation.

Data determines the structure of economic organizations and their decision-making models. Data can help organizations adjust their organizational structures and decision-making models, formulate more effective performance evaluation and incentive mechanisms, and improve employee motivation and work efficiency.

Data determines the way value is created and realized. Data can help economic agents formulate more effective strategies for value creation and realization, develop more innovative and competitive products and services, assess the market potential and return on investment of products, and formulate more effective investment strategies and profit models.

7.2 Characteristics of Decision-Making in the Digital Age

In the digital age, economic decision-making has undergone significant changes, with the most notable features being data-driven, precision, automation, and real-time aspects. These features not only affect the decision-making behaviors of economic agents but also alter their competitive strategies, resource allocation methods, division of labor, cooperation modes, organizational structures, and decision-making models.

First, being data-driven is the core feature of economic decision-making in the digital age. Data has become one of the most critical resources, with economic agents utilizing extensive data collection, analysis, and mining to make more scientific and accurate decisions. For instance, businesses employ big data technology to analyze market trends and consumer behaviors, thereby formulating more precise marketing strategies and product development plans.

Second, precision is an important characteristic of economic decision-making in the digital age. With the support of digital technology, economic agents can acquire more comprehensive and in-depth data and process it using advanced analytical tools and algorithms, leading to more accurate conclusions and predictions. This not only enhances the competitiveness and profitability of economic agents but also meets consumer demands, thereby increasing customer satisfaction.

Third, automation is one of the significant features of economic decision-making in the digital age. With the development of digital technology, many decision-making processes can be automated, reducing labor and time costs while improving decision-making efficiency. For example, in the fields of production and logistics, automated systems can optimize production and logistics plans in real-time based on market demand and sales data.

Last, real-time capability is another important feature of economic decision-making in the digital age. With digital technology tools, economic agents can access and process data more quickly, enabling decisions to be made in real-time. This helps economic agents to promptly grasp market dynamics and consumer demands, enabling them to make rapid decisions and adjustments to maintain a competitive edge.

In conclusion, data-driven, precision, automation, and real-time aspects are four important characteristics of economic decision-making behaviors in the digital age. These features not only change decision-making behaviors but also profoundly influence competitive strategies, resource allocation methods, and organizational structures among economic agents. With the continuous development of digital technology, these features will continue to drive the transformation and innovation of economic decision-making behaviors. Therefore, economic agents need to fully utilize digital technology to continually improve the precision and real-time capabilities of decision-making, achieving more efficient, scientific, and intelligent economic decisions.

7.3 Information as the Foundation for Decision-Making in the Digital Age

In the digital age, the core basis of economic decision-making is information because it has the ability to compress decision uncertainty and is an important input in the decision-making process. In this era, the volume of information is exponentially increasing, coming from diverse sources and in various forms. Therefore, how to acquire, process, and utilize information becomes a critical link in economic decision-making.

Regarding the costs of economic decision-making in the digital age, they mainly include information acquisition costs, information processing costs, and opportunity costs in time.

First, information acquisition costs refer to the expenses incurred in obtaining the necessary information, including determining information sources, specifying information indicators, selecting information acquisition tools, and storing information. Determining information sources involves identifying where to obtain the required information, such as the internet, databases, or social media. Specifying information indicators involves defining the specific indicators and content of the required information, such as market trends, consumer demands, or competitor situations. Information acquisition tools and usage involve using appropriate tools and techniques to obtain the required information, such as search engines or data collection software. Information storage involves storing the acquired information for subsequent processing and analysis.

Second, information processing costs refer to the expenses incurred in processing the acquired information, including data cleaning, integration, calculation, result output, interpretation, and utilization. Data cleaning involves cleaning and organizing the acquired information, removing invalid, erroneous, or duplicate data. Data integration involves integrating information from different sources into a unified data format and structure. Data calculation and result output involve performing calculations and analyses on the integrated data and outputting results. Interpretation and utilization of results involve interpreting and utilizing the results of calculations and analyses to support decision-making.

Last, opportunity costs in time refer to the opportunity costs incurred owing to the time spent on information acquisition and processing. In the digital age, both information acquisition and processing require time, and the opportunity costs of time are also significant. When economic agents spend time acquiring and processing information, they may miss market opportunities or lose competitive advantages.

Therefore, economic agents need to balance between the time and opportunity costs of information acquisition and processing.

In summary, the core of economic decision-making in the digital age is information, and the related costs mainly include information acquisition costs, information processing costs, and opportunity costs in time. Economic agents need to fully understand and manage these costs effectively in the decision-making process to improve decision efficiency and accuracy. Meanwhile, the development of digital technology provides economic agents with more information and data resources, making economic decision-making more scientific and precise. However, it is essential to pay attention to the quality and reliability of information and data to avoid decision-making errors caused by false or incomplete information and data.

7.4 The Changing Environment of Economic Behavior in the Digital Age

The rapid development of digital technology has brought about significant changes in the information environment for economic decision-making. In the digital age, the information environment for economic decision-making exhibits three main characteristics: drastic changes in the informational attributes of data elements, substantial upgrades in the functionalities of available decision-making tools, and a significant increase in the complexity of decision-making problems. These changes profoundly affect the precision and efficiency of economic decision-making. Below, we will elaborate on these characteristics and their impacts on economic decision-making.

First, there have been significant changes in the informational attributes of data elements. In the digital age, almost all economic activities generate vast amounts of data, including transaction records, browsing history, social media activities, and more. Through the collection, storage, and processing facilitated by digital technology, decision-makers are provided with abundant information support. The informational attributes of data elements have changed as follows:

Large-scale information: With the development of the internet, mobile devices, and sensor technologies, the volume of data has witnessed remarkable growth. We are now able to collect and process data on an unprecedented scale, providing a solid information foundation for economic decision-making.

Multi-dimensional information: Data not only comes in large volumes but also covers various dimensions. For instance, a consumer's purchasing behavior may involve aspects such as geographic location, purchase timing, types of purchased goods, prices, and more. These multi-dimensional data provide decision-makers with a more comprehensive and in-depth perspective.

High complexity of information: In the digital age, the speed of data generation and dissemination has increased, leading to greater complexity and uncertainty in data. For example, tasks like sentiment analysis on social media and search engine ranking algorithms require handling complex data and models.

High real-time nature of information: With the development of technologies like the Internet of Things and cloud computing, the real-time nature of data has significantly improved. Decision-makers can access market and consumer information in real-time, facilitating timely decision-making.

High demands in information processing: Owing to the large scale, diverse dimensions, and complexity of data in the digital age, higher demands are placed on the processing and analysis of data. Nowadays, various advanced data processing and analysis tools are required to handle massive amounts of data swiftly and effectively.

Second, there has been a substantial upgrade in the functionalities of available decision-making tools. With the advancements in artificial intelligence and machine learning, an increasing number of analytical tools and algorithms can assist in understanding and predicting market trends, consumer behaviors, and competitive situations more accurately. Using various data analysis tools, people can quickly and effectively conduct in-depth analysis of massive data, providing more accurate data support and business intelligence for decision-making. For instance, tools such as chatbots, recommendation systems, and prediction models help businesses better understand consumer demands and market trends. Additionally, artificial intelligence can automate some decision-making processes, such as automated trading and customer service, thereby enhancing efficiency and accuracy.

Last, the complexity of decision-making problems has significantly increased. Digital technology has accelerated the speed of information dissemination and communication, allowing global markets and economic conditions to be influenced by different perspectives and information in an instant. Globalization and digitalization have made the environment for economic decision-making more complex, necessitating considerations of factors such as global market trends, cultural differences, and policy changes. The application of digital technology has also made economic decision-making problems more complex, requiring the handling of more data and information, and more precise prediction of market trends and consumer demands. Emerging economic formats such as e-commerce, the sharing economy, and customized production also pose more challenges to economic decision-making.

In summary, the information environment for economic decision-making has undergone significant changes in the digital age, profoundly impacting economic decision-making and demanding a more scientific, precise, and efficient decision-making process. At the same time, it also imposes higher requirements on decision-makers, requiring a deep understanding of digital technology, accurate grasping of market and consumer behaviors, and swift decision-making.

7.5 The Mechanism of Decision-Making in the Digital Age

In the digital age, economic decision-making is characterized using information processing tools and follows a pattern of human–machine collaborative division of labor. Owing to the complexity of economic phenomena in the digital age, the complexity of decision data and tools makes it difficult for decision-making processes to be completed solely by human effort. Therefore, relying on intelligent information systems to assist decision-making and selecting decision behaviors based on their output results becomes inevitable.

In understanding the basic principles of economic decision-making in the digital age, it is crucial to recognize that being data-driven is its core approach. Although in the digital age, economic decision-making still follows the principle of cost–benefit analysis, unlike traditional economic frameworks, the cost–benefit analysis in the digital age involves the comprehensive costs and benefits of individuals acquiring and processing information. In the past, economic decision-making assumed that information acquisition and processing incurred no costs, but this assumption does not hold. Information acquisition costs and the costs of processing massive amounts of information are particularly important in the digital age because economic agents need to extract useful information from vast amounts of data and engage in complex and time-consuming computational processing to effectively evaluate decision risks.

The costs of decision-making in the digital age consist of both implicit costs, such as decision costs, and explicit costs, such as transaction costs. This means that the costs of decision choices in economic behavior include not only explicit transaction costs but also implicit information acquisition and processing costs.

In the digital age, cost–benefit comparisons still follow the marginal analysis method because economic agents still face situations where marginal costs are increasing. Therefore, economic agents still determine the optimal economic choices based on comparing marginal costs with marginal benefits.

7.6 The Mindset for Economic Decision-Making in the Digital Age

In the digital age, economic decision-making relies on digital technology tools to collect and analyze information to make rational choices. Owing to the complexity of decision problems and tools in the digital age, decision-makers need to possess nonlinear thinking capabilities to handle a large number of nonlinear relationships and complex issues, adapting to the iterative optimization requirements of human–machine collaborative division of labor.

In the digital age, economic decision-making needs to have the following four characteristics:

Holistic Thinking: Given the rapid pace of information dissemination and market changes, decision-makers need to analyze problems from a broad perspective, including market trends, competitive environments, technological developments, etc., to make more accurate decisions.

Data-Driven Thinking: Data becomes a crucial basis for decision-making, and decision-makers need to be driven by data, analyzing and mining to gain deeper insights and enhance the scientific and accuracy of decisions.

Complexity Thinking: Decision-making involves a large amount of information and relationships, and decision-makers need to deal with complex information and relationships to find optimal solutions, including balancing uncertainties and multiple interests.

Iterative Thinking: Considering the rapid changes in the market, decision-makers need to continuously optimize decisions based on market feedback, adapting to the competitive environment.

The standards of economic decision-making in the digital age have shifted towards information processing efficiency. Information processing efficiency standards cover both the ability and efficiency of information processing, becoming fundamental selection criteria. Improving information processing capabilities implies solving more complex problems, creating more powerful products, and providing more development possibilities choices, thereby enhancing environmental adaptability.

Decision efficiency has also become a consideration and requires the adoption of information processing efficiency standards. This standard considers the level of information processing capabilities and efficiency, problem-solving abilities, and time resource costs. Considering various factors, decision-makers need to find optimal solutions and make the most efficient decisions under resource and time constraints.

Economic decision-making in the digital age requires nonlinear thinking capabilities such as holistic, data-driven, complexity, and iterative thinking, while emphasizing the comprehensive consideration of information processing efficiency and decision efficiency and effectiveness. Only in this way can decision-makers make accurate and scientific decisions in the complex and ever-changing digital age, adapting to market changes and competitive environments.

In the digital age, economic decision-making involves several steps:

Understanding the Problem: Deeply understanding the decision problem, clarifying goals and scope, defining the problem clearly, and determining decision objectives.

Information Collection and Processing: Gathering relevant information, including structured and unstructured data such as user behavior data, sales data, social media comments, etc., and analyzing and processing it.

Choosing Suitable Algorithms and Tools: Selecting appropriate algorithms and tools for processing and analysis based on the problem and data structure, such as machine learning, clustering analysis, etc.

Evaluation and Validation of Results: Scientifically validating and evaluating the analysis results, considering uncertainty and risk, and further analyzing the accuracy and reliability of model results.

Formulating Decision Solutions: Developing decision solutions and implementing and tracking them, such as formulating marketing strategies, optimizing product design, etc.

Iterative Optimization: Reflecting and providing feedback, summarizing experiences and lessons learned, continuously developing and improving decision-making methods, for example, continuously optimizing decision models and methods through user feedback, sales data, etc.

These steps require decision-makers to possess various thinking abilities such as holistic thinking, data-driven thinking, complexity thinking, and iterative thinking. Additionally, decision-makers need to continuously learn and adapt to new ways of thinking and skill requirements to address the challenges and opportunities of the digital age.

Chapter 8
New Phenomena in the Digital Economy

The emergence of the digital economy has brought about a series of new phenomena that were previously unseen in traditional economies. These phenomena represent the new characteristics and development trends of the digital economy, holding significant practical significance. Among them, the most notable are the emergence of "super individuals" and "internet celebrities", who are not only enthusiastic about live-streaming sales and lifestyle sharing but also highly active in the dissemination of information and knowledge. This phenomenon of a new economic form at the level of fame is the result of ordinary individuals' sudden surge in economic value under the empowerment of digital technology, attracting a large influx of capital to create their own "super individuals" or "internet celebrities". Although many regard this as the future and long-term trend of the digital economy, it is only an initial phenomenon in the digitalization of the economy, representing the early dividends of individuals leveraging digital empowerment to realize new value monetization or creation in their respective industries. The future sustainable development is constrained by the impact of digital technology applications on the redefinition of the social and economic value of individuals. And these "super individuals" or "internet celebrities" all need to rely on platform companies and society for communication and interaction to realize their commercial value.

Therefore, this chapter will delve into the "super individuals", "internet celebrity economy", and "platform economy", where the former two reflect the digitalization of individuals and its impacts under the empowerment of digital technology, while the latter demonstrates the ways in which digital technology empowerment is reshaping the socio-economic model.

Y. Yu and Y. Jiang, *Understanding the Digital Revolution and Its Influences*,
https://doi.org/10.1007/978-981-97-4939-3_8

8.1 The "Super Individuals"

Regarding the phenomenon of "super individuals" in the digital economy, there are five aspects of issues worthy of exploration:

First, what is the essence of "super individuals"? In other words, what is the fundamental nature of "super individuals"? This is a thought-provoking question. While many people believe that the development of "super individuals" is the future of the digital economy and reflects a long-term trend of future development this is only an initial phenomenon in the digitalization of the economy. The emergence of "super individuals" is primarily the early dividends of individuals leveraging digital empowerment to realize new value monetization or creation in their respective industries. However, the sustainability of future development of "super individuals" will be constrained by the redefinition of the socio-economic value of individuals owing to changes in the division of labor between humans and machines under the application of digital technology.

Second, we need to explain what contributes to the emergence of "super individuals", that is, the reasons behind the creation of "super individuals". Third, we need to explore the impact of "super individuals" on individuals and society to understand the essence of their influence. Fourth, we need to elucidate the distribution characteristics of "super individuals" to evaluate the developmental characteristics of "super individuals" more objectively. Last, we need to explain the general pathways for ordinary individuals to become "super individuals" and discuss common ways to become "super individuals" at present.

8.1.1 The Essence of "Super Individuals"

The emphasis on "super individuals" lies more on their social influence, highlighting the significant differences in influence boundaries and speed compared to traditional ordinary individuals. The impact of "super individuals" in the digital economy landscape on society has surpassed the imagination of past eras. Therefore, "super-individuals" are essentially individuals with significant influence in society.

As digitalization progressed to the rise of social networks, the concept of "key opinion leaders" (KOLs), a unique term in the internet sphere, gradually gained wide acceptance and became an important feature of the internet economy with the development of social networks. However, "super-individuals" are not unique to the internet. In every era of history, whether agricultural or industrial, individuals with high status and fame have belonged to the category of "super individuals". However, the difference lies in the fact that past "super individuals" were often the result of organizational empowerment, while "super individuals" in the digital age are more often the result of digital technology empowerment. In the past, "super-individuals" could leverage the power of organizational systems to exert influence far beyond individual capabilities, but once they left their organizational systems, their personal influence was no different from that of other ordinary individuals. In the digital age, "super-individuals" are empowered more through the network connections of digital technology, enabling them to potentially connect with all individuals in society, thus gaining immense social influence and wealth through their performance in the digital virtual world.

Currently, "super-individuals" choose various monetization methods to gain sufficient wealth. For example, in the field of live-streaming sales, many successful "super individuals" have emerged. These individuals have accumulated huge wealth in a short period, becoming prominent examples of the growth of "super individuals" in the digital age. However, although the phenomenon of "super individuals" is currently very hot, it is only the initial dividends of individuals leveraging digital empowerment to realize new value monetization or creation in their respective industries. The sustainability of future development of "super individuals" will be influenced by the redefinition of the socio-economic value of individuals owing to changes in the division of labor between humans and machines under the application of digital technology. For example, the success of large generative language models like ChatGPT may lead to the rise of many virtual "super individuals", posing a significant challenge to existing real-life "super individuals". Virtual "super individuals" have the potential to disrupt the business value realization methods of traditional "super individuals" owing to their low risk, low cost, high efficiency, and high capability.

8.1.2 What Contributes to the Emergence of "Super Individuals"

The fundamental reason for the widespread emergence of "super individuals" is the empowerment of ordinary individuals by digital technology, enabling individuals to connect with the entire world and thus gain the potential to influence society. In China, the application of many large-scale platforms boasts hundreds of millions of users, resulting in particularly pronounced economies of scale. This means that individuals' activities on platforms, in terms of potential, can connect with hundreds of millions of people. Once market resonance is formed, the commercial value generated is unimaginable compared to the past.

There are mainly two reasons for the success of "super individuals": first, the lowering of the threshold empowered by digital technology allows every participating individual the opportunity to become a "super individual". Second, the extraordinary returns have stimulated the initiative of individuals in society.

In China, with the increasingly perfect digital infrastructure, the application of various intelligent technologies continues to enhance individuals' digital capabilities. The continuous iteration and upgrade of various mobile applications for shopping, socializing, entertainment, making friends, and sharing knowledge enable people of all ages to easily access the convenience and joy brought by digital technology. This establishes a connection between the whole society and the internet, forming a vast digital market, which provides the foundation for the emergence, survival, and development of "super individuals".

Once becoming a "super individual", the individual's ability to allocate social resources will undergo explosive growth, accompanied by a significant increase in wealth, bringing enormous, previously unimaginable returns.

The vast market, low entry barriers, and potential for tremendous success and returns motivate many people to eagerly pursue becoming "super individuals" in the tide of the times. This has led to the emergence of remarkable "super individuals" in various fields, becoming one of the most prominent and widespread phenomena of the digital age.

8.1.3 The Impact of "Super Individuals"

Currently, "super-individuals" are predominantly viewed from the perspective of their social influence, emphasizing their "super" characteristics. Compared to traditional ordinary individuals, their influence boundaries and speed have significantly increased, and their impact on society has surpassed past imaginations. For example, on social platforms such as Weibo and Douyin, "key opinion leaders" (KOLs) with tens of millions or even hundreds of millions of followers can rapidly influence a wide audience with their words and actions, some of which can even trigger social resonance and become social phenomena. The impacts brought about by these social phenomenon-level events often extend beyond mere news reporting to potentially catalyze societal changes and evolution. In the economic and social system, the impact of "super individuals" is noteworthy, mainly manifested in two aspects:

Weak interdependent cooperative relationships form a new mode of the division of labor: Once becoming a "super individual", their social super influence is associated with their unique labels or specific personas. Therefore, although achieving social super influence and wealth monetization depend on platform companies, this process can also be achieved independently of specific platform companies. This situation makes the ecological relationship between "super individuals" and platform-type companies fundamentally different from the employer-employee relationship of the industrial age, being merely a weak interdependent associative relationship. In this stage of the social division of labor, organizational attachment of individuals decreases, while social attachment significantly increases.

Weak interdependent division of labor model promotes the emergence of gig economy: In the digital age, individuals can leverage their knowledge and skills from multiple avenues without relying on a specific organizational structure. This makes the gig economy one of the important modes of the division of labor, leading to the emergence of the "gig economy". In the "gig economy", individuals can freely choose work projects and flexibly participate in the social division of labor, no longer constrained by fixed employment relationships. Digital platforms play an important role in employment matching and payment, facilitating communication and cooperation between employers and gig workers.

Lowering the threshold to become "super individuals" can promote socioeconomic equality: If monopolization of digital information resources and technological resources can be avoided, and if the threshold for ordinary individuals empowered by digital technology to become "super individuals" continues to decrease, it can break the class stratification phenomenon caused by resource polarization in the industrial age and promote intergenerational mobility in society. Owing to the low ownership impact of digital resources and their low replication costs and strong positive externalities, individuals can more freely utilize and reconfigure digital resources, thus achieving high mobility enabled by digital empowerment. Therefore, by empowering ordinary people through digitization to become "super individuals", the egalitarian ideals of the internet can also be realized.

The emergence of "super individuals" not only reflects the new characteristics of the digital age but also has profound impacts on the socio-economic system. Therefore, their development trends and impact mechanisms deserve continuous attention.

8.1.4 The Distribution Characteristics of "Super Individuals"

The disproportionate return on investment compared to potential gains in the market of "super individuals" has attracted increasing resources, leading to intensified competition and a rise in specialization. In such a competitive environment, individuals aiming to become "super individuals" with significant societal influence and achieve sustainable development often require team support across various stages such as information content creation, dissemination, and monetization. Otherwise, they risk being eliminated in the competition.

In practice, the influence of "super individuals" conforms to a Zipf distribution. This means that the contribution of top "super entities" in the market is far greater than that of ordinary "super entities". Zipf distribution is a universal law, observed not only in linguistics but also in areas such as city size, individual income, number of downloads of network music, and number of video views.

In the field of the internet, Zipf distribution is also considered a manifestation of the long-tail distribution. The long-tail distribution implies that a vast majority of the market is occupied by popular projects, but although the number of niche projects is small, their total quantity remains considerable and maintains a relatively stable level. This phenomenon arises owing to the richness of choice sources. When the sources of choice are abundant enough to satisfy all demands, the long-tail phenomenon occurs.

Based on the theory of the long-tail distribution, ordinary individuals have the opportunity to become "super individuals" as long as they position themselves reasonably and provide information supply that meets market demand. To become a leading member of "super individuals", however, one needs to target larger market scales and offer distinctive and appealing digital information supply.

Therefore, in the digital age, individuals can become top "super individuals" in the market and gain significant influence and profits by differentiating their positioning and providing attractive information supply.

8.1.5 Pathways to "Super Individuals"

From current practices, individuals typically have two typical approaches to becoming "super individuals":

1. Independent Exploration and Innovation: Individuals can gain social recognition through independent exploration and innovation. This approach is suitable for pioneering new fields or markets, avoiding intense competition in existing mature markets. Individuals need to fully utilize the potential of digital empowerment to establish high-quality social connections and unique labels, thereby building their influence in social networks. However, once individuals reach a certain level of influence and find monetization methods, they often choose to form teams to maintain their community influence. Therefore, corporate operation remains one of the sustainable development approaches for "super individuals".
2. Joining MCN Organizations: Individuals can choose to join various MCN (Multi-Channel Network) organizations and become part of their value creation process. This approach is suitable for individuals operating in mature markets. MCN organizations can provide various support, but individuals need to face the challenge of intensified market competition, as market competition has entered a stage of competing in professional levels and service differentiation.

Regardless of the approach individuals choose to participate in the "super individuals" market, they will face fierce competition and unpredictability in market changes. The branding development model of "super individuals" will become increasingly popular, and individuals' social responsibility awareness and capabilities will become increasingly important. Recent events have shown that individuals may face risks in the development process, so they must manage relationships with stakeholders and can handle unexpected events. Socialization will not only contribute to the birth and development of "super individuals" but also become a potential risk point for their development.

8.2 The "Influencer Economy"

The rise of the influencer economy is a significant example of how "super individuals" monetize their influence and commercial value. Through methods such as live streaming sales, influencers (or internet celebrities) leverage their accumulated influence and trust within their communities to integrate product sales and brand advertising, thus transforming social value into economic value. The popularity of this business model can be seen as "super individuals" attempting to convert their social influence into economic value.

8.2.1 The Characteristics of the Influencer Economy

The influencer economy indeed exhibits the characteristics described above, with widespread influence and visibility being one of its core features. Internet celebrities attract many followers through their activity and appeal on social media platforms, thus becoming targets for brand collaborations. By partnering with brands to promote products or services, internet celebrities can enhance and monetize their commercial value. This business model emphasizes conversion efficiency, namely turning followers' attention into actual purchasing power. Collaboration methods are diverse and include paid partnerships, sponsored collaborations, revenue sharing from advertisements, among others. Meanwhile, the internet celebrity economy also emphasizes authenticity and interactivity, as internet celebrities share genuine life experiences and opinions on social media platforms, fostering closer relationships with their followers.

However, the influencer economy also faces some challenges, such as false advertising and integrity issues in commercial collaborations. Consumers need to approach internet celebrity endorsements rationally, discerning between truth and falsehood, and ensuring that their consumption decisions are based on objective information and genuine needs.

8.2.2 The Rise of the Influencer Economy

The rise of the internet celebrity economy can be attributed to three main factors: consumer upgrading, the output of industrial production capacity, and the arrival of a new consumption era.

First, consumer upgrading manifests as personalized consumption becoming a mainstream trend. With the increase in income levels and the rise of the Y generation (born between 1980 and 2000), consumer demands have continuously upgraded, leading to a shift in consumer attitudes. The pursuit of individual characteristics has become fashionable. The widespread application of the internet and digital technology has accelerated the development of social networks, making social information exchange more convenient and promoting the flourishing of the community economy. The rise of this community economy has provided the basis for information exchange to meet personalized demands, thereby driving the development of the internet celebrity economy. The application of digital technology has made consumer demand scenarios more fragmented and diversified, and consumer touch points have become more diverse, further promoting innovation in consumer goods tailored to niche demands. Additionally, the convenient communication brought by digital technology has made individual trust a significant factor in consumer choices.

Second, the development of industrialization has entered a new stage, leading to new outlets for production capacity. With the basic completion of industrialization in China, industrial overcapacity has become a common phenomenon. The widespread application of flexible and intelligent production lines enables enterprises to complete personalized orders at lower costs and higher efficiency. At the same time, the development of e-commerce platforms such as Taobao, JD.com, and Pinduoduo has made the product supply more diversified and product information more transparent, providing supply and information conditions for the development of the internet celebrity economy.

Third, the arrival of a new consumption era signifies that social consumption has entered a new stage. With the continuous increase in income levels among the Chinese population, the younger generation born in the 1980s, 1990s, and 2000s has gradually become the mainstream of society. Particularly, the so-called Z generation has begun to lead consumption trends. The updating of consumer attitudes has led to the arrival of a new consumption era, reflected in changes in the judgment of consumption values. Japanese bestselling author Miura Hiroshi summarized Japan's consumption process since 1912 into four stages in his book "The Fourth Consumption Era". Today, Japan has entered the fourth consumption era, emphasizing a "sharing" society. China's consumption philosophy, led by the Z generation, is becoming increasingly similar to the fourth era described by Miura. This new consumption philosophy emphasizes sharing, quality, and comfort, while also taking into account emotional and inner satisfaction. For example, on the Xianyu platform, over 60% of users are born after 1990, showing characteristics of more trust in others, more love for gatherings, and more love for interaction, indicating that the new generation of consumers increasingly values sharing, leading to the rise of new idle consumption models.

This shared, and interactive consumption philosophy has gradually gained broader recognition, not only giving rise to various entrepreneurial hotspots in the sharing economy but also becoming the ideological foundation for the development model of the internet celebrity economy. The "fourth consumption era" described by Miura is not only occurring in Japan and China but also in many other countries, including the United States.

8.2.3 The Influencer Economy in the Developing Age

The development of the internet celebrity economy can be attributed to three main factors: the increase in individual income levels leading to a rise in personalized demands, the industrialization entering a new stage resulting in surplus industrial production capacity seeking new outlets, and the arrival of a new consumption era.

On the demand side, the development of the internet celebrity economy can be summarized as the flourishing of community-based internet celebrity economy driven by the increase in personalized demands under the rise in individual income levels. On the supply side, industrialization entering a new stage has led to surplus industrial production capacity seeking new outlets, thereby promoting the development of personalized product supply. Additionally, the updating and development of consumer ideologies have led to the widespread social acceptance of the personalized, shared, and emphasized interpersonal relationship consumption model of the internet celebrity economy, further promoting its deepening development. It's worth noting that the shared consumption model and personalized consumption are not contradictory but complementary. Personalized demands reach a consensus within specific groups and provide market conditions for the shared consumption model, with the two playing complementary roles in regulating the relationship between surplus output supply and demand.

Currently, the development of the digital economy is still in its infancy, with significant room for improvement in both the production process on the supply side and the level of digitization in various aspects. The development of the internet celebrity economy can be regarded as a manifestation of the laws of development of the digital economy. By exploring the characteristics of the current internet celebrity economy and the differences between its business models and traditional business models, we can better understand the trends in business and economic development supported by digital technology.

The current internet celebrity economy has adopted a community-based economic development model; whether based on WeChat-based microbusinesses or short videos or live streaming, all attempt to facilitate the connection between people and products through the relationships between people, thereby achieving product sales. In this business model, the trust relationship established between sellers and consumers drives consumers' choices and purchases of products, which is essentially no different from the traditional economic model that uses "celebrity endorsements" to promote consumption. It's just that now, the so-called "internet celebrities" have replaced the "celebrities" of the past, lowering the entry threshold, but fundamentally, it is still a process of commercial value realization based on information asymmetry. Therefore, the internet celebrity economy can be regarded as a manifestation of the traditional "star effect economy" in the digital economy era. It is worth noting that with the development of intelligent technology and platform competition, the living space of the information asymmetry business model will gradually shrink. The competition in the current internet celebrity economy is already fierce, and top internet celebrities will gain a competitive advantage by controlling more aspects of the industrial chain, such as optimizing the supply chain and further improving product production. However, in the long run, the information asymmetry business model is difficult to sustain a competitive advantage. Because digital empowerment enables individuals, making technological impacts rapid, information dissemination and influence rapid, and the time and space gap for information arbitrage minimal. Therefore, information asymmetry should not be the source of social value creation and will be replaced by business models based on the creation of information value in the future.

8.3 The "Platform Economy"

The platform economy is a novel economic model characterized by its support for information dissemination and transaction completion between two parties. Its main functions include collecting transaction data, providing advisory services, and conducting classification. The development of this economic model encompasses internet models, two-sided models, three-party models, models with technical services, and social economy models. The internet model creates virtual logical relationships through the collaborative creation of information resources, the two-sided model achieves bilateral selection, the three-party model revolves around information collection and maintenance, the model with technical services focuses on designing fair, secure, and efficient service channels, while the social economy model fully leverages the advantages of social networks to realize diverse social capital gains.

With the development of the digital age, platform economy has been widely applied, exemplified by the emergence of digital platform companies such as Facebook, Amazon, Taobao, and Tencent. The successful business models of these platforms benefit from their ability to create new value through the scale-based realization of the social division of labor network, thereby reducing costs and forming a more competitive development trend. In addition, platform-based companies internalize the positive externalities of different super-individuals participating in the social division of labor, gaining supernormal profits and achieving rapid development, becoming giants in the economic system.

The rise of the platform economy is attributed to various reasons. First, the rapid development of information technology accelerates information dissemination and improves information acquisition efficiency. Second, there exists a large-scale supply and demand of resources, but there are difficulties in matching, communicating, and cooperating between the two parties. Platforms can serve as intermediaries to facilitate resource sharing and communication. Additionally, changes in user demand, changes in business models, optimization of resource allocation, application of big data and artificial intelligence technology, innovation in profit models, and policy support are all important reasons for the rise of the platform economy.

The platform economy has a series of characteristics, including strong economies of scale, quasi-public attributes, the importance of data elements, high interactivity, real-time transactions and immediate feedback, and network effects. These characteristics make the platform economy an important part of the digital economy era and will continue to grow rapidly with the continuous development of internet, data, and artificial intelligence technologies. In the future, the platform economy will pay more attention to user needs and interactions, improve efficiency, intelligence, and globalization. At the same time, issues such as platform credibility and data protection will also be emphasized, and regulatory and security issues will be strengthened.

Chapter 9
Business Operation and Value Creation of the Digital Economy

9.1 The Systematic Changes in the Business Environment

The rise of digital technology has provided individuals with more choices and room for action, profoundly impacting the realization of individual social value. With changes in individual decision-making behavior, economically organized forms have had to adapt to the development needs of the digital economy. These economic organizations are able to more fully utilize the new business value creation capabilities and development opportunities brought about by digital technology. This change inevitably reshapes the existing economic structure, accelerating the comprehensive digitization of the economic and social system. This transformation starts from the grassroots level, driving the comprehensive transformation of the economic and social system, leading to systemic changes in the business development environment and a comprehensive renewal of business development dynamics. New business models and organizational forms in the digital age are evolving and transforming rapidly in various fields with unstoppable momentum.

The empowerment of digital technology has generated new dynamics and opportunities. Digital technology gives rise to the success of a series of high-tech enterprises based on digital technology. In China, well-known companies such as Baidu, Alibaba, Tencent, JD.com, Meituan, Pinduoduo, and ByteDance have penetrated into various aspects of our lives, becoming outstanding representatives of digital technology empowerment. These companies have accumulated tremendous corporate value and scale at unprecedented speeds while serving ordinary individuals, gradually becoming core components of the economic system. Their market capitalization often reaches hundreds of billions or even trillions, with annual revenues in the hundreds of billions, and employee numbers reaching tens of thousands, serving millions of customers. This rapid achievement of such enormous commercial success in a short period is unprecedented in the industrial age.

All of this stems from the empowerment of digital technology for enterprises. Under the influence of digitization, these companies rapidly expand their markets

Y. Yu and Y. Jiang, *Understanding the Digital Revolution and Its Influences*,
https://doi.org/10.1007/978-981-97-4939-3_9

and integrate resources through the internet, utilizing the viral effect of links. The financial system developed during the industrial age has also provided a boost to their development, allowing them to accumulate commercial resources at an exponential rate from their inception, accelerating the enhancement of their commercial value and scale. This unprecedented momentum and development space reflect different development laws and characteristics from the past. Fundamentally, all of this is because the human society is rapidly entering a new era of digital business civilization, providing new dynamics and laws for business development.

9.1.1 The Rise of New Formats in the Digital Economy

The empowerment of digital technology is driving the economic and social system towards digitization, making enterprises empowered by digital technology the mainstream of the economy. The development of the digital economy has become the main driving force of the economic society and the most significant characteristic of the digital age. The rise of new formats in the digital economy shows different economic development laws from the industrial age.

There are significant differences between the formats of the digital economy and those of the industrial age in terms of the source of commercial value, economic form, decision-making methods, and organizational forms, determining the development process of the new business civilization formats of the digital age.

9.1.2 The Source of Commercial Value

In the agricultural era, the production of agricultural products was the cornerstone of social development, while the industrial era established manufacturing as the primary industry for wealth creation. Both eras relied on physical product production as the main source of wealth. Therefore, "how to produce" and "what to produce" became crucial factors determining the potential wealth of society, and the boundaries of production potential determined the society's ability to transform and the efficiency level of information processing. The commercial value was mainly determined by the scarcity of products, with the key lying in the ability to integrate resources, and the bottleneck being the social supply of the scarcest resources.

In the digital age, industrial technology has highly developed, and the production process has matured, with significant improvements in standardization, modularization, and automation levels. The economies of scale of industrial technology have led to product supply exceeding effective demand, so product scarcity is no longer the primary determinant of commercial value. Instead, resource optimization allocation becomes crucial, and the ability to integrate resources on the demand side becomes the decisive factor for commercial value. The business civilization of the digital age has fundamentally changed from the past, with significant changes in the basic conditions for forming commercial value, and demand-side resource integration and supply–demand integration becoming the dominant factors. Data integration has become the core of forming commercial value, while the decision-making process relies entirely on data acquisition and processing. It is worth noting that in the digital economy, data has unlimited supply and is non-depletable, which is drastically different from the past where there were physical constraints on economic factors.

9.1.3 The Economic Forms

The empowerment brought by digital technology leads to the comprehensive digitization of economic forms, and the result of digital development is the increasing trend of virtualization in economic forms. Economic transactions increasingly rely on digital tools, and economic transaction objects also exist more in digital forms. Digital resources are easy to replicate, disseminate, and use, often with external effects. The production and optimization allocation of these digitalized and virtualized economic elements no longer follow the rules of physical form economic elements in the industrial era. This is because the replicability, ease of dissemination, and non-depletion of digital production factors (such as data information, technical knowledge, etc.) affect the definition of rights and interests of these virtualized elements in the digital economy. It is difficult to form effective market incentives, resulting in operational difficulties in the production and circulation of related elements.

Addressing the challenges of determining and transferring the value and rights of digitalized and virtualized economic elements in the digital world requires the use of digital technology tools. Currently, Non-Fungible Tokens (NFTs) in innovative applications of blockchain technology are potential new technological tools. NFTs utilize the immutability of blockchain technology through timestamps, consensus mechanisms, and encryption algorithms. Their unique encoding can represent the uniqueness and scarcity in the digital world, marking digital assets with digital certificates to assert their ownership rights. Currently, NFTs are popular in fields such as art and gaming, with the value of NFTs exceeding $42 billion as of early January 2022, and they will be applied in the entire digital economy field in the future.

The application of NFTs in the digital economy demonstrates that the development of the digital economy requires digital technology development that matches institutional reforms. Corresponding applications of digital technology will change the original laws of economic operation and form new characteristics of economic development in the digital age.

9.1.4 The Decision-Making Methods

In the digital age, the economy and society have undergone comprehensive digitization, where digital information becomes the determining factor in resource allocation.

Information is abundant, even redundant, disrupting the traditional concept of information scarcity. The amount of information required and obtained for economic decision-making far exceeds human processing capabilities. Effective decision-making relies on intelligent machine systems to process information, thus achieving a mode of human–machine collaborative decision-making.

Economic decision-making no longer merely pursues profit maximization but also considers decision costs and efficiency. Optimal decision-making choices depend not only on returns but also on the upfront investment costs. In the digital age, effective decision-making requires the collection and processing of vast amounts of information and intuition alone is insufficient. Decision-making without sufficient information can lead to high-risk behavior, exposing companies to the risk of elimination.

Decision-making has transitioned from being solely reliant on individual human agents to being a collaborative effort between humans and machines. Therefore, adjusting the mode and process of human–machine collaboration is crucial for enhancing decision-making efficiency, improving competitiveness, and realizing societal value.

9.1.5 The Organizational Forms

In the digital age, the speed of information transmission and decision-making determines decision efficiency and shapes the boundaries of decision-making power and the forms and operations of organizational structures.

The complexity and scale of information in the digital age have overturned the characteristics of decision-making formed in environments of information scarcity, thereby changing the way economic decisions are made and leading to adjustments in economic organizational structures. Different organizational structures imply different information processing processes, corresponding to different economic decision-making methods.

To cope with the requirements of efficient information processing and the constantly changing environment, there has been a qualitative change in the division of labor between humans and machines. In the division of social labor, people need to adapt to the functional requirements of machines, but individual learning and growth are difficult to keep up with the iterative optimization speed of intelligent systems. Therefore, economic organizations in the digital age must choose more open organizational forms to attract talents with strong subjective initiative to improve information processing efficiency and promote the flow of organizational talent.

These talents with strong subjective initiative can form highly efficient organizational forms with strong self-organization capabilities, achieve parallel information processing, and greatly enhance information processing efficiency and decision adaptability. Therefore, economic organizations in the digital age exhibit open forms and flat management styles, adopting distributed decision-making models to adapt to the vast and complex information processing needs and the changing environmental trends.

The development of the digital economy is built upon the foundation industrial civilization.

Compared to the industrial age, digitization empowers enterprises to create more business value by integrating resources from the demand side, rather than just the supply side. In the agricultural and industrial ages, the development of business civilization mainly relied on the integration of supply-side information and resources to meet market demands and obtain returns on social value.

With the completion of industrialization and the maturity of industrial production systems, the production processes of many social necessities have become standardized, modularized, and automated. This renders the integration of information and resources on the supply side no longer a constraint on social development, laying the groundwork for economic virtualization. However, in the industrial age, the efficiency of information processing mechanisms was not high, mainly relying on the organizational optimization of human resources. Consequently, the level of integration of resources on the demand side was relatively low, leading to inefficient supply–demand matching and high costs for the effective circulation of product value, with high intermediary transaction costs.

With the improvement of industrial product quality and the increase in production capacity, the Great Depression of the 1930s revealed the problem of total supply exceeding total demand caused by industrial development, resulting in the unsustainability and systemic issues of the economic system. Therefore, the integration of resources on the demand side became increasingly important, becoming a key goal of the development of the new business civilization. This also prompted the emergence of government as the regulator of the economic system, undertaking the function of regulating the economic system. Therefore, the development of business in the digital age needs to be based on the full development of industrial civilization and the integration of resources on the demand side.

9.1.6 New Characteristics in the Digital Economy

The fundamental characteristic of the digital economy is based on advanced industrial capabilities, where the economies of scale in industrial technology led to the fundamental feature of supply and demand: total supply significantly exceeds effective total demand.

In the digital age, human industrial production capacity has reached its limit, and the social supply capacity of industrial products often exceeds total social demand. Data from 1971 to 2018 show that the average annual growth rate of GDP per capita exceeded the average annual growth rate of net per capita adjusted national income by 0.139%. GDP represents the final market value outcome of production activities of a country or region during a certain period, reflecting the market supply capacity of the economy's products and services, while national income represents market demand capacity. Over the long term, the imbalance between total supply and total demand has been accumulating.

Especially since the deepening of globalization since the 1980s, with China becoming the world's factory, global product supply capacity far exceeds demand capacity. This has led to a continuous decline in the global annual inflation rate, further exacerbating the cumulative imbalance between total supply and total demand. The outbreak of the 2008 subprime mortgage crisis was one of the deep-seated reasons for this imbalance. The influence of Keynesianism led to deep government intervention in economic operations, taking a series of policies to regulate the state of total supply exceeding total demand, avoiding the risk of long-term deep economic recession globally.

In the new business civilization of the digital age, the situation where total supply exceeds total demand has become a basic premise for discussing the rationality of business logic and the development characteristics.

The phenomenon of total supply exceeding total demand not only stems from the high flexibility of industrial mass production technology but is also influenced by the continuous slowdown in the growth rate of total demand compared to total supply. The sluggish growth rate of total demand is mainly due to slow real income growth for the majority of people and the widening gap between the rich and the poor. For example, in the United States, from 1974 to 2018, the share of income held by the lowest income 20% of the population decreased from 6.2% to 5.2%. In contrast, the share held by the highest income 20% increased from 41.8% in 1974 to 46.9% in 2018, a growth of 5.1%. Particularly noteworthy is that the share held by the top 10% of income earners increased from 26% in 1974 to 30.8% in 2018, a growth of 4.8%. This indicates that the increase in the share of income for high-income groups mainly comes from the population at the top of the income distribution pyramid. This phenomenon is also prevalent in developed European countries such as Germany and the United Kingdom. China is no exception. Since the reform and opening-up, despite continuous economic and income growth, income inequality persists. In 1990, the income share of the lowest 20% income group in China was 8.3%, which decreased to 6.5% in 2016. Meanwhile, the share of the highest 20% income group increased from 40.8% in 1990 to 45.3% in 2016, an increase of 4.5%. The share of the top 10% of income earners increased from 25.5% in 1990 to 29.4% in 2016, an increase of 3.9%. This situation is very similar to that of the United States, indicating a more significant increase in the income share of the population at the top of the income pyramid. Owing to the diminishing marginal propensity to consume among the wealthy, the expansion of total demand cannot keep pace with the growth of total supply, resulting in a contractionary market competition. This affects the value circulation in the process of product reproduction, and competition among products becomes increasingly fierce.

9.1.7 Imbalance in Supply and Demand Sparking Escalating Competition

The cumulative effect of total supply consistently surpassing the growth of total demand has led competition to gradually evolve into a state of stock competition. When industrial technology reaches a certain level and people's basic living needs are largely met, many so-called product innovations often only bring about stock substitution effects rather than expansive incremental effects. This business environment has become a common condition for the development of most enterprises, leading to "involution" becoming a widespread phenomenon in modern the social division of labor and cooperation.

The term "involution" was initially proposed by American anthropologist Gilts to describe the state of struggle and internal consumption caused by excessive competition in a certain field. In contrast, "evolution" refers to the development of a system to a higher state, while "involution" refers to the phenomenon where system energy is consumed internally without pushing it towards a higher state of development. In the long run, any phenomenon that cannot push the system to a higher stage of development or break through the existing state can be called "involution".

The popularization of digital technology has accelerated information exchange, eliminating the constraints of information asymmetry on cooperative production business models. However, as the creation of new value from information and the increasing marginal cost of innovation have risen, the space for creative growth has become increasingly difficult for individuals to achieve. Therefore, "involution" has become the only choice for survival for the majority of individuals. In East Asia, including China, Japan, and South Korea, "involution" has become the norm for the general population, and the same is true in Western countries. The phenomenon of involution highlights the contradiction between individual development opportunities and social distribution mechanisms. Society cannot provide sufficient resources for individuals to promote cooperation, forcing individuals to seek survival through competition, thereby causing the social system of the division of labor to enter a state of internal consumption. This indicates that the current social system is facing a bottleneck in information processing efficiency and urgently needs the emergence of technological innovation and new development models to promote a renewed innovation of the social system of the division of labor.

The universality of the phenomenon of "involution" in modern society has led to widespread discussion and recognition of this concept. Its fundamental reason lies in the fact that the social system of the division of labor driven by technological change no longer matches the needs of social development, and social resource inputs no longer play a role in promoting social development. Young people lack choices under the current socio-economic conditions and can only make choices among existing opportunities, forcing everyone to choose "involution" as a way of survival. Stock development is the root cause of involution, and only through incremental development can the problem of involution be fundamentally resolved. Through incremental development, everyone can have other opportunities, and young people can see hope, thereby no longer being forced to choose involution as a way of survival.

9.1.8 Digital Technology Accelerating the Transformation of the Social Division of Labor

Currently, the application of digital technology has triggered revolutionary changes in the social division of labor, exacerbating the impact of stock-based development. Empowered by digital technology, the efficiency of information processing in the economy has greatly improved. This has led to the replacement of traditional brick-and-mortar business models by e-commerce online business models, the substitution of production workers by smart robots on production lines, and the substitution of white-collar workers by intelligent machine systems in offices, among other phenomena. The establishment of these substitution relationships follows the principle of efficiency first, adopting a new and more efficient economic form, replacing old economic forms in a stock-based manner. This mode of stock-based development has driven people from all walks of life into a continuous state of internal competition. The root cause of internal competition lies in the macroeconomic background where total demand has long been lower than total supply, and this imbalance in distribution is a result of the value evaluation system of the social division of labor.

To eliminate the trend of internal competition, it is necessary to promote the transformation of the system for forming, evaluating, and exchanging social values, stimulate the potential space for innovative division of labor cooperation, and reduce the probability of competitive division of labor. At the same time, it is necessary to reevaluate the social value of individual division of labor and adjust the value evaluation system of the social division of labor to prevent individuals from falling into irretrievable marginalization once abandoned by the social system of the division of labor. Improving the social security system and re-education system is crucial for the survival and development of ordinary individuals because everyone's ability to relearn is limited and faces the risk of being replaced by new technologies.

The digital age must explore the sustainable development logic and ethical relations of the new business civilization, promote the improvement of the overall information processing efficiency of society. This means establishing symbiotic competitive relationships, fully utilizing the principle of comparative advantage, and forming a division of labor and cooperation between people and machines. At the same time, existing social distribution methods also need to be adjusted, redefining the ways in which factors participate in economic activities and the way in which their value is evaluated. The government plays a crucial role in this regard and must use digital technology tools to define the functions of the economic and social sectors and intervene in economic and social activities, becoming the main guarantee for achieving sustainable development of the economy and society in the digital age.

The application of digital technology is expected to change the irreversible state of internal competition in society. Through the empowerment of digital technology, not only can the effective supply of social labor be increased, but also the diversity of demand and the generation of new demand can be promoted, thereby providing opportunities for incremental development to society. Therefore, expanding the new development space for digital technology applications, promoting diversified development of demand, will be a business opportunity in the digital age and the greatest commercial opportunity for digital technology innovation and development. Enterprises and innovative entrepreneurs should focus on how to utilize the innovation of new organizational cooperation and division of labor systems more effectively between people and machines, promote the development of new demand space and innovative diversified development of demand. This will be the main source of creating new business value in the digital age.

9.1.9 A New Perspective on the Evolution of New Business Civilization Under the Digital Economy

The widespread application of digital technology has created a completely new development environment for humanity. In this environment, the new business civilization of the digital economy and its evolutionary logic differ significantly from the economic laws of the industrial and agricultural eras, which requires us to re-examine. We must adopt a completely new perspective to examine the development conditions and opportunities of the future new business civilization. Past theoretical frameworks often limit our identification of opportunities for development in times of change because each theory is a product of its era and cannot transcend its temporal and spatial limitations.

Economic theories are constrained by the limitations of their time as they evolve. With changes in the major systems of the era, existing theories may become obsolete, necessitating new theoretical frameworks to respond. For the development of the new business civilization of the digital age, the changing conditions of the economic system itself make theoretical innovation urgent and necessary. Only through innovation at the theoretical level can more development space and possibilities be won for the new business civilization.

In the era of digital economic development and transformation, we need to be aware of the cognitive limitations of the existing economic theoretical framework in understanding new economic phenomena. Especially when considering business logic, we need to be mindful of potential constraints. In the digital age, we must break out of the framework of existing business logic and pay attention to an important systemic economic condition change: the continued weakness of labor distribution rights under the existing value distribution system leading to long-term total demand lower than total supply. In this changing environment, entrepreneurs must reassess the sources and driving mechanisms of business value in the digital age.

Viewing the social system of the division of labor or the economic and social system from the perspective of the unity of human reproduction process and the value circulation of product reproduction process will help us better understand economic activities, analyze the impact of technological innovation on the economy, and identify the sources of social value created by different economic entities.

9.2 New Paradigms for Business in the Digital Economy

The social value of a company lies in whether its business logic aligns with the needs of social development. With changes in socio-economic conditions, companies need to reshape new business logic by adjusting their business models to adapt to the requirements of social development. To better understand the sources and driving forces of business value in the digital economy era, it is necessary to review the sources of business value creation and key driving forces in the industrial age.

9.2.1 New Drivers for Business: From the Supply Side to the Demand Side

The shift in business drivers has transitioned from supply-side to demand-side. With the continuous development of industrial technology, many industrial consumer goods now offer product experience functionalities beyond human physiological perception. In many fields, such as high-definition televisions and digitalized transportation services, product functionalities have reached a level sufficient to meet people's needs. For example, in the television industry, with the introduction of 4K and 8K television products, the richness of colors and resolution of television screens has surpassed human physiological limits; further improvements in visual physical indicators have minimal impact on sensation. In the transportation sector, the services provided by airplanes and high-speed trains can meet the travel needs of most people, enabling them to cross time zones within a single day. The proliferation of the internet has made digital communication a daily occurrence, and digital visualization conferences allow people to communicate in real-time from different locations, overcoming limitations of time and space. Meanwhile, digital products such as smartphones and computers interact through the internet, generating and outputting information beyond the processing capacity of the human brain, making information redundancy a new challenge. Therefore, from the perspective of consumer demand, these hardware devices can basically meet individuals' daily life needs. This implies that the scarcity of industrial products is gradually disappearing with the development of industrial and digital technologies.

9.2.2 *Value Creation in the Industrial Era: Reconfiguration of Supply-Side Resources*

(1) Integration of Supply-side Resources in the Industrial Era

The development of industry has propelled human civilization into a new stage, where large-scale industrial production allows for the efficient and cost-effective manufacturing of a wide range of products to meet various needs such as food, clothing, shelter, and transportation. With technological advancements, the capacity for product production has continuously increased, leading to a growing phenomenon of overcapacity, particularly with the proliferation of intelligent unmanned factories. The emergence of automated, unmanned intelligent factories demonstrates that the complex knowledge required for manufacturing products has been fully integrated into systems, and the production process has been materialized. The commodification of vast amounts of production knowledge implies that knowledge for product production is no longer a high-value scarce resource. As the scarcity of supply-side resource integration capabilities decreases, so does social value, leading to a decline in the returns from supply-side resource integration. This gradual bottlenecking of supply-side development means that the creation and realization of social wealth increasingly depend on the integration of demand-side resources. Only through the integration of demand-side resources can enterprises on the supply side efficiently produce products that meet genuine social needs, achieve more effective integration and utilization of social resources, enhance wealth creation capabilities, and reduce wealth creation costs.

In the industrial age, entrepreneurs primarily invested in the production process by reconfiguring various factors and related knowledge and information on the supply side. For example, if an entrepreneur aims to create value for society and generate profits by establishing a business, they might choose to produce televisions or similar products to meet people's entertainment needs. In this process, they would need to collaborate with financial institutions to obtain funding, then establish factories, import production equipment, and hire technical personnel and workers. This is a process of aggregating and reconfiguring industrial product knowledge and various production factors under the guidance of capital. Subsequently, they would establish sales channels for the product, possibly selling it to consumers through shopping malls or a chain store network. In this process, entrepreneurs mainly control the reconfiguration of various factor resources and related knowledge and information on the supply side of product production, while having limited direct influence on the specific consumption demands of individual consumers.

In the industrial age, the commercial value of enterprises mainly stemmed from entrepreneurs' understanding of demand in the market and the production process. Leveraging the power of capital, they integrated various resources and knowledge information on the supply side of product production, manufactured relevant products, and obtained profits through sales, thereby realizing commercial value. Although the realization of commercial value of enterprises is concentrated on the demand side of the market, its roots lie in the integration of information resources on the supply side and the aggregation of factor resources. Therefore, understanding the value of enterprises requires starting from the perspective of enterprise organization.

Economists have proposed different theoretical explanations for the social value sources and foundations of enterprise organization, among which two important theories are the theory of firm capabilities and the theory of firm contracts. The theory of firm capabilities was first proposed by Adam Smith, emphasizing that firms increase social wealth creation capacity by improving labor efficiency through specialization. Penrose (1959) further elaborated on the theory of firm capabilities in "The Theory of the Growth of the Firm", arguing that firms are collections of productive resources, and management decisions determine the allocation of resources and the creation of value. The theory of firm contracts, on the other hand, originated from Coase's research on the nature of the firm, emphasizing that firms exist as a form of organization to reduce transaction costs. These two theories respectively explain the existence of firms from the perspectives of the characteristics of firm production and transaction costs.

Despite profound theoretical analyses, economists still have divergent understandings of the value of enterprises. Part of the reason is the diversity and dynamic nature of the forms of enterprise development, as well as the complexity of their business activities. Moreover, economists have relatively limited knowledge of the actual operation of the economy. Some successful investment gurus, such as Buffett, adopt different theoretical logics when evaluating the value of enterprises, indicating significant discrepancies between existing economic theory frameworks and the actual operation of the economy. Although economic theory is attempting some theoretical breakthroughs, the current level of change in economic theory is still insufficient.

(2) Successful Investment Philosophy Focused on Supply-Side Integration

As a successful investor, Warren Buffett insists that the commercial value of a company mainly comes from its ability to integrate resources on the supply side. His investment career, dubbed the "Oracle of Omaha", saw remarkable success. Over a span of 42 years from 1965 to 2006, the net asset growth rate of his holding company, Berkshire Hathaway, averaged 21.46% annually, with a cumulative growth of 361,156%. In comparison, the annual growth rate of the S&P 500 index components during the same period was 10.4%, with a cumulative growth of 6479%. His successful investment philosophy is known as value investing.

Buffett's "economic moat" theory, which evaluates the commercial value of companies in the industrial age, is widely applied in the selection of investment targets. The concept of an "economic moat" first appeared in his shareholder letters in 1993, was elaborated upon at the Berkshire Hathaway annual meeting in 1995, and further emphasized at the 2000 shareholder meeting. Buffett believes that a company's economic moat is its most important, stable, and enduring competitive advantage, and the source of its value. He sees the sources of the economic moat as the company's brand strength, product uniqueness, sales power, and franchise rights.

In his book "The Essays of Warren Buffett", Pat Dorsey further interprets Buffett's "economic moat" theory, categorizing it into four types: intangible assets, customer switching costs, network effects, and cost advantages. Among these sources of structural competitive advantage, intangible assets, customer switching costs, and network effects are closely related to demand-side resources, while only cost advantages pertain to the supply side, highlighting Buffett's emphasis on demand-side factors.

Guided by Buffett's "economic moat" theory, his company gained a $4.9 billion profit during the 2008 financial crisis, and his long-term holding, Walmart, rose against the trend by 2% in 2008. Such achievements underscore the significance of the "economic moat" theory. Buffett's investment philosophy differs fundamentally from the perspectives of economists studying enterprises, who typically analyze from the supply-side perspective, whereas Buffett and other practical economists place greater emphasis on the impact of demand-side factors.

Warren Buffett's investment in American Airlines provides a notable case study. During the 1980s and 1990s, American Airlines experienced rapid expansion, continuously adding flights, and the industry flourished. However, investors found it challenging to profit from this growth. Buffett believed that the airline industry suffered from severe homogenization of services, intense competition, price-sensitive customers, and consequently, low profitability. Moreover, the monopolistic supply of aircraft led to high maintenance costs, further hindering profitability. This example illustrates that resource integration on the supply side is unlikely to be a source of new value creation in the post-industrial era, even in monopolistic industries.

Comparing the differences between theoretical economists' theories such as the theory of firm capabilities and the theory of firm contracts and investment masters' economic moat theory, we can observe that theoretical economists focus more on the impact of the supply side and transaction processes, while Buffett places greater emphasis on the impact of the demand side. Practical evidence has shown that this understanding can lead to significant economic returns. This difference arises because theory always lags practice. The theories of firm capabilities and firm contracts originated during the prosperous industrialization phase while Buffett's successful investment experiences began in the 1960s and peaked in the 1980s. By this time, the United States had entered the post-industrial era, and the relative surplus of industrial goods became increasingly apparent. Thus, the demand side determined the value of enterprises. In a macro environment where total supply exceeds total demand, the development trend of supply–demand contradictions is determined by the demand side. The efficiency of resource allocation on the demand side determines the overall efficiency of economic operation and becomes the main source of commercial wealth realization. Therefore, in the post-industrial era, emphasis on the demand side is a strategic issue that every enterprise must take seriously.

(3) Attempts at Integrating Demand-Side Resources in the Industrial Era

Before the digital age, integrating the demand side was a highly costly task, nearly impossible to accomplish. This was because, during the industrial civilization period, with the abundant supply of industrial products, production was carried out through centralized planning. By integrating production-side resources, companies could produce various scarce industrial products, ensuring almost guaranteed sales as long as the products were produced. However, a dilemma existed: the demand for industrial products was not centralized, and entrepreneurs could only know that their products were valuable and scarce at the societal level, but they could not determine the distribution of this value and scarcity among individuals in society, nor could they determine how much individuals were willing to pay for their products.

Furthermore, consumers had their own preferences for industrial products, making them willing to spend time and effort to find products that met their needs. Therefore, early and subsequent product sales usually took place at fixed locations, where consumers would go to purchase rather than companies actively engaging in individual sales pitches. This approach could address the problem of asymmetric product information because fixed locations served as a form of quality assurance in sales, alleviating consumers' concerns about product quality without companies needing to exploit their advantage in product knowledge information to deceive consumers, nor did consumers need to spend extra effort and cost to identify product information.

As a result, the realization and circulation of product value only required the dissemination of product sales information, without the need to explain the various kinds of complex professional information involved in the product production process. In this way, the decision costs and transaction costs for the entire society were lower, making the department store sales model a popular sales approach.

After the emergence of direct sales models, companies began actively engaging in individual sales pitches targeting specific individuals through personal social networks. This approach shifted the trust cost of product information from trust in fixed capital investment in sales points to trust in relationship capital between individuals. By leveraging trust between individuals, companies can reduce decision costs and transaction costs when purchasing products, thereby saving society's information processing resources. Particularly, this approach tends to have higher supply–demand matching and can more easily reduce decision costs related to information discernment.

When choosing a sales method, companies typically assess the costs and benefits of different sales methods based on their product characteristics. Generally, lower-priced daily necessities are more likely to choose a direct sales model. Regardless of the sales model adopted, companies construct their own product sales channels, allowing customers to actively purchase products to drive sales. However, this model also has two significant characteristics: first, companies produce a large number of products but need to deal with a widely distributed base of consumers themselves, making it difficult to determine their location, specific demands, and purchasing power. This is detrimental to product production planning and continuity and controllability of production. Second, the company's products are sufficient to motivate consumers to willingly invest their own time costs and other search costs to satisfy their consumption desires. Therefore, in the early stages, companies usually lack the ability and motivation to achieve effective integration of demand market resources, and a significant cost of achieving supply–demand matching is the cost of information dissemination.

With the intensification of competition among enterprises and the advancement of information dissemination technology, companies can directly target the entire social community through broadcasting, television, and other information dissemination channels, thereby reducing the cost of information dissemination. Leveraging these economies of scale in dissemination, companies began to network their sales points, covering a broader consumer base. Through retail channels such as chain supermarkets and hypermarkets, companies can proactively understand consumer demand information, and analyze product market characteristics as well as consumer purchasing power and preferences. This greatly enhances the company's ability to integrate demand-side resources, thereby improving the targeting and planning of production plans, subsequently increasing production efficiency, and saving costs.

At this stage, companies began to exploit consumers' desires, influencing their cognition and preferences through branding, thereby establishing their monopoly position, and gaining more profits. By insightfully understanding consumer demographics, companies can cleverly shape consumer values, creating differentiation in market competition and consequently earning more profits. This has also directly propelled the development of modern marketing and become a primary driving force for humanity's entry into the information society.

However, during the stage of enterprise branding development, the integration of demand-side resources by companies remains relatively rudimentary. Although companies have begun consciously collecting, producing, and disseminating relevant information, attempting to increase their dominance over consumer demand, the consumption process still entails consumers bearing all decision-making costs and transaction costs. Therefore, this integration approach essentially remains a passive adaptation of demand-side to supply-side products, where the outcome of the company's product production still dictates customer choice opportunities and potential demand satisfaction, making it difficult to fully meet customers' true underlying needs.

9.3 Business Value Creation in the Digital Economy: Reconfiguration of Demand-Side Resources

In the digital age, the industrial economy has entered a new stage of development, with the digital economy being its digitized version. One characteristic of this stage is that industrial products are gradually becoming standardized, and modular production methods have formed robust supply chain systems. This has made industrial production more elastic and flexible, enabling the supply side to provide a more diverse range of products at lower costs. However, owing to supply capacity far exceeding effective demand, this has led to intensified competition, especially in the consumer goods sector.

Taking China as an example, Chinese industrial enterprises generally face the challenge of low profit margins, with net profit margins typically below 5%. This indicates that Chinese industrial enterprises are in a highly competitive state, but it also reflects the efficient production efficiency and robust supply chain systems of Chinese industrial enterprises. Despite the low profit margins, China's industrial system continues to operate well under various economic and financial crises and economic cyclical fluctuations, demonstrating its resilience and adaptability.

Overall, the industrial economy in the digital age faces new challenges and opportunities, requiring industrial enterprises to continuously innovate and improve efficiency to adapt to market changes and diversifying demands.

The development of the digital economy has ushered in new ways of integrating demand-side resources. Against the backdrop of China's efficient manufacturing sector, businesses in terms of product supply have become increasingly challenging. Internet platform companies like Alibaba have leveraged the well-developed internet infrastructure and the widespread adoption of smartphones in China to drive the rise of the internet economy. These platform companies attract consumers to their platforms, concentrating consumer demand onto a single online platform, thereby achieving autonomous integration of consumer demand.

This approach differs from the early industrial era when the process of social reproduction was driven by optimizing supply-side information and knowledge. In the digital economy era, optimization of demand-side information and knowledge began on the foundation of industrial civilization, aiming to integrate information more effectively from both the supply and demand sides, thereby enhancing the overall efficiency of information processing in society and promoting the improvement of resource utilization efficiency.

In conclusion, the development of the digital economy era provides new pathways and possibilities for integrating demand-side resources. Through internet platforms and similar means, the exchange of information between consumers and producers has become more convenient and efficient, thereby driving economic development, and promoting more effective utilization of social resources.

According to the developmental history, the reconfiguration of demand-side resources will become a new battleground for value creation. The main reason is the increasingly fierce competition on the supply side. The development of industrial technology has solved the scarcity problem of basic human living needs, leading to supply surplus becoming the norm in industrial sectors. Especially after China joined the global industrial supply chain, this trend has become more evident. To gain an advantage in competition, product manufacturers must design and produce products according to the requirements or orders from the demand side. Only by possessing the ability to integrate demand-side resources can the problem of resource reconfiguration under supply surplus conditions be solved, thereby obtaining core competitiveness. For example, if a company producing televisions continues to produce black and white TVs instead of meeting the demand for high-definition color TVs, it will not receive the expected returns and will eventually be eliminated from the market. Therefore, the process of integrating demand-side resources inevitably reduces the overall operating costs of the economy and society and enhances the welfare of the human society. In the future, the optimization of demand-side resource reconfiguration will be closely related to the optimization of supply-side resource reconfiguration to achieve the optimization benefits of supply–demand matching. This integration essentially involves the integration of demand-side information and supply-side information, representing an improvement in the efficiency of social information processing.

The innovation of digital technology has become the driving force behind the continuous optimization of demand-side resource reconfiguration. With the continuous development of digital technology, achieving optimized allocation of demand-side resources has become technically feasible and economically acceptable. Digital technology enables consumers on the demand side to easily gather on various platforms, such as social platforms, e-commerce platforms, and video platforms, demonstrating diverse interests, social relationships, and demand satisfaction. This allows product producers to obtain demand-side information at lower costs and in a more precise manner, and to match demand through e-commerce platforms or social groups. In the digital age, platform operators can analyze user characteristics and potential needs based on diversified information such as user browsing behavior and browsing objects. With the help of big data technology, platform operators can gain deep insights into the potential demand characteristics of individual users, even better than the users themselves, thereby recommending products and prices that are more acceptable, making demand resources more controllable, and optimizing supply–demand matching. At this stage of development, algorithms still passively provide products on the market based on demand-side requirements, achieving supply–demand matching. Therefore, at this stage, the demand characteristics of the demand side still dominate.

The development of digital technology is leading to a breakthrough transformation in demand-side resource integration. With the continuous accumulation of data and the ongoing optimization of algorithms, supply–demand matching is entering a new stage. Through the introduction of upgraded knowledge graphs and deep learning algorithms, the algorithms used by platforms will be able to actively understand consumers' innate needs and higher-level demand goals, providing them with more proactive satisfaction solutions. Algorithmic recommendations can also help demand-side users optimize their own demands, actively guiding demand trends, thus taking demand resource integration to new heights. The ability of algorithms to actively gather demand information and forecast demand trends enables platform operators to clearly identify users' real needs, gather demands from different groups in an orderly manner by providing demand optimization solutions based on big data and artificial intelligence technologies. This process makes the process of demand satisfaction orderly, effectively combining the orderly process of demand orders with the orderly process of production, reducing the systemic costs of information dissemination, identification, and matching in the market price mechanism adjustment process of the socio-economic system. Therefore, many standardized products will achieve goal-oriented, orderly production at lower resource costs and be efficiently and accurately delivered to users.

In this phase, platform operators, through demand aggregation, transform demand orders into scaled production orders, thereby securing lower price levels for demanders. For producers, obtaining clear scaled orders means eliminating market demand volatility risks, making production plans clearer, and fully leveraging economies of scale in industrial production. This allows producers to lock in raw material demand at lower costs, reduce uncertainty costs in the production process, and decrease product inventory costs. Additionally, they can more clearly determine investment scales based on demand volume. These benefits enable producers to organize production-side resource matching at lower costs and achieve scaled production. Therefore, when algorithms begin to help demand-side users actively provide optimized product demand solutions, both demand-side users and production-side enterprises can share the low-cost benefits of economies of scale and the eliminated risk costs, eliminating the phenomenon of demand–supply information asymmetry. This phase does not lead to product homogenization, but rather achieves flexible production with low-cost conversion through intelligent system-supported production lines, allowing the production of various types of products without cost escalation.

During this period, the integration and matching of social product production processes with demand processes can truly enhance social resource utilization efficiency. Business competition will focus on providing demand solutions that are more intelligent and better able to help consumers achieve their pursuit of a better life. Economic entities with large-scale data and powerful algorithm development technologies will become the hub of social resource allocation, like the role of financial institutions in modern economies. The role of such economic organizations in the economic system will far exceed that of the industrial age, and their impact on the economic system will be more profound. However, this also brings about some externalities, so the public sector will inevitably enact legislation and regulatory measures to avoid the risk of misallocation of social resources caused by adverse algorithmic recommendation schemes. During this period, the optimization of demand-side resource reconfiguration will become the primary driving force for social development, and the critical role of data as a production factor will become more prominent.

The transformative shift in the driving force of social development in the digital age is poised to usher in an era of opportunities. With the deepening digitization of the socio-economic landscape, various economic entities are leveraging digital empowerment to emerge as new forces reshaping the business world. This transformation is giving rise to new business logics and fostering new formats of business civilization. A prerequisite for this change is that enterprises are beginning to possess the genuine capability to integrate demand-side resources, thereby achieving seamless and precise alignment between demand and supply. Empowered by digitalization, enterprises can utilize the Internet and various digital technologies to gather, process, and extract value from diverse and multi-sourced information in a cost-effective and low-latency manner. Consequently, consumer demand information becomes readily collectible, enabling enterprises to establish direct contact and interaction with consumers, and produce precise and effective demand information that was previously difficult to obtain. Through the fusion of diverse data technologies and the analysis of big data, enterprises can gain deeper insights into the characteristics of consumer demand than individual consumers themselves, making it easier to identify high-value service targets and provide products and services with higher profits. This shift redirects the monopoly power of enterprises from controlling product supply elements to controlling consumer intrinsic demands, purchasing power, and willingness, compelling enterprises to focus more on integrating and optimizing demand-side resources. In this process, enterprises pay greater attention to multi-channel collection of consumer demand information to form a more effective data foundation for demand-side resource integration and leverage their advantages in information acquisition and processing capabilities to build the foundation of their core competitiveness and sustained monopolistic position.

9.4 The Rise of New Business Models in the Digital Economy

With the development of the digital economy, new business models focusing on demand-side integration are emerging. In the early stages of Internet applications, when the digital economy was just beginning to rise, the integration of demand-side resources became the foundation for constructing business models. Initially, Internet business applications attempted to send information and advertisements to the demand side through the integration of information resources, to inform potential consumers about product information. Portals such as Yahoo, Sohu, and NetEase were representatives of this phase.

As digital technology hardware and software continue to advance, platforms directly collecting product information have begun to emerge. First-generation e-commerce platforms such as Alibaba and JD.com have become gathering places for product information, attracting consumers from the demand side. In the fierce competition among hundreds of e-commerce platforms in China, innovators like Alibaba and JD.com have explored innovations to improve industry standards, forming a low-cost and guaranteed shopping model. This passive integration of demand-side resources has contributed to their success. Platform economy is essentially economies of scale, like industrial mass production, achieved by evenly distributing high fixed inputs on a large scale. The boundaries of the digital economy exceed billions of calculations, allowing for the application of more complex and powerful information processing technologies.

Statistical data from 2022 shows that China's online retail sales of goods reached 13.8 trillion-yuan, accounting for 27.2% of the total retail sales of consumer goods, an increase of 2.7 percentage points over the previous year. However, e-commerce platforms still face development pressures, mainly from the uncertainty of consumer demand, leading to rising operating costs for product management. E-commerce companies are unable to achieve stable demand docking. After realizing the monopoly role of their information platforms, e-commerce platforms began to use their monopolistic position to implement various service policies on platform operators, leading to a continuous increase in operating costs for product sellers. The e-commerce development model has gradually evolved into an electronic store in the Internet era. Consumer complaints or costs mainly stem from the difficulty of information search and identification in e-commerce shopping. To increase traffic and user base, e-commerce platforms have chosen to import demand externally through methods such as investing in Weibo platforms or conducting live streaming sales. These efforts and attempts can be seen as explorations of proactive integration of demand-side information resources.

9.4.1 The Example of Pinduoduo in China: A New Stage of Demand-Side Integration

Pinduoduo, as an emerging e-commerce platform, has adopted a different business model from traditional e-commerce to integrate demand-side resources. Founded in September 2015, Pinduoduo is a third-party social e-commerce platform focused on C2M group buying. Its uniqueness lies in users initiating group purchases with friends, family, neighbors, etc., to buy high-quality products at lower prices, aiming to harness the power of collective buying for a better shopping experience. Based on the social concept formed through communication and sharing, Pinduoduo has developed a unique new social e-commerce mindset.

According to Pinduoduo's 2019 annual report, its revenue reached 301.4 billion yuan, with 580 million active buyers, a year-on-year growth of 40%, far exceeding its peers. Such achievements have allowed Pinduoduo to emerge as a new giant in the fiercely competitive e-commerce market in less than four years. Particularly noteworthy is that on October 25, 2019, Pinduoduo's market value surpassed that of JD.com for the first time, demonstrating the capital market's recognition of its development model and expectations for the future.

Despite receiving recognition from investment institutions in the capital market, Pinduoduo also faces some skepticism. It is believed that its promotional development model relying on subsidies is unsustainable, and there are concerns about excessive reliance on the WeChat social platform, low average order values, counterfeit and inferior products, payment systems, consumer protection systems, inadequate after-sales services, and the lack of high-value-added products. However, these doubts have not substantially affected Pinduoduo's development. The success of Pinduoduo lies in its development reflecting a new stage of demand-side integration. Although its development model is still in the early exploration stage, it has already matched supply and demand information in a more efficient and sticky manner, becoming the cornerstone of its rapid growth.

Pinduoduo's supply–demand matching model embodies its unique characteristics as a social e-commerce platform. Among Pinduoduo's user types, there are roughly three categories: those who initiate group purchases, those who receive invitations to join groups, and platform merchants. In Pinduoduo's product model, users can initiate group purchases with friends, family, neighbors, etc., to buy high-quality products at lower prices. This group-buying model formed under the social concept has become the unique development model of Pinduoduo's social e-commerce.

Compared to platforms like Taobao, which rely more on Weibo traffic diversion models, Pinduoduo relied more on groups with close social relationships, especially in the early stages of development. These groups share similar characteristics and relatively consistent demands, making it easier to integrate and meet their needs. As the platform accumulates users, the integration of social relationships gradually becomes less important because the platform has accumulated a deep understanding of users' consumption and demand characteristics through extensive data, enabling proactive demand integration through algorithmic recommendations. Based on these social relationship-based recommendation algorithms, Pinduoduo can efficiently achieve demand integration, promoting its rapid development.

Currently, Pinduoduo's demand integration is still in the stage of data accumulation, namely the user segmentation stage. The next step will be the integration of the supply-side resources and achieving effective connection with the demand-side integration. In the future, the pre-order model may become the main way to meet consumer demand, where consumers can obtain lower prices through pre-orders, and the platform can aggregate many scattered demands based on supply-side recommendation algorithms and place orders with suitable production companies. This model can utilize economies of scale to reduce production costs, eliminate market promotion and sales costs, and improve the efficiency of socio-economic operations.

9.4.2 Livestreaming Sales: A Transitional Approach to Demand-Side Integration

Live streaming e-commerce has become a major hotspot in the e-commerce market in recent years, with its popularity experiencing a significant surge during the COVID-19 pandemic. Live streaming e-commerce provides users with a direct and real-time shopping experience through real-time and intuitive product displays, along with strong interactive advantages. In 2020, owing to the impact of the pandemic, many industries came to a halt, leading to an influx of more people and capital into the live streaming e-commerce market. Monitoring data from the Ministry of Commerce shows that in the first half of 2020, there were over 10 million live e-commerce sessions nationwide, with over 400,000 active hosts, over 50 billion viewers, and over 20 million products listed. By 2022, these numbers continued to show a significant upward trend. According to monitoring data from business big data, in 2022, the cumulative number of live e-commerce sessions monitored on key platforms exceeded 120 million, with a total of over 11 trillion viewers, over 95 million live stream products, and nearly 1.1 million active hosts. In 2022, the cumulative sales of live streaming e-commerce reached 144.5-billion-yuan, accounting for 20.8% of the total online sales. These data indicate that live streaming e-commerce has become an indispensable sales channel in the e-commerce market, playing an important role in economic vitality.

The popularity of live streaming e-commerce comes from its provision of vivid real-time shopping experiences that can create a more intuitive and interactive shopping environment for consumers. Through live streaming, consumers can directly watch product demonstrations, interact with hosts, and receive real-time product information and purchase recommendations, thereby enhancing their confidence and shopping experience. Additionally, live streaming e-commerce provides consumers with the opportunity to participate in the shopping process, allowing them to experience the joy and satisfaction of shopping, thus increasing their desire to purchase and satisfaction.

However, as a sales channel, live streaming e-commerce is only a transitional method of demand-side integration. Although live streaming e-commerce can bring sales growth and user stickiness to e-commerce platforms or video websites, it fundamentally relies on consumer demand and participation, rather than changing the structure or resource allocation of the supply side. Therefore, while live streaming e-commerce is an important part of the e-commerce industry at present, its position in the entire business model remains transitional. In the future, with the advancement of supply–demand matching technology and the evolution of business models, live streaming e-commerce may gradually evolve into a more mature and perfect form, but its essence will still be to better meet consumer demand.

The popularity of live streaming e-commerce can be attributed to the following reasons:

1. Real-time Interaction: Live streaming e-commerce allows consumers to interact directly with hosts, ask questions, and express opinions, enhancing their participation and experience in shopping. This interactive approach enables consumers to gain a deeper understanding of products and strengthens trust in hosts and brands.
2. Trust: Hosts in live streaming e-commerce typically have a certain level of influence and a fan base, which instills a sense of trust in consumers. By authentically showcasing products, sharing personal experiences, and recommending discounts, hosts enhance trust in the products and increase the desire to purchase.
3. Entertainment Value: The format of live streaming e-commerce is entertaining, with hosts captivating the audience's attention through performances, storytelling, interactive games, etc. This provides a more enjoyable shopping experience and increases audience engagement.
4. Real-time Promotions and Limited-time Offers: Live streaming e-commerce often combines with promotional activities and limited-time offers, providing exclusive benefits such as coupons, group-buying prices, and flash sales. This creates a sense of urgency and prompts viewers to take immediate action to purchase products.
5. Product Showcase and Demonstration: Live streaming e-commerce allows for real-time product demonstrations, enabling consumers to gain a more intuitive understanding of product features, usage methods, and effects. Hosts can demonstrate products, answer questions, and assist consumers in making purchase decisions.

6. Cost Reduction: Live streaming e-commerce provides businesses with the opportunity to directly promote products, facilitating quick transactions and eliminating the distribution costs and time consumption associated with traditional sales channels. It also enhances brand image and promotional effectiveness.
7. Exploring New Marketing Models: Live streaming e-commerce integrates online and offline channels, leveraging celebrity endorsements or collaborations with merchants to directly promote products. This forms a powerful combination of "internet celebrities + live streaming + product promotion" innovating and advancing online shopping experiences and brand promotion methods.

Live streaming e-commerce offers various advantages in sales, providing consumers with a better and more convenient shopping experience, hence it has become popular among consumers and a significant trend in the e-commerce market.

However, the deeper reason lies in why various platforms and MCNs are so persistent in promoting live streaming e-commerce. On the one hand, the existing e-commerce development model has encountered growth bottlenecks, with the previous high growth becoming unsustainable. The market has shifted from incremental growth to competing for existing market shares, prompting everyone to seek new development opportunities and market potentials. Live streaming e-commerce, as a form of online video sales, brings new hope to these platforms.

On the other hand, with the widespread adoption of 4G networks and the saturation of social media platforms, live streaming e-commerce has broken through the traditional internet business model of charging advertising fees, becoming a new model for monetizing traffic. This leads all participants to believe that the internet economy has ushered in new opportunities, viewing it as an industry breakthrough that can bring substantial profits and share the dividends of industry development. This perception has attracted a large influx of capital into the industry, creating a bustling scene with the establishment of numerous MCN agencies and the emergence of many prominent hosts.

While the capital influx may seem unstoppable, it's likely to collapse soon. Although live streaming e-commerce has contributed to improving the efficiency of supply–demand matching by integrating demand-side resources, its role is limited. The primary value of live streaming e-commerce lies in hosts using their expertise to identify category information and product quality and functionality for demand-side consumers, and then leveraging consumer trust and low prices to make sales. However, the information selection value of hosts in this process is limited because of their limited understanding of demand-side characteristics. Unless they can rely on platform data and algorithm support to target the right audience for promotion, live streaming e-commerce based on personal experience may only lead to temporary trust from consumers. Therefore, the return rate of live streaming e-commerce is high, indicating that consumer acceptance of promoted products is uncertain, not just because of unstable demand, but because of the limited role of product information asymmetry in demand integration.

For the live streaming e-commerce model to truly develop, it must find a way to reduce the cost of social information collection, processing, or dissemination, or establish a more powerful mechanism for processing supply–demand information, thereby improving social information processing efficiency. This requires live streaming e-commerce to intervene in demand-side information processing with more comprehensive and systematic information, seeking innovation, reducing the costs of information processing on the supply or demand side, or improving processing efficiency.

China's development pace in the field of live streaming e-commerce surpasses that of other developed countries owing to several key reasons:

First, China boasts a well-developed internet application domain with abundant supporting resources, coupled with a strong sense of innovation and drive. The government's advocacy of "mass entrepreneurship and innovation" has ignited enthusiasm for internet innovation, leading to widespread acceptance and promotion of internet innovation in China, far surpassing other developed countries. Particularly in recent years, innovation in areas such as short videos and live streaming has led global trends, while diverse monetization methods have further propelled the rapid development of live streaming e-commerce models.

Second, with a population of 1.4 billion and a sizable middle-class demographic, China's demand is diverse and sizable, providing a broad domestic market for internet innovation. The Chinese market can accommodate various types of innovative businesses, absorb the costs of failure, and provide an environment conducive to the growth of innovative businesses.

Third, over the past 40 years of reform and opening up, China has accumulated substantial capital, with active investment in related sectors. According to monitoring data, in 2020, 23 platforms in China's live streaming e-commerce field received financing totaling over 1.17 billion RMB, providing crucial support for the industry's rapid development.

Last, China possesses the world's most efficient and complete supply chain system, capable of effectively supporting the practical implementation of internet innovation businesses. With the rise of the express delivery industry alongside e-commerce development, the efficient supply chain system supports the matching of supply and demand in the Chinese market, providing reliable assurance for the actual delivery of various internet innovation businesses.

9.5 Conclusion

The digital age marks a new stage in the development of the industrial age, which is the result of the transformation brought about by digital technology. After more than two hundred years of industrial development, the business environment in the digital age has undergone fundamental changes compared to the past. Information scarcity is no longer the fundamental constraint on economic and social development, and the scarcity of supply of products and services has also undergone a thorough transformation. Humanity has entered a new path of development in the digital age, characterized by a new business civilization.

The new business civilization in the digital age differs significantly from the business civilization of the industrial age in terms of the source of commercial value, economic forms, economic decision-making methods, and economic organizational methods. Empowered by digital technology, the primary value creation of the new business civilization will shift from the integration of supply-side resources to the integration of demand-side resources, ultimately achieving integrated transformation of supply and demand. Therefore, forms like "live streaming e-commerce" essentially represent transitional forms of demand-side resource integration, while new business models are continuously being explored and developed.

Chapter 10
Evolution of Enterprise Organization in the Digital Age

The empowerment of digital technology has led to a fundamental transformation in the social division of labor between individuals and between humans and machines. This implies that the cooperative relationships in the division of labor within the economic system have also undergone fundamental changes. As the basic unit of the division of labor in society, the forms of economic organization must naturally undergo transformation as well. This transformation brings about new opportunities and challenges for economic development, presenting different characteristics and development patterns.

The empowerment of digital technology is profoundly driving the evolution of economic organizations. For instance, corporate governance structures with different equity holdings are becoming popular, and the development model of business ecosystems has also become one of the mainstream choices. Understanding these changes and trends holds practical significance for economic organizations seeking to adapt to the changing dynamics of the digital age. Understanding the drivers of change and common trends enables organizations to actively adapt to the significant changes of the digital age guided by their own consciousness, seize developmental opportunities, and avoid becoming "loners" or "obsolete entities" in the era of transition.

10.1 Technological Advancements and the Corporate Structure

Economic organizations refer to units such as households, enterprises, and companies that organize factors of production in a certain way for production and business activities. They are complete organic entities composed of certain social groups, ensuring the normal operation of the economic cycle system through the allocation of rights and responsibilities and corresponding hierarchical structures.

Y. Yu and Y. Jiang, *Understanding the Digital Revolution and Its Influences*,
https://doi.org/10.1007/978-981-97-4939-3_10

These organizations are mainly involved in activities such as production, exchange, distribution, and consumption, aimed at achieving optimal allocation of social resources and operational efficiency of organization. Economic organizations bear primary responsibility for economic activities and are interconnected with the entire social economic system, encompassing the rights, responsibilities, and interests among participants.

Economic organizations are dynamic entities that require continuous information processing for various activities. The flow of information is a key factor connecting the units within economic organizations, determining the direction of fund and resource flows, and shaping the structure of economic organizations. Achieving efficient allocation of resources and efficient organizational operation requires economic organizations to have efficient information processing capabilities. Therefore, the efficiency of information processing will determine the form of economic organizations.

10.1.1 The Efficiency of Information Processing: A Determinant of the Form of Economic Organization

The efficiency of information processing determines the scope and form of economic organizations. The value of any economic organization lies in its ability to provide products or services needed by society more efficiently and at lower costs than its competitors. This requires a higher level of resource integration and information processing capabilities, namely high-level information processing efficiency, compared to competitors. To achieve this state of capability, economic organizations need to have economies of scale and internal structural forms that match their technological level. Only in this way can higher levels of information processing efficiency be ensured.

From a societal perspective, the capacity to create social wealth depends on the supply capacity of product production and service provision. Supply capacity depends on the efficiency of factor allocation (reflecting information integration capability) and the production efficiency of products and services (reflecting information processing capability). Therefore, how efficiently a society integrates and processes information, namely the level of information processing efficiency, determines the potential for creating social wealth.

The creation of social wealth is the result of cooperation among people, and the formation of economic organizations is the fundamental unit of this wealth creation. Only organizational forms that adapt to the technological characteristics of the times can possess the corresponding efficiency and capacity in the allocation of economic factors. This includes determining economic decision-making, selecting information processing processes, and completing the process of economic resource integration and disposal.

Each era requires appropriate economic organizational structures and forms to meet the demands of technological development for the social division of labor and to fully exploit the potential of information technology at that time. This is necessary to realize the potential for creating social wealth and to establish the most efficient way of allocating economic resources for the era. The architecture and form of economic organizations determine their mechanisms for information collection and processing, as well as the level of efficiency in information processing.

Whether it is the selection of social and economic resources entering the system of the social division of labor or the guidance of resource allocation, it depends on the decision-making choices of economic organizational forms in collecting, analyzing, and responding to environmental information. Only organizational forms with the highest efficiency in integrating and processing environmental information can solve the most challenging issues of deepening division of labor in the era in the most economical way and stand out in competition.

Therefore, we should understand the development trend of the transition from the industrial age to the digital age organization from the perspective of information processing efficiency and efficiency in adapting to environmental information. This will help us better grasp the changing trends of organizational structures in the digital age.

10.1.2 The Evolution of Corporate Structure in the Industrial Era

The improvement of information processing efficiency is the fundamental driving force and direction of the evolution of the social division of labor. With the enhancement of information processing efficiency, the social system of the division of labor can operate more economically and efficiently, thereby increasing the capacity for wealth creation and enhancing the ability to resist risk shocks.

The history of human social development can be seen as a history of the division of labor and cooperation among individuals. From the gender division of labor within early tribes, to the division of labor based on labor between privileged classes and slaves in slave societies, to the division of labor based on land between landlords and tenants in agricultural societies, and the division of labor model of free cooperation partnership in the capitalist era and the modern corporate system, different division of labor models correspond to different organizational forms and information processing processes. The evolution of these organizational forms unfolds with the development of production modes and technologies, and its fundamental driving force is people choosing organizational forms that maximize cooperative benefits based on the technological conditions and characteristics of the elements they possess, in order to achieve a higher efficiency of the social division of labor cooperation through information integration and processing. Therefore, the continuous improvement in the level of social information processing efficiency reflects the organizational forms that maximize the economic potential of social resources.

In the industrial era, with the increasing demand for mass production driven by industrial technology, the degree of socialization of economic organizations has continued to rise. Particularly as the complexity of production technology and market uncertainty increase with the expansion of market scale, more efficient and standardized forms of economic organization are needed to meet production and consumption demands and to cope with the continuously rising requirements of information processing efficiency. This has led to the continuous transformation and innovation of economic organizational forms, enabling new economic organizational forms to better adapt to market demands, improve production efficiency, and achieve greater advantages in market competition.

To meet the high requirements of resource allocation in economic organizations, the mainstream economic organizational structure of the industrial era shifted from proprietorship and partnership to the corporate system. Corporate economic organizations, with the company as the main entity, are funded by shareholders who share profits and bear limited liability. Their characteristics include:

1. Broad sources of capital enable large-scale production.
2. Shareholders have limited liability, reducing investment risks.
3. The company has independent legal property rights, ensuring the independence, continuity, and integrity of enterprise decisions.
4. Ownership and management rights are separated, laying the foundation for scientific management.

Modern corporations are highly socialized enterprises and represent an institutional innovation of the industrial era, superior to proprietorship and partnership. The emergence of corporate economic organizations has greatly promoted the development of social productivity. It can be said that corporate economic organizations have achieved a high degree of socialization of capital, making capital widely available and easily raised, with standardized management and strong organizational capabilities. Although the organizational structure is relatively complex, corporate economic organizations can achieve their organizational goals with higher socialization capabilities and information processing efficiency.

10.1.3 The Limited Liability Company Structure: Primary Economic Organizational Form of the Industrial Era

Over the past few centuries, with the development of the Industrial Revolution, the modern corporate system, characterized by limited liability, has gradually become one of the most important forms of economic organization worldwide, serving as a key driver for the prosperity and development of economies around the globe. N.N. Butler, former president of Columbia University, pointed out that the limited liability company system transcends inventions like the steam engine and electricity. Adopting the limited liability company system enables large-scale social cooperation necessary for industrial production to proceed in an orderly and efficient manner.

In modern society, economic entities generally opt for the organizational form of modern corporations mainly because, in fiercely competitive market economies, market demand becomes the guiding principle for achieving economic interests. However, the unpredictability and adaptability challenges posed by demand variations imply an increase in information uncertainty and complexity in market information. Consequently, economic organizations are required to possess more efficient market information integration and processing capabilities to remain competitive and achieve sustainable development.

Therefore, separating corporate management rights from ownership has become a rational choice. This separation reflects the higher-level requirements of market competition for social cooperation driven by industrialization technology. The independence and socialization of corporate management rights enable operators with entrepreneurial spirit and capabilities to utilize their professional economic strategic information processing capabilities to gain more control over social and economic resources. This approach enhances the overall economic information processing efficiency of society. Essentially, the socialization of corporate management rights leads to the separation of corporate management rights and ownership, allowing companies to attract high-quality decision-making resources from society in an open manner, thereby ensuring the effectiveness of corporate decision-making and enhancing the organization's level of information processing efficiency.

Furthermore, the modern limited liability company system not only reduces the risks for participants but also facilitates risk transfer, promotes market-oriented trading of interests, encourages investment, and thereby enhances the socialization level of enterprises. By introducing high-quality decision-making resources, this organizational form lowers the probability of business failures. Therefore, the modern limited liability company system not only plays a role in separating ownership and management rights of corporate organizations but also promotes highly socialized industrial operations, driving the development of socialized mass production.

10.1.4 Characteristics of Limited Liability Company Structure: From the Perspective of Information Perspective

In the industrial era, the limited liability company system regarded capital as its adhesive, bringing together various factors of production onto one platform, facilitating large-scale cooperation between different types of labor factors (skills or positions) and capital factors (funds and machinery). This model was in line with the large-scale industrial production mode. The reason capital became the adhesive of the limited liability company system lies in its ability to reveal information at the lowest cost.

Owning capital means having the potential to allocate social and economic resources, enabling other factor owners to trust and form social cooperative relationships with them at a lower cost. Therefore, capital became the foundational resource for socialized production and could integrate socialized economic resources at a lower information cost. This is particularly evident in credit-based economies, where, with the development of industrialization, the financial system becomes increasingly complex and prosperous, forming an integral part of the interrelated social system of the division of labor with industrial economic organizations, thus becoming a core force in resource allocation in modern economic society.

In the cooperative production model of the limited liability company system, owing to the planned nature of industrial production, the risks and returns of each participant are relatively predictable, resulting in lower costs of information integration for economic resource reallocation and higher processing efficiency. This enhances the stability of enterprise organizations, especially large-scale companies demonstrating more pronounced advantages, further promoting the development of economic financialization. The widespread application of industrialization technology has made the limited liability company system a key economic organizational form in modern economic systems, with the resulting economic ecosystem matching the processes and value realization of large-scale industrial production. It is worth noting that the initiators of modern limited liability companies are typically the capital parties, possessing the lowest information integration costs, enabling other economic resources to form the social division of labor cooperative relationships through them. Therefore, capital plays a crucial role in the formation of modern limited liability company organizational forms and consolidates this power through legal means, forming corresponding capital-dominated cognitive consensus, which is further strengthened with the continuous growth of capital. Consequently, the limited liability company system has become the most important and common economic organizational form since the industrial era.

10.2 Digital Technology as a Driving Force of the Evolution of Enterprise Organization

10.2.1 The Changing Nature of Organizational Costs and Its Impact on Organizational Structure

The existence of economic organizations inherently incurs costs, and changes in the maintenance costs of specific economic organizational forms can affect their evolutionary processes. Each type of economic organizational form has its operating and maintenance costs, and its information integration and processing efficiency are limited by the efficiency of organizational information processing technology and the efficiency of organizational structure operation. To ensure stable existence and sustainable development, the structure and operation mode of economic organizations need to match the technical characteristics and business characteristics they apply. This principle applies to economic organizations in any era and is an important logic for understanding the diversity of real economic organizations.

With the development and widespread application of digital technology, the vast and diverse digital information has led to an exponential growth in the demand for decision-making information processing and complexity, which has exceeded the boundary of employees' information processing capabilities under the corporate system at every position. Almost no employee can keep up with the increasingly growing information processing requirements, and employees must rely on intelligent machine systems to meet the changing demands of their positions. The social division of labor between humans and machines is beginning to replace the social division of labor between humans, becoming the main factor determining the dominant form of the division of labor. Therefore, the organizational form of the limited liability company system based on the division of labor and cooperation between people, such as the information processing architecture of shareholders' meetings, boards of directors, and supervisory boards, is gradually becoming mismatched with the information processing requirements of the digital age. In an environment of complex and massive information, the organizational form of the limited liability company system exhibits a trend of decreasing information processing efficiency, continuously increasing maintenance costs, and increasing the risk of decision-making errors, leading to an increasing possibility of organizational failure. This means that the organizational form of the limited liability company system is no longer suitable for current information processing requirements and cannot meet the demands of intensified competition in the digital age, necessitating imminent transformation.

10.2.2 The Emergence of Technological Capital

The primary characteristic of the data age is the fundamental change in the scarcity of social information, where the volume of information required for decision-making has dramatically increased, and the difficulty of processing information has grown exponentially, necessitating reliance on new digital technology tools for effective decision-making. As the role of technological elements in creating social value becomes established, the traditional economic organizational models based on capital dominance must continuously evolve with the development of the new economic ecosystem brought about by new technology applications. In particular, the transformative impact of digital technology applications on information integration and processing capabilities is beginning to challenge the information efficiency advantage of existing organizational forms. Additionally, the deepening of globalization and the intensification of competition have led to returns on industrial capital and commercial capital gradually falling behind those on technological capital and risk capital closely associated with new technologies. Technological capital is gradually gaining dominance in the new economic ecosystem, and new economic organizational forms are becoming increasingly linked with the development of new technologies.

In both China and the United States, the highest-valued companies have shifted from traditional financial institutions to emerging digital technology companies, such as Alibaba, Tencent, Apple, Google, Microsoft, Amazon, and Facebook. Taking DJI as an example, this Chinese technology company, with its leading position and technological advantages in the drone market, once proposed financing through a bidding process, allowing financial capital to compete to maximize profits. The fundamental reason for this phenomenon lies in the strengthening dominance of the discourse system of technological capital. In the past, technology entrepreneurs had to continuously pitch to financial capital to obtain financing approvals, but now financial capital competes to invest in technological capital opportunities.

On a global scale, in 1990, the top ten companies by market value were primarily dominated by financial institutions. However, by the end of 2022, there was a fundamental shift in this scenario, with the list being largely dominated by high-tech companies represented by digital technology, including Apple, Google, Microsoft, Amazon, Facebook, as well as Chinese companies like Alibaba and Tencent leading the pack. This global transformation of economic entities forced the limited liability company organizational form, which has evolved alongside industrialization, to adapt to the demands of the times. These companies are adjusting their organizational structures and business models to meet the new requirements brought about by the application of digital technology, particularly in terms of integrating and processing information within the social system of the division of labor, in order to adapt to the trend of improving social information processing efficiency.

Therefore, it is precisely because economic organizations inherently incur costs, and the application of digital technology has changed the information costs in economic organizational decision-making, that economic organizational forms must change with the application and development of digital technology.

10.3 Adapting to the Digital Age: Evolution of Organizational Structure Within Enterprises

10.3.1 The Declining Importance of Capital in the Social Division of Labor

In the digital economy era, the organizational form of the limited liability company has gradually shown discrepancies with the requirements of digital age development. This is mainly because the rapid advancement of digital technology has enhanced information processing capabilities, challenging the advantage of limited liability companies in information integration and processing. In emerging technology-driven economic organizations, particularly in industries represented by internet applications, the vast and complex information processing demands have made digital technology play a decisive role in enterprise development, becoming a prominent feature of the digital age.

As we enter the digital age, capital is no longer a scarce resource. After more than two hundred years of accumulation since the industrial revolution, the information costs and efficiency advantages of capital in integrating other economic resources into social cooperation relationships are being challenged. Therefore, the corporate organization of limited liability companies no longer follows the decision-making and profit-sharing models of one share, one vote as it did in the past. Increasingly, emerging internet companies have adopted a partnership model because the business development and value creation of these high-tech enterprises primarily rely on research and development capabilities and the ability to acquire intellectual property rights, with their future commercial returns guaranteed by the modern financial system. Consequently, the position of technology stakeholders in companies is gradually being recognized by the capital market, and the concept of dual-class shares is also gaining acceptance, challenging the absolute dominance of capital.

10.3.2 Equal Rights with Different Shares: A New Choice for Economic Organizations in the Digital Age

The concept of dual-class shares includes various forms such as multiple voting shares, restricted voting shares, non-voting shares, priority voting shares, and shares with larger or exclusive director nomination rights. This practice deepens the separation of management rights and ownership rights in modern corporate governance, leading to further differentiation of management rights at the governance mechanism level. This process essentially reflects the self-differentiation of capital elements under the influence of technological elements and is the result of the evolution of internal organizational governance mechanisms of limited liability companies in response to the needs of emerging industries and the digital economy era. This differentiation is essentially the result of the market position game between technological elements and capital elements. More importantly, owners of technological advantages often possess strategic information processing advantages regarding the technological development path of the industry, which determines the ultimate value of the enterprise. Therefore, for capital, it should choose owners of technological elements with profound insights into industry development as cooperation and investment partners.

To meet the financing needs of high-tech industries and improve the quality and valuation of listed companies, some mainstream financial institutions, such as the Hong Kong Stock Exchange and the Singapore Stock Exchange, have begun to accept the dual class share corporate organizational model and have accordingly amended their articles of association. In fact, Nasdaq, which has the most internet companies listed, allowed this model as early as the 1980s. It is worth noting that the concept of dual-class shares has gradually been accepted with the development of the times and has now become the primary organizational governance model for many high-tech companies. The establishment of this model is closely related to the increasingly rapid pace of technological innovation and the increasingly complex technological development environment. In this environment, owners of technological elements with the ability to strategically choose the development path of the industry can survive in the market and gain a voice when forming cooperative relationships with capital.

10.3.3 The Origin of Dual-Class Share Structures

The concept of dual-class shares originated in the early twentieth century in the United States when some family businesses and banks began issuing non-voting preferred shares and common shares to maintain control over the company. In 1925, the Dodge Brothers Company issued 150 million shares of non-voting Class A common stock to the public, raising approximately $130 million; and issued 2,500,001 voting Class B common shares to its controlling shareholder, the Dillon, Read & Co. The company's stock was soon listed on the New York Stock Exchange. The listing of the Dodge Brothers Company triggered strong public reactions, leading some state governments to withdraw approval for the issuance of non-voting shares, and the Investment Bankers Association's Industrial Securities Committee also opposed the issuance of non-voting shares. Starting in 1926, the New York Stock Exchange refused to list non-voting shares, and from 1940, it refused to allow companies issuing non-voting shares to trade on its listing. The New York Stock Exchange adhered to the principle of "one share, one vote" for a long time, until recent decades. However, in the competition between different exchanges, after 1980, the U.S. Stock Exchange and Nasdaq became more lenient towards "dual-class shares", attracting many companies to list their stocks on these two trading systems. Faced with competitive pressure, the New York Stock Exchange later abandoned its long-standing principle of "one share, one vote."

The corporate governance model of dual-class shares is also known as the Controlling Minority Shareholder (CMS) structure. This corporate structure fails to provide adequate investor protection and lacks the primary mechanisms to limit agency costs, leading to potential significant agency costs. As time passes, these potential costs increase, while potential returns decrease, making it difficult to effectively supervise company controllers. Nevertheless, domestic internet giants such as Alibaba, JD.com, Pinduoduo, as well as foreign giants like Google, Amazon, and Facebook, along with venture capital and investors, still endorse this model.

10.3.4 Dual-Class Share Structures: Becoming the Mainstream Choice for Emerging Enterprises in the Digital Economy

To pursue stronger control, an increasing number of startup enterprises in emerging technology applications are opting for the dual-class share model. Clearly, this new economic organizational form is a result of the evolution of social development and the product of long-term interactions among various participating entities. In the digital economy era, the acceptance of "dual-class shares" by mainstream economics is essentially an internal evolution and adjustment of the limited liability company system to meet the demands of digital economic development.

In the "dual-class shares" model, venture capital and investors are not necessarily seeking operational or control rights; rather, they are concerned with whether they can follow the trend of the times and enjoy the rapid and high returns brought about by new technological applications. In the internet age, technological changes are rapid, and emerging technology companies can grow rapidly owing to technological empowerment, leading to rapid changes in the economic ecosystem. This makes investors more willing to bear the potential agency costs risks than to miss the opportunities for development in the era.

It can be said that the successful application of digital technology brings much higher returns to participating capital than the application of industrial technology. This encourages venture capital and investors to bear the potential agency costs and risks associated with the existence of enterprises under the dual-class share structure. The high returns of emerging enterprises are entirely the result of the empowerment of digital technology in their business operations. Currently, the dual-class share organizational form is still in its nascent stage of digital technology application. It is a product of the combination of emerging technologies and traditional capital driving forces, reflecting the new demands of the digital age for the social division of labor cooperation, information integration, and processing efficiency.

10.4 Adapting to the Digital Age: Evolution of Organizational Structure Outside Enterprises

10.4.1 The Increasing Openness of Economic Organizations in the Digital Age

Under the impact of digital technology, the existing limited liability company system is no longer entirely suited to development requirements. Consequently, corporate governance has initiated a self-adaptive adjustment towards the "dual-class share" model at the internal governance level to accommodate the critical role of technological elements and their high-risk, high-return nature in the development of the high-tech industry. Meanwhile, these emerging high-tech companies are increasingly opting for more open approaches in their business operation models to seek development opportunities and competitive advantages, balancing the relationship between organizational element integration efficiency and risk, thereby further enhancing the efficiency of the social division of labor information integration and processing. Major companies like Apple, Google, Facebook, Amazon in the United States, and Alibaba, Tencent, JD.com, Baidu, and Xiaomi in China, both domestically and internationally, have coincidentally chosen to build their own business ecosystem by establishing close connections with suppliers, intermediaries, and consumers to expand their business, strengthen their competitiveness, and increase potential future development space.

The openness of economic organizations in the digital age differs significantly from that embodied by economic organizational forms in the industrial age. The openness of economic organizations in the industrial age primarily manifests in the separation of operational rights and ownership within economic organizations, attracting high-quality social decision-making resources into the internal economic organization to enhance information processing efficiency and strengthen the adaptability of economic organizations to the environment. In contrast, the openness of economic organizations in the digital age is more comprehensive, involving the full openness of business processes and development directions of economic organizations, making an economic organization an indispensable part of its economic ecosystem, thereby achieving high-quality social resource introduction throughout the entire business process, enhancing information processing efficiency, and improving environmental adaptability.

10.4.2 From Theory to Practice: The Concept of Business Ecosystems

The term "business ecosystem" was first proposed by the renowned American economist Moore in 1993 in the Harvard Business Review.[1] However, the origin of this concept can be traced back to 1977 when Hannan and Freeman first examined the adaptability issues of enterprises from an ecological perspective, proposing concepts such as organizational ecology and corporate populations.[2] Since the concept of business ecosystem was put forward, it has triggered a large amount of academic research, mainly divided into two perspectives: ecological perspective and network perspective.

---

[1] Predators and prey: a new ecology of competition. James F Moore. Harvard Business. 1993.

[2] The Population Ecology of Organizations [J]. Michael T. Hannan, John Freeman. American Journal of Sociology. 1977 (5).

The ecological perspective emphasizes that the internal of a business ecosystem is an economic community composed of numerous enterprises with symbiotic relationships, creating value through cooperation.[3] In contrast, the network perspective emphasizes the relationships between enterprises, suggesting that the business ecosystem is a network of internal enterprises providing resources and market information to each other. In subsequent research, systems theory was introduced to emphasize the adaptability of business ecosystems.[4]

The original intention of proposing this concept was to try to consider enterprises as part of the economic and social system, exploring the adaptability issues of value creation by enterprises. However, enterprises did not truly attempt to autonomously form business ecosystems. The business ecosystems discussed by researchers are merely an examination and interpretation of the close and mutually influential economic development relationships among enterprises in the market economy from a systemic perspective, with no explicit development goals for business ecosystem development.

It was not until the advent of internet applications and the rise of the digital economy that enterprises began consciously promoting the construction of business ecosystems. Today, various large technology companies have become the core enterprises of their respective business ecosystems. These technology companies, based on digital technology, dominate the current economic development process through business ecosystems and profoundly and extensively influence the entire path of socio-economic development.

10.4.3 The Development Model of Business Ecosystems and the Complete Socialization of Economic Organizations

The reasons behind the choice of developing a business ecosystem model by these large technology companies warrant further exploration. Generally, people attribute this model to large companies attempting to raise industry entry barriers and strengthen their monopolistic position through enclosure strategies in the face of market competition. However, if we only understand this change from a competitive perspective, we may only emphasize the passive choices of enterprises caused by changes in the external environment. Similarly, if we only understand it from the perspective of cooperation networks, we may only emphasize market choices under the constraints of resource scarcity. These two perspectives fail to truly reveal the inherent inevitability of its development.

---

[3] The Roles of Information Technology in Business. Kim H, Lee J N, Han J. Communications of the ACM. 2010.

[4] Entrepreneurship and strategic thinking in business ecosystems. Zahra, S, Nambisan, S. Business Horizons. 2012.

The development of the business ecosystem model should be seen as a result of the mismatch between the current limited liability company organizational form and the digital age environment, as well as the characteristics of digital technology development. We should understand the emergence and development of business ecosystems from the perspective of enterprise choices, resource organization goals, and environmental relationships. Building a business ecosystem is a high-cost investment decision for enterprises, which is the autonomous choice of these large companies considering comprehensive industry development information and their own resource constraints.

Therefore, the development of the business ecosystem model should be regarded as an external evolutionary result of the limited liability company organizational form. In the digital age, the choice of economic organizations to construct business ecosystems is essentially an attempt to adapt to the breakthrough changes in the digital age information environment and the requirements of information processing efficiency in a comprehensive and thorough socialized manner, reflecting the evolutionary law of the survival of the fittest.

10.4.4 The Fundamental Logic Behind the Operation of Business Ecosystems

In the industrial age, the organizational form of limited liability companies provided an efficient platform for a broad social group, allowing different types of capital to jointly take on challenges and risks. This form's high efficiency in information integration and processing enabled various economic entities to collaborate comfortably to complete complex product order processes. However, with the widespread application of digital technology, the complexity of market information and the rapid changes in the environment have limited the capabilities of limited liability companies, leading some enterprises to face uncertainties. In the digital economy era, businesses require more social resources and broader information processing capabilities to adapt to the rapid changes in the market and the challenges of globalization competition.

As a result, many large technology companies have chosen the business ecosystem model to pursue the right to use resources rather than ownership. This model enables enterprises to gain advantages in resources, costs, and risks in a competitive environment, achieve new changes in corporate governance, and balance the relationship between limited liability company governance models, rapidly changing environments, and enterprise development goals.

However, the evolution of business ecosystems in the digital age is still ongoing. With the digitization and virtualization of the economy, especially in the field of blockchain applications such as the Ethereum ecosystem, new models different from traditional entity-based economic organizational business ecosystems have emerged. These new types of business ecosystems are entirely realized through blockchain technology to achieve participation consensus and value creation and circulation, allowing for more efficient handling of business process information and potentially higher levels of information processing efficiency. Therefore, such blockchain ecosystems may represent one of the potential trends in the future development of the digital economy.

10.5 Conclusion

The evolution of economic organizations began with the empowerment of digital technology, which gradually transformed the mode of the social division of labor. The importance of human–machine division of labor has become increasingly prominent, surpassing the influence of human-to-human division of labor. This shift has sparked new characteristics in the evolution of economic organizations, moving from a model focused on human-to-human relationships to one that emphasizes the evolving human–machine division of labor.

With the breakthrough changes in the scarcity of information in the digital age, traditional economic organizational information processing architectures and mechanisms have become inadequate to meet the growing demands for information processing efficiency. Therefore, economic organizations have initiated a process of autonomous evolution. Internally, economic organizations have elevated the status of technological capital, allowing technological elements to play a more important role within them. Externally, economic organizations are becoming increasingly open, adopting the construction of business ecosystems to achieve comprehensive socialization of business processes and resource sharing. This enhances their level of information processing efficiency to adapt to the digital age environment and seize opportunities for future development.

These changes have become an integral part of the new business civilization format and will continue to evolve with the deepening of the digital economy and the acceleration of the comprehensive digitization and virtualization of the economy.

Chapter 11
Summary and Conclusion

11.1 The Digital Economy: Unveiling New Business Logics and Development Models

Starting from the characteristics of digital technology and taking the development issues of the human society as a starting point, from the historical evolution of the social division of labor under individual empowerment to understanding the digital age from the perspective of human nature attributes—the storage and processor of environmental information, we can clearly perceive that the digital age is nurturing a new business civilization. We can already see that the development of the digital economy is showing new business logics and development patterns.

First, digital technology is overturning the old business logic. With the continuous accumulation of the achievements of the industrial revolution, the economy has entered a stage of relatively abundant and relatively surplus supply, and the application of digital technology has made economic information supply sufficient. In the past, business value creation was based on the scarcity of products and information, and the business value creation mode based on information volume is no longer effective. The old logic of business development, whether based on information advantage on the supply side (i.e., how to manufacture products) or demand-side information advantage (i.e., how to meet market demand), is facing challenges. This is also the fundamental reason for the "internalization" of development in various fields. With the development of digital technology, especially the advancement of artificial intelligence technology, the possibility of machines replacing humans has increased, leading to a fundamental change in the scarcity conditions of labor. The change in information, labor, and supply scarcity means that the scarcity of inputs (information and labor) and outputs (supply) of business development has fundamentally changed, and the source of business value and business logic has been completely overturned. This change in the scarcity of factors and outputs will shift the focus of the social division of labor from optimizing resource allocation to ensuring fairness.

Y. Yu and Y. Jiang, *Understanding the Digital Revolution and Its Influences*,
https://doi.org/10.1007/978-981-97-4939-3_11

Second, the capital-dominated economic pattern is shifting towards an information-dominated economic development pattern. In China, the digital economy has made significant progress. With the government's rectification of platform monopolies in 2020, it signifies the end of the "traffic economy development model", and the digital economy is entering a new stage. The previous "traffic economy" model and its various derivative platforms essentially used the volume of information as a way of economic resource allocation. In this model, economic development was mainly based on the quantity of information, while overlooking the role of information processing efficiency and information value. Therefore, in the digital age, this model has lost its competitiveness. Under the traffic economy model, various platform companies often maintain their market position through monopolies rather than relying on the creation of social value and innovative development. Although the "traffic economy model" is in the initial stage of digital economic development, it has obvious shortcomings. This model heralds the departure of a new business civilization from the capital-dominated economic development model to an information-dominated economic development model. In this model, capital must be transformed into information flow to generate corresponding economic benefits because the pure form of capital can no longer directly create new value. The flow of information elements and information processing efficiency will determine the direction, mode, and efficiency of economic resource allocation.

Last, the institutional rules of the new business civilization are continuously being constructed and improved. Countries are exploring the establishment and improvement of new institutional rules of business civilization to establish a sustainable economic development model in the digital age. Regulatory measures taken by regulatory authorities in various countries against platform monopolies and data privacy protection in the digital economy are government responses based on the systemic instability risks caused by the existing development model to the economic society. This reflects the imperfection of the early stage of digital economic development and indicates that government intervention has become an important factor affecting the development of digital business civilization. The formulation and exploration of these regulatory measures can only meet the needs of sustainable development of digital economic formats if they conform to the characteristics of digital technology development. Owing to the powerful externality of digital technology, public authority needs to intervene in the process of digital economic development. In the format of the new business civilization, the logic of business value creation and the business ethics relationship will be jointly negotiated and defined by market forces and public authority. The characteristics of digital technology applications determine that the results of the game between market forces can no longer meet the needs of a sustainable economic development model. Opposition to the monopoly of digital economic platforms has become a consensus among governments worldwide, meaning that humanity is consciously exploring the way of constructing new rules of business civilization in the digital age to find a suitable, stable, and sustainable development model.

We perceive the new business civilization from the perspective of the historical evolution of human development. The origin of modern business civilization can be traced back to the Industrial Revolution triggered by the steam engine technology transformation, along with the corresponding social, legal, ethical, and organizational forms. This main axis has remained largely unchanged for over two centuries. However, in the past three decades, the development of digital technology has been deepening globally, especially in the past decade, where China's practice has made its breakthrough impact increasingly evident. We increasingly believe that the changes brought about by the digital age are not just technological changes but systematic disruptions to the foundation of modern business civilization. In the digital age, the economic functions of enterprises, individuals, and governments will all be reshaped. The challenges of this transformation are comprehensive and profound, and the new business civilization is emerging.

The reason why the new business civilization is called "new" lies in the fact that the creation and circulation of business value depend on the application of digital technology, which changes the basic conditions of the original business operation. The conditions of information scarcity and labor scarcity have been completely changed, and the social division of labor model and the way of achieving business value have begun to reshape, forming a new economic organizational form. Therefore, we need new ways to define and analyze business value, new business ethics concepts to coordinate the division of labor and value distribution among individuals, to redefine the functional positioning of different economic entities, and new institutional arrangements to enhance the overall information processing efficiency of society, promote the sustainable development of the economic and social system, and enhance the possibility space for future development.

The formation of the new business civilization is the result of the innovative development and widespread application of digital technology, as well as the comprehensive digitization of the economy and society in the digital age of the human society. Currently, the early form of the digital economy—the "traffic economy model"—has not completely faded away, and the traffic determinism is essentially a determinism of information volume, bearing many similarities to the past asymmetrical information's commercial value logic. This indicates that the formation of the new business civilization is still ongoing. Therefore, it is necessary to explore the laws of future development of the new business civilization and analyze its driving forces and characteristics.

11.2 Digital Technology: Transforming the Business Value Creation

The profound changes brought about by the digital age stem from the characteristics of digital technology that fundamentally alter the process of creating business value and redefine the source of economic value.

In the digital age, digitized information becomes the primary form of economic decision-making. Digital information, characterized by clear definition and easy storage, leads to exponential growth in various types of information. The rapid development of digital technology hardware and software makes digitized information easy to store, integrate, and process, resulting in an exponential increase in the complexity of information, surpassing the processing capacity of traditional cognitive tools. Digitized information is easy to share and disseminate, thus rapidly and widely impacting the economy and society. Additionally, digital technologies like artificial intelligence possess self-iterative optimization functions, enabling machines to far exceed human biological potential in information processing efficiency. Moreover, the speed of digital technology innovation and iteration, coupled with the rapid decline in the barrier to entry, makes technology empowerment more accessible to ordinary individuals and organizational forms, fundamentally changing the human–machine division of labor model. The human–machine decision-making division of labor pattern has become the fundamental driving force behind the current evolution of the social division of labor. The application of digital technologies such as blockchain makes information more transparent, thus altering the mode of cooperation between individuals.

Therefore, in the digital age, the scarcity of information quantity decreases, inevitably leading to a fundamental change in the business development model that was previously primarily driven by information asymmetry. Particularly when the volume of information exceeds human processing capacity, the scarcity of effective information processing capabilities becomes increasingly prominent, and the standard of information processing efficiency becomes the primary criterion for measuring efficiency and value. The creation and formation of economic value increasingly depend on the level of information processing efficiency. Therefore, in the new business civilization of the digital age, the allocation of economic resources will shift from price-guided mechanisms to information-guided mechanisms. The volume of information and information processing efficiency will jointly determine the direction of resource allocation, while decision-making costs and transaction costs will become key cost factors in economic operations.

11.3 Transformation in the Social Division of Labor: Prompting the Development of a New Business Civilization

The perspective of the social division of labor, as we have consistently emphasized, systematically illustrates how the transformation of the social division of labor under the influence of digital technology has given rise to the development of a new business civilization.

A profound aspect of Marx's work lies in his recognition of the irreconcilable contradiction between the cooperative mode of production in capitalism and the characteristics of production technology. He pointed out that the contradiction between socialized production and the private ownership of capitalist means of production is the fundamental contradiction of capitalism, which leads to the instability of the capitalist production system and a lack of sustainable development. This insight reveals that production technology must be compatible with the mode of the social division of labor cooperation; otherwise, it may lead to systemic risks and hinder sustainable development.

In the digital age, digital technology empowers individuals with greater capabilities, enabling them to have greater capacity for problem-solving and wealth creation. This changes individuals' social independence and possibilities for choice, reshaping their capacity for social value creation and cooperation. Therefore, changes in the social division of labor relations between individuals will drive the transformation of social production processes and value creation processes, thereby prompting systemic changes in the social system of the division of labor.

In the digital age, significant changes have occurred in the division of labor within society, with one of the most crucial changes being the empowerment of individuals by digital technology. This has not only triggered a transformation in the division of labor among individuals but, more importantly, it has led to a qualitative change in the division of labor between humans and machines, shifting from a mode of production cooperation to a mode of decision-making cooperation. In this era, the division of labor between individuals inevitably relies on the human–machine division of labor mode, and the decision-making division of labor mode between humans and machines determines the efficiency of the social division of labor and the competitiveness of the economy. However, in the digital age, the substitutive effect of machines on humans no longer creates more job opportunities in other areas as it did before; instead, it directly leads to a reduction in valuable job positions within the economic and social system, altering the status of labor scarcity in economic development. Consequently, the unity of value circulation between the reproduction of labor (labor factor) and the reproduction of products in the economic and social system will disintegrate, and economic value creation and orderly sustainable circulation will be unable to unfold, leading to the breakdown of the social distribution system that sustains the operation of the division of labor system.

Therefore, the new the social division of labor relationships formed by digital technology cannot match the existing forms of economic organization and economic institutional arrangements. Particularly under the empowerment of digital technology, individual choices have strong externalities, and the mechanism of economic development driven by the individual pursuit of profit in the market economy must be subject to necessary restraint. In addition to necessary institutional arrangements, it is more important to align new values and wealth concepts with the new capabilities possessed by individuals, making individual self-restraint even more critical. It is imperative to redefine the value of individuals in the division of labor according to the information processing efficiency standards of the digital economy, determine reasonable division of labor cooperation mechanisms based on the requirements of human–machine division of labor, and adjust the forms of economic organization based on the new characteristics of the division of labor between individuals. Consequently, the logic and definition of business value realization will inevitably change, and new forms of business civilization will emerge and mature accordingly.

11.4 Trends in the Development of the New Business Civilization

It is evident that the emergence of a new business civilization in the digital age will bring about changes in various aspects such as the forms and dominant modes of the social division of labor, economic organizational structures, and information processing mechanisms, as well as the sources of value and competition standards owing to the application of digital technology. There are two key points to consider regarding the development of this new business civilization: the formation and development of new values, and the shaping and evolution of new economic organizational forms. These two aspects are closely interconnected and interact with each other.

11.4.1 Formation and Development of New Values

Indeed, human behavior is often driven by internal values and beliefs, and the new business civilization of the digital age presents individuals with new demands, thus requiring corresponding new value concepts to match this change.

In the digital age, individuals have gained stronger socio-economic value creation and realization capabilities owing to the empowerment of digital technology. However, they also become more dependent on digital technology, which may weaken their independence in social value creation and lead to a sense of fragmentation and anxiety. Therefore, individuals urgently need new values and development concepts to adapt to this reality, to maintain consistency between behavioral choices and cognition.

The new business civilization is the dynamic development of the collaborative ecology between individuals in the digital age, where the value of individuals is reflected in these collaborative relationships. Therefore, the determination of value standards is crucial. In the information-driven digital age, information processing efficiency becomes the most important criterion for defining value. New value concepts should be based on the contribution to enhancing information processing efficiency to measure the value of the division of labor cooperation, rather than simply based on the amount of factor ownership. The social value evaluation method of the new business civilization will shift from static factor ownership to dynamic incremental value creation, emphasizing the contribution to economic value growth and dynamic development.

Therefore, the value concept of the new business civilization will pay more attention to how to contribute to the socioeconomic value cake, rather than just focusing on how to distribute the cake fairly. This transition highlights the significance of gradually adding value and embracing flexible development approaches. It's pivotal to move away from the restrictive nature of the "zero-sum" development model, where gains for one party necessitate equivalent losses for another.

11.4.2 Formation and Development of New Organizational Forms

In any economic setup, organizational structures act as conduits for economic activities. Each structure aligns with a specific level of information technology, facilitating efficient information processing and decision-making to enable effective collaboration and attainment of economic goals.

In the digital age, digital technology offers robust capabilities in information handling, from acquisition to analysis and transmission. The extraction of value from information emerges as a crucial driver of economic value creation. Information elements play a pivotal role in economic decision-making and resource allocation. The emerging commercial landscape in the digital economy is marked by three significant characteristics:

Openness: Economic organizations' survival hinges on their openness and inclusivity. Rapid technological advancements necessitate a receptive stance, fostering continual absorption of new technological and knowledge elements to maintain competitiveness. Moreover, capital no longer reigns supreme; instead, it becomes subordinate to technological and knowledge capital. The traditional capital-centric organizational model gives way to more dynamic socio-economic structures.

Autonomy: In the digital age, individuals strive for autonomy in decision-making. The evolving business civilization reflects humanity's pursuit of autonomous development. In the human–machine division of labor paradigm, individuals must enhance their autonomy in learning and decision-making processes. Consequently, individual, and organizational autonomy becomes the primary driver of progress.

Network Effects: Connectivity-driven network effects emerge as pivotal determinants of economic value. Value creation shifts from resource supply to demand, magnifying the externalities of economic organizations' decision-making processes. Therefore, fostering stronger autonomy becomes imperative for economic entities to mitigate development risks and costs. This necessitates the adoption of new business ethics, wherein economic entities perceive themselves as integral components of the socio-economic ecosystem, making decisions aligned with societal interests.

In essence, the evolution of the new business civilization entails the emergence of novel economic organizational structures and ethical frameworks characterized by openness, autonomy, and adaptability. These adaptations are vital to navigating the economic shifts and societal demands of the digital age effectively.

The challenges mentioned are indeed significant issues facing the development of the new business civilization in the digital age. Under the new man–machine division of labor model, shaping new outlooks on life and values, as well as avoiding excessive competition and ensuring the sustainable flow of value reproduction and product reproduction, all require the collective efforts and deep reflection of the entire society.

Raising the overall efficiency of information processing in society and promoting the enhancement of human autonomy are also important tasks facing the digital age. This requires continuous improvement in the application of digital technology, strengthening education and training in information technology, and promoting the deep application of informatization in various fields, in order to enhance the overall competitiveness and sustainable development capability of society.

Furthermore, traditional models of social governance are indeed facing new challenges brought about by the development of the digital age, requiring timely reform and adjustment. The modernization of national governance capabilities will be built on a profound understanding of the development of the digital age, requiring close attention to the trends in digital economy development, and the formulation of corresponding policies and plans to promote the healthy development of the new business civilization and provide important guarantees for the long-term prosperity and stability of society.

SPRINGER NATURE

GPSR Compliance

The European Union's (EU) General Product Safety Regulation (GPSR) is a set of rules that requires consumer products to be safe and our obligations to ensure this.

If you have any concerns about our products, you can contact us on ProductSafety@springernature.com

In case Publisher is established outside the EU, the EU authorized representative is:

Springer Nature Customer Service Center GmbH
Europaplatz 3
69115 Heidelberg, Germany

The manufacturer's authorised representative in the EU is Springer Nature Customer Service Centre GmbH, Europaplatz 3, 69115 Heidelberg, Germany. If you have any concerns regarding our products, please contact ProductSafety@springernature.com

Printed and bound by CPI Group (UK) Ltd, Croydon, CR0 4YY
01/10/2026
02225849-0002